CHANAKYA NITI
KAUTILYA ARTHSHASTRA

Methods of management and the art of governance

Acquire the art of management from Chanakya, become a successful leader achieve self-control and be a leader of groups

The complete text of Chanakya Niti, Chanakya Sootra and Kautilya Arthashastra

The peerless economist;
business management Guru;
destroyer of Empires and
architect of nation;
moralist and definer of ethical values;
dynamic director and leader;
mass psychologist;
liquidator of foes and
imperious political strategist;
Awaken the enlightenment by the philosophy of
Chanakya to realize your potential and acquire
wisdom, science and art of management!

Prof. Shrikant Prasoon

V&S PUBLISHERS

Published by

V&S PUBLISHERS

F-2/16, Ansari Road, Daryaganj, New Delhi-110002
☎ 011-23240026, 011-23240027 • *Fax* 011-23240028
Email info@vspublishers.com • *Website* www.vspublishers.com

Regional Office Hyderabad
5-1-707/1, Brij Bhawan (Beside Central Bank of India Lane)
Bank Street, Koti, Hyderabad - 500 095
☎ 040-24737290
E-mail vspublishershyd@gmail.com

Branch Office Mumbai
☎ 022-22098268
E-mail vspublishersmum@gmail.com

Follow us on **t** **f** **in**

For any assistance sms **VSPUB** to **56161**

All books available at **www.vspublishers.com**

© **Copyright** V&S PUBLISHERS
ISBN 978-93-505716-3-7
Edition : 2014

Printed at Param Offseters Okhla New Delhi-110020

Publisher's Note

We feel immensely proud and honoured to present to the readers the precious work called **Chanakya Niti and Kautilya Arthashastra.** This book is a treasure trove of knowledge and learning. The reader will be able to bring in changes in his daily life upon reading this book. After reading this book, the reader will be able to easily grasp Chanakya's illuminating thoughts and ideas.

The book describes Chanakya's philosophies and Kautilya's economic theories. The entire content has been explained in simple language for easy comprehension. Chanakya's Ethics is an invaluable gem in Indian history. There are seventeen chapters in it. The novel Chanakya Niti comprises 17 chapters specifically chosen from the great treatise Kautilya's Arthashastra by the venerable Chanakya himself and named as Chanakya Niti by himself.

Kautilya's Arthashastra is the world renowned work of Pandit Chanakya. In this book along with the description of the doctrines of administration, the fine essence of administrative management has also been incorporated. The greatest speciality of this literary composition is the beautiful connection between the doctrines and their usage, between idealism and actuality and between knowledge and action.

This book contains Chanakya's life and the important incidents which occurred in his life. There are also illustrations on his acquired knowledge and his thoughts on how to lead a life happily and fruitfully, coupled with his pieces of advice on them. The book is filled with ideas on how to become a ruler, how to make a ruler, how to establish a kingdom, how to strengthen that kingdom, how to administer that kingdom and how to increase its wealth.

The book is written in simple yet lucid language so that those who read it will be benefitted enormously from it.

Dedication

Chanakya – Procedure of Administration and the Art of Ruling

This book is dedicated to all those, who, with utmost determination and dedication, coupled with industry and devotion wish to scale the pinnacle of eminence and remain there.

To my two very close Publishers of Indian Publishing Services

Sri. Amitabh Verma

Sri. A.K.Upadhyay

–Prof. Shrikant Prasoon

Contents

Preface.. *9*
Chanakya's Prayers *10*
Vedic Prayers... *11*
Chanakya's Immortality *12*

SECTION-1
Solemn Oath, Personality, Life History

Chanakya – The Master of Administration 17
Life, Thoughts and Knowledge...27
Chanakya – Accomplishment with Multifaceted Talent 35
Chanakya's Firmness 41
Niti and Kautilya's Arthashastra 49
Chanakya's Commentary on Women.....................................54

SECTION-2
Methodical Man and Society
Complete Policy of Chanakya

Chapter – 1 63
Chapter – 2 66
Chapter – 3 69
Chapter – 4 72
Chapter – 5 75
 Chapter – 6 78
Chapter – 7 81
Chapter – 8 84
Chapter – 9 87
Chapter –10 89
Chapter – 11 92
Chapter – 12 95
Chapter – 13 99
Chapter – 14 102
Chapter – 15 105
Chapter – 16 108
Chapter – 17 111

SECTION-3
Self, Time, Things-Methodical

Chanakya's Rule 115

SECTION-4
Thoughts on Management, Kautilya's Arthashastra

First Case – Courtesy 151
Second Case – Publicity of Rules 158
Third Case–Righteousness..169
Fourth Case – Difficultiesin Reformation....................................172
Fifth Case – Plan of Conduct..174
Sixth Case – Origin of Spheres 180
Seventh Case – The Six Qualities 184
Eighth Case – Addiction to Vices 195
Nineth Case – Duty of Practice..200
Tenth Case – Association 207
Eleventh Case – Plan of Society 208
Twelfth Case – Weakness...209
Thirteenth Case – Longevity of Fortress/Organization.................210
Fourteenth Case – Treatise...212
The Fifteenth Case – Bases of Principles 213

SECTION-5
Immortality and Salvation, Remaining Story

Chanakya's Steadfast Activity 217
Chanakya—Journey & Salvation..232

Preface

Chanakya did not write anything in his younger days. It was not in tradition then. Only after stepping down from the position of a minister did Chanakya begin writing in the fourth phase of his life. He wrote on the science of politics, the principles of politics and the science of economy. He wrote a lot, he wrote for all and he wrote very well. The purpose of publication of this book is to help the reader in not only improving self administration but also the quality of universal administration.

Chanakya wrote the treatise keeping a developed nation as the pivot and wrote for the safety and development of existence. Hence this book is for every thinker, trainer, organization, student, government officer and common reader.

The words and examples of modern methods of management have been used wherever possible in order that the reader can easily comprehend.

The book has been classified into business management and administrative management for the reader's benefit so that by reading them he can come to a self realisation.

This book contains Chanakya's life, important incidents of his life, his achievements and his thoughts on leading a comfortable, accomplished and happy life. The book is filled with ideas on how to rule a country, how to create a ruler, how to establish a kingdom and strengthen it, how to administer that kingdom judiciously and how to increase the wealth.

It is left to the readers' level of interest on how they learn it, assimilate its thoughts and use it dedicatedly. Their acquisition of this knowledge will be revealed only when they apply it and use it in an enlightened manner.

For the all round development, complete prosperity and unequalled joy of everyone,

May good fortune be bestowed on all!

– Prof. Shrikant Prasoon

Chanakya's Prayers

Pranamya shirasa vishnum trailokyadhipathim prabhum.
Naanashaastra uddhrutham vakshe rajaneetisamucchayam.

Bowing reverently to Lord Vishnu, the Lord of three realms – the Earth, the Heaven and the Hell, who is omnipotent and omnipresent, I describe the science of government after compiling thoughts from various shastras.

❖ ❖ ❖

Adhityedam Yathasastram naro janaati sattamaha
Dharmopadesha vikhyatam karyakarya shubhaashubham.

Eminent men will duly learn and understand the kind of actions fit to be performed and not fit to be performed and the actions which result in fortune or misfortune.

❖ ❖ ❖

Tadahamsampravashyami lokaanam hita kamyaya.
Yasya vignana maatrena sarvagnatvam prapadhyate.

Hence desiring the welfare of mankind, I wish to explain this knowledge in depth which will help the man become more knowledgeable.

❖ ❖ ❖

Namah shukra bruhaspatibhyaam.

The learned master Chanakya started writing the book on the science of economics [arthashastra] after seeking the blessings of Bruhaspati, the venerable teacher of Devas [Gods] and the blessings of Shukracharya, the revered teacher of the Danavas [demons]. He has explained how to control the wealth available on this Earth, how to augment that wealth, how to safeguard it in order to establish an administration so that happiness is obtained, so that there is all round development, so that generation after generation will live happily, so that respect and prestige is maintained till the attainment of salvation.

Vedic Prayers

Abhayam mitraad abhayam amitraad abhayam gnaataad abhayam puro yah.
Abhayam naktam abhayam diva nah sarvaa asha mama mitram bhavanthu,

Oh Lord! We shall not take fear from either our friends or foes!

Release us from the fear of known people.

Release us from the fear of all things.

May we not live in fear either during day or night.

Let there be no reason for fear in any country.

May we find friends and only friends everywhere!

❖ ❖ ❖

Bhadram no api vaataya mano dakshamuta kartrum.

O'Lord! Give me a compassionate heart,

Give me work which helps in the welfare of people,

Give me an abundant strength of charitable heart.

❖ ❖ ❖

Vaisvanarajyothihi bhuyasam.

O'Lord! Keep us engrossed in your bountiful splendour!

Chanakya's Immortality

On accumulation of wealth or affairs of security, the worldly guru Chanakya's thoughts were outstanding. Meaningful, refined words filled with dignity, and language so mature and so synthesised. Though moved far away we are from our wealth, culture, knowledge-tradition, and firm foundations. The ideas of Chanakya keep us on the summit, make us administrators extraordinaire.

Student of Taxila, teacher, master, progressive, ready and renowned. Reached Taxila, saw, assessed the country with pure heart, speech and action. Calculating, analysing, predicting the future course of action came Chanakya. But humiliated by Dhananand, became exceedingly wrathful and vowed to wreak destruction to them.

The teacher of Chanak- Why will he bear the son's humiliation and misconduct?. Why will he remain mum? Calm? Why not tell the truth correctly?. No greed, nor avarice, why then douse the raging fire?. Why not destroy the rotten empire? Why will he remain silent?

Remained drowned in thoughts day and night, no peace or rest for Chanakya. Tough it was to fulfil the vow, only one inclination- work and more work. Search for soldiers, implements, arms and ammunition- to collect them in large numbers. The days and nights used to merge- all the while he was striving and striving.

Young eager, attentive soldiers did Chanakya prepare, gave them such a training. Country bumpkin became fit to be a king, happened as he planned. Without himself resorting to cruelty, he retaliated cruelty with unqualled strength of mind. Chanakya destroyed the race of Nandas, as they sowed, so did they reap.

Such was the conflict, such was the war that the soldiers were the personification of war. Virtue emerged as sapling, grew with flowers, thorns, scents attracting the bees. Yet he took nothing, always gave, only saving, lifting, lengthening in each step. Winning through daring actions, revolutionary ideas, Chanakya became immortal.

Excellent science Chanakya created, science of government and science of diplomacy. Style of creation was cold, calculative, venomous, yet having excellent conduct. The good became fearless and the evil turned fearful. Provoked the strength in all while promoting astounding love too.

Physically frail, yet mentally strong, Chanakya roared loud and ferocious. His depth was immeasurable, his breadth unspannable. The secret spell of his success was – patience, steadiness, permanence. Single minded focus on the objective while all encompassing vision on four directions.

Admonished for the abandonment of inferior thought and inferior action. Chanakya used to ponder and speak, act, taking the right step at right time. Balanced was his thinking, decision-arithmetical, success guaranteed. Intelligent, well behaved, thinker extraordinaire, why will he totter? Fear?

Self motivated for social service, engaged himself in penning an exemplary science of ethics. Brimming with cleverness and cunningness, thus completed Kautilya Arthashastra. Bound it in the yarn of experience in order that life turns golden and aromatic. Maintained impeccable, the dignity of his clan, this bright lamp of his clan.

Gave us the complete safe system, before Chanakya left on his final journey. Easy, natural, educational path-which gives us wonderful success. Never erred and never allowed others to err, never made a tepid plan. Became rhythmic, absorbed in the melody, this master an invaluable treasure.

Noble Chanakya was, a foe to wrong doings, a supporter of fate. Compiled knowledge, without wasting even a moment. For the kingdom and for the society, he lived, breathed, stood or died. Made his life meaningful with honesty and dedication.

Gave the generation a peerless, boundless, practical knowledge. With which one could follow an excellent path and gain wisdom and awakening. Wrote, taught, the advantages of enterprise, of acquisition. Such was his wonderful steadfastness, that he completed his journey successfully.

Like this, so many, are seers and sages born and blossomed in tradition. Chanakya's thoughts, ideas and knowledge can never become displaced. Seen, understood, eternal, path denoting salvation which if comprehended and followed. Automatically and voluntarily, will place the great Chanakya's glory in eternal niche.

* 15 *

No amount of praise is enough to eulogize the noble Chanakya.As he was the complete circumference, all circles inside and the central axis too. He was with the time, the time walked with him supporting and protecting. For those who accept and follow it, none of their desires will remain unfulfilled.

SECTION-1

SOLEMN OATH, PERSONALITY, LIFE HISTORY

CHANAKYA – THE MASTER OF ADMINISTRATION

LIFE, THOUGHTS AND KNOWLEDGE

CHANAKYA – ACCOMPLISHMENT WITH MULTIFACETED TALENT

CHANAKYA'S EMINENCE AND RESOLUTION

ECONOMICS AND KAUTILYA'S ARTHASASTHRA

AN ACQUAINTANCE TO CHANAKYA'S POLICIES

Chanakya – The Master of Administration

Great personalities are born on the earth at powerful times when exemplary forces of natural and supernatural collide. These men are able to direct the time's historical flow according to their desires using their complete strength of knowledge through intellect and through exhaustive intelligence and create a new kingdom thereby creating a new history. Such men are so powerful and strong that history turns according to their desires, various incidents occur as they obey their orders and public obeys their commands/instructions.

These men act according to the age as they are the men of that age. Therefore time/age becomes compatible with them. As a result, even after they shed their mortal body and leave this mortal world, their glory remains immortal and eternal. Time keeps them in its bosom providing warmth and keeping them alive in spirit even centuries after centuries. Just like they were responsible in refining and keeping the society renowned during their time, they remain responsible for the evolution and progress of the society through ages. Thus they become the public treasure, they become every one's and loom larger than man and society. They become invaluable to the future generations. They decorate and adorn the future making it secure and safe for the others.

Undoubtedly Chanakya was such a famous, successful, scholarly statesman that he became a historical figure during his time itself. There has never been any personality both in the past and the present who can come close enough to Chanakya in his level of knowledge, in practical thinking, in character, in virtue, in esteem, in firm mindedness, in dedication and in single minded following of his deeds.

The most surprising fact is that Chanakya lived like a sage, apart from acquiring knowledge he did not acquire anything else. Fame and glory came to him naturally by themselves. All that he ever did was for the welfare of others. He strived for the welfate, progress, peace, prosperity, safety, knowledge, improvement and salvation of the others, the society and the country and this great being brought the entire Bharat under one rule and made it a vast, wealthy, peaceful and pleasant country.

Chanakya is the personification of knowledge. He is usually symbolised as clad in a simple dhoti with a shawl wrapped round his shoulders, his hair tied at the back of his head looking like an ornament, having a broad and bright forehead, big lustrous eyes, holding two books in his hands. Thus is sage Chanak's son Chanakya portrayed filled with self-confidence, firm determination, knowledge and intellect. Therefore even to this date, Chanakya is considered as a living progressive thinker and a quick and strong pointer of rightful path.

Dedicated Administrator

Chanakya did not remain just a practical thinker, but translated those thoughts into action very rapidly and quickly. He was not only a sharp and effective orator but also a very obstinate, unbending and stubborn man, was a teacher, guru, dutiful minister of the state. He was pure, blemish less, kind, single minded and firm administrator, a successful strategist. Though he had mastery over a plethora of destructive forces within him, he portrayed only his creative strengths. He was an amalgamation of common sense and emotions, used to receive more respect from others than he ever gave to others. He was obstinate but not pig headed. He was the object and the verb of dedication and morality, hence he could bring the complete downfall of a well established, strong kingdom and was able to unify many kingdoms and tie the entire Bharat under one regime. Though he wreaked destruction very swiftly, he brought in reformation and reorganization more swiftly as he had already commenced the task of reformation even before the destruction. His deep sense of belief and his mind's eye had already known that whatever he said or wished, would only happen. Such a firm resolution cannot be seen in anyone else.

Whatever Chanakya did, he did it with mental strength and the strength of character. Thus he always used to display enviable qualities. He never left any task half done, never failed in any task because he used to complete any task with complete dedication and sincerity, thus being very close to perfection.

The reason was not just because Chanakya was a preceptor or teacher in Taxila. In fact he had resigned from his post and had gone on a tour to various kingdoms traversing from down below south to the high above north. He saw the atrocities committed by the Nandas and vowed to destroy their race. To succeed in this endeavour, he transformed himself so quickly- which is not possible even by the learned men despite sever penances. He became self sufficient in all ways and planned on the destruction of a kingdom while simultaneously preparing for the establishment of another one.

A Vow – Almost Impossible

Any kind of destruction will result in the ruin of a society, but in the planned, methodical manner Chanakya went about bringing change, there was no ruin at all infact there was development and progress with a change in the kingdom and administration. He began this by making necessary changes from all directions and in every department and reaching the central administration finally. Before the third part of the night was over and even before the breaking of dawn, he had brought in complete transformation. It is difficult to even gauge how intensive and quick he was in bringing about this change and how thoughtful and peaceful this change was. A complete effect of administrative reforms! Filled with blessings! Elegant! Exemplary and praiseworthy! This transformation was done with complete dedication and earnestness.

Chanakya brought in this change while being unaware of the place and population and while the people did not have any knowledge about him. All alone! he brought it alone! no place or house! no friends or foes! Had no money, no army, no soldiers, no arms, no commander-in-chief. Had mental strength and was conscientious, had strength of charater, knowledge. These attributes of his helped a village lad become a king and training others similarly in arms and warfare, made them into an army and a commander-in-chief thus making an impossibility, a reality.

Complete Annihilation

Chanakya was able to do this because he was taught that the enemy has to be destroyed completely. Even if any quarter of the army remained, in due course of time it could become strong, retaliate and destroy them.

An important incident occurred in Chanakya's life which proved that he did not have even a slight tolerance for his enemies. He preferred a clean route sans any difficulty. A peaceful is one being safe, without enemies and being brave. Only then can one move to the path of spiritual glory. He wanted to completely raze a ramshackle house in order to build a completely new building which shines and glows, so that there can be novelty in progress of tradition, there can be new creation, where profit and development are visible. One incident clearly reveals his inner anxiety and firm determination which is described in the following paragraph.

Kush is a plant with thorn like roots and when poked is very painful and the pain persists for a long time. But it is used by people for rituals and rites. Once, a kush twig got entangled in Chanakya's foot. In some books it is also said that this twig pricked the feet of Chanak, Chanakya's father and he died due to this reason. Chanakya completed his father's funeral rites but neither forgot nor forgave the kush root.

Whatever the reason, Chanakya decided to destroy kush root completely from its place. Each day he used to go there with a pot of buttermilk, pull the plant including the root and used to pour the buttermilk in that place in order that no new plant sprouted there.

This was the method employed by Chanakya- to show his rage and to take revenge on his enemies.

People were surprised to see a youngster going everyday with buttermilk, pulling out Kush plant and pouring the buttermilk over that place. Some did not like this, some even opposed this but it didn't bring any change in Chanakya. One day a few village elders headed by a minister came there. Chanakya was busy with his daily chore. His attention never wavered. The minister politely questioned him, "What are you doing and why?" Chanakya's reply was crystal clear. "I can't bear if anything upsets humans and humanity, hence I'm completely uprooting and destroying these thorns which prick them. If anybody goes against humans and humanity, I will eliminate that person."

His lustre and steadfastness was liked by the minister. The minister did not like King Dhananand and was plotting to uproot him. As he was not capable, he thought that this being would be able to do that great work. Knowing that Dhananand and Chanakya cannot stand each other, the minister invited Chanakya to a feast hosted by Dhananand. He was sure that something would happen which will result in the destruction of the king. Thus Chanakya entered the court of Dhananand.

Chanakya used to either conceal his thoughts within him or reveal them frankly. He never forgave anyone. He remained quiet because he thought that in case the word spread even before the completion of work, then it could create complications. He has also quoted thus

Manasa vichintyayet vachasa na prakashayet.

Explanation: It seems truly impossible that one can achieve the pinnacle of glory without creating enmity with some because there is hatred everywhere in large number and it seems impossible for anyone to reach the pinnacle of success when there are so many enemies. Hence it is imperative to face and destroy the enemy at appropriate time and forge forward. One must spend much time, labour and power in it.

Effect: The enemy who gets entrenched becomes stronger and stronger. Then he starts attacking with increased strength and hatred. Hence when an opportunity arises, the enemy has to be completely routed.

Every Night – Work and only Work

Chanakya believed only in punishment and not in forgiveness for any mistake. The punishment could be harsh or mild but he never allowed anyone go scot free. This was an important cause for fearing Chanakya. One when one escapes punishment will one repeat the mistakes, repeat the faults. But when there is no respite from punishment, then one will spend all the time in trying not to commit mistakes and won't even have time to think of committing a crime. This lesson was learnt by all his disciples. The villagers who passed byu his hermitage were witness to an incident one morning.

The fisher men, the washer men, the gardeners who had left home at dawn to catch fish, wash clothes or pluck flowers were filled with wonder seeing an unusual sight. They stood in stunned silence in the mangrove. This was the same hermitage they used to frequently hear and discuss. Master Chanakya was returning from the river carrying two pots of water. This was not the usual custom. Chopping wood, filling water and cleaning were the work of the disciples. The teacher did not perform these physical tasks, hence the surprise. The unanswered question was why the master was fetching the water.

An unusual incident occurred then which made every one burst into unrestrained laughter. The master first placed both the pots on the ground, lifted on and went to the place where his disciples lay slumbering and muttering something poured the water all over them. The boys shot up awake and ran helter-skelter towards the river with their dhotis falling, their shawls slipping. There was utter chaos. The master returned, took the second pot and turned towards the place where his disciples had lain. The villagers doubled with laughter because not even one disciple remained there. Continuing to mutter, the master kept the pot there. The villagers could only hear the sound of anger but could not listen to the words.

The spectacle being over, the villagers continued towards their work spots laughing and appreciating the master.

Explanation: Despite not having resources, despite not being physically strong, one can succeed if one works hard tirelessly and with complete dedication. The difference will be visible through dedicated work. If you repeatedly chafe a delicate thread on a rough stone, it will leave its mark on it.

Effect: A man can increase the length of day as well as work by getting up early and going to bed late. He can get a sound sleep from ten at night to five in the morning. Those who go late to bed and wake up late will remain listless and inactive.

Modernization – Boon or Bane

Chanakya brought out the feelings of both respect and fear in all because he was never greedy or avaricious nor did he seek redemption for the acts done. Hence though he was fearless, people feared him. The surprising fact was that Chanakya always taught everyone to be fearless. But one can be fearless only when one is free from unethical habits. Then being fearless would mean always following ethical practices.

One who is evil has no worry of losing his prestige or has no fear of any danger. *Naastya maanabhyaam anaryasya.* One who is intelligent and industrious has no fear in work or profession. *Na cheta navataam vrutthi bhayam.* One who has complete control over his senses has no fear of downfall. *Na jitendriyanan vishaya-bhayam.* One who is honest and duty bound has no fear of any man or of death, doesn't fear anything at all. *Na krutharthanaam maranam bhayam.*

If there are such people and if the society is without fear, only then will all be able to live fearlessly and the evil and wrong doers will skulk and lurk and not throw bombs in the areas filled with population. Then there won't be any rapes or displays of nudity in women, no disturbances, no bank robberies, no murders, no accidents and no untimely deaths.

In the modern days students are punished without any rhyme or reason. And trials are conducted on teachers too. This situation has worsened in the last 30 years. Before that one had not even heard of such ruin. Today characterlessness is more powerful and firmly embedded in the system, turning everyone characterless and does not allow anyone to point fingers at it calling it shameless. Such people even get five star treatment in the prisons and now it is said that they get to meet their wives in another cell in the same prison. Under such circumstances why won't a criminal continue to lead a decadent life in the prison? No one is afraid of imprisonment now. Chanakya has written a verse which says that one must not live in a country where there is terrorism and fear of terrorism. Today terrorism is rampant and terrorists are everywhere and people are forced to live with this fear. There is no security to common man even though we have security from A to Z category.

Earlier fire used to burn in stoves, but now it burns the huts. Fire strikes like lightening and despite safety measures thousands perish in it and crores lose their wealth. Earlier in Delhi, two persons used to be killed in road accidents, now five are killed! Today there isn't any safe place and any place free from corruption. Other than the accusers, all have become corrupt and for the greed of money are prepared to do any menial crime. We have progressed a lot after independence! So much that neither the people and the country were under debt during the independence are debt ridden now. If the national debt is divided among its one hundred crore people, each person owes thirty three thousand. Since we have forgotten to count beyond crores, whatever said has to be in crores only.

And the condition of America, supposed to be the most developed country, is that every year it has to pay one hundred and ninety two billion dollars as just annual interest. Wow! What a progress!

Today it is useless to describe education field or any other field. It is sheer waste of time and effort because of the anarchy prevalent there which was not envisaged during the independence or after. On one hand the marks of the students are enhanced by adding marks of various exams so that there is uniformity, on the other hands ten thousand to forty thousand students fail in exams every year. There is hardly any exam where question paper is not leaked out beforehand. The situation of nominations is such that the honorary nominees have to pay lakhs and crores as donations apart from paying the required remuneration. Most of the universities have become exam centres rather than being centres of learning. All they do is filling nominations, filling exam forms, distributing exam papers, entrance papers or degrees. But what is the necessity of describing this when all of us are aware of this malaise?

Development has to be done by those who have no interest in all these things. The others require money, in whatever way they get. Ask someone what is the greatest thing in life, one will answer 'wealth', another 'house', one more 'wife-lover' and yet another 'car'. Nobody knows the common yet real answer, does not think that the greatest thing in life is 'life' itself. The moment breath leaves the body, our kith and kin – dad, son, brother burn us in the pyre or bury us under the ground. At that moment how the wealth – house, wife, car or items of luxury be useful to us? Just as the life and the creation of life is certain, old age and death is also certain. It cannot be postponed, yet everyone is preoccupied in the quest for immortality and eternal youth and enjoyment of the pleasures. They get easily chained in the arms of people who make money in unscrupulous ways. In reality we are cheating ourselves. But nobody wants to accept it despite knowing the fact. They live moaning, groaning and suffocated. People kill themselves, kill others but are incapable of leading a happy, peaceful, comfortable, healthy and joyful life.

Chanakya – A Treasure Trove of Knowledge

Chanakya did not have the strength of wealth, strength of arms and ammunition, strength of army. He had only the strength of knowledge. Only a knowledgeable person will be able to recognize the strength of wisdom and announce it strongly. *Buddhihi yasya balam tasya nirbudhestu kuto balam.* One who has knowledge has strength, where will an ignorant have any strength? Only such a person can become the master of administration and administrators and provide a good situation and see that this wonderful situation continues for a very long time. A ruler can achieve this only if he takes his master's advice.

A minor incident which took place in Nanda's court made Chanakya change the history of India and has been incidental in changing and revolutionising the thoughts of people through the ages.

Vow

There are various versions of the incident related to Chanakya. Narrators have interspersed with the facts, their imagination while narrating in order that his philosophy, his teachings remain as effective now as it was before. There are various versions as to when and how Chanakya took his vow. Whether at the behest of the minister, or by himself, Chanakya went to the court of Nanda, the King of Magadh. The most commonly described fact is that he attended the feast hosted by the king Nanda, honouring an invitation extended to him by the minister.

It is difficult to say whether the day was dark and dismal or bright and beautiful. Maybe it was dark and dismal to the king and his race, but bright and beautiful to the human race.

Seeing Chanakya seated among the invited Brahmins, King Nanda laughed and said, "Is this man a Brahmin? If he is a Brahmin he cannot be dark in complexion and if he is dark, then he cannot be a Brahmin."

Chanakya did not like this mockery and he retaliated but none paid any heed. The minister was content that things were going the way he envisaged they would. He took the side of the king which enraged Chanakya. The situation became very tense. Though many did not like the disgrace shown to the Brahmin, they kept quiet. But Chanakya did not remain quiet. The king was arrogant but why should he bear the brunt of the king's arrogance? He was mocking at the Brahmin and the brahmin's courage was eager to break the barrier and flow out.

Then Dhananand lost his temper and ordered that Chanakya be thrown out of his court. This broke Chanakya's dam of restraint and he was beside himself in rage. He rained curses on both the king and the kingdom. No one was able to stop both of them. The rage of Chanakya sky rocketed with the taunts of Dhanananda. The soldiers caught him, which was humiliating to him. Freeing himself from their hold, Chanakya loosened his locks and roared loudly. " Dhananand, I came to show you the righteous path and wean you away from the wrong path, to unshackle you from wine and women. It didn't happen, you did not heed to the voice of wisdom. You have insulted me. I take a vow in the presence of everyone in the court that I will annihilate you and your race. I will not breathe easy till you are completely ruined. I will not tie my locks until I destroy you completely."

Saying this, Chanakya walked out of the court seething in rage while all stood in shocked silence.

Chanakya fulfilled his vow in due course of time.

Explanation: None of us should take a vow or an oath, but if we take it, we should fulfil it at any cost. We should use our complete knowledge, strength in fulfilling the oath and then we become worthy of being respected. If we fail in fulfilling it, we become a laughing stock. The victory will help in blossoming of self confidence and provide us utmost happiness.

Effect: We progress from within. Our organs develop from within. Knowledge increases from inside and thoughts are born there. Internalisation is pure and complete power. We have to become powerful so that we get instant and complete success.

In doing this, Chanakya rose to the stature of a mountain which could not be scaled, a deep ocean which could not be measured, a moving storm which could not be halted, a superhuman being who could not be defeated. Chanakya was larger than a shalya tree, safe as a cave, bright as rays illuminating the path and safe guard it.

Chanakya is both feared and venerated because he is the only knowledgeable person who is both a peaceful, gurgling brook and also an erupting volcano. If we comprehend and follow his teachings, we will greatly benefit from it.

Individual Expenditure and Expenditure of Kingdom

Just one incident is enough to portray Chanakya's historical height and depth, hisfame, action and behaviour. One incident is enough to bring to light his purity, his detachment which makes it very clear about his greatness and potentiality.

Once he welcomed a stranger into his house dousing one lamp and lighting another. This incident has been described by Megasthenes in his journal describing his journey to India. Megasthenes was also a part of this incident. Megasthenes had come to India and had heard a lot about Chanakya. He wanted to meet this pious personality. It wasn't a difficult task to meet Chanakya. Request was sent, permission was granted and Megasthenes was directed to the house of Chanakya.

It was dusk when Megasthenes entered the house and darkness was slowly pervading all around. Chanakya was seated on a carpet writing something with the light from a lamp. He lifted his head, welcomed the stranger and asked him the purpose of his visit. The foreigner replied that he had come to meet Chanakya, know more about him and discuss some personal matter with him.

Chanakya requested him to wait and doused the lamp he was using after lighting another lamp. He requested the stranger to take a seat. Megasthenes sat on the same carpet and watched the lighting and dousing of lamps with curiosity. The master was easily able to comprehend the thoughts of Megasthenes, yet the guest questioned him the reason for changing the lamp when both gave out the same illumination.

Chanakya replied, "Before changing the lamps I asked you the purpose of your visit and found out that you have come to meet me on personal work. Therefore I lit the lamp which has oil bought from my income and doused the lamp which has the oil purchased from the royal exchequer. I cannot spend from royal exchequer for my personal work.

The stranger did not know how to react and respond. He knew that Chanakya was the pivot of Mauryan empire. Any arrogant person could have belittled this great act. But Megashtenes bowed and said softly that this is your special strength.

Explanation: It is dangerous to use money kept aside for some purpose for some other work. It will affect the internal relations and the work which has rto be done and the completion of the said work will also be doubtful. As it is one project will be incomplete, the other one will also be incomplete. Instead of transferring funds from one treasury, different treasury should be created for different projects thus both projects can be completed.

Effect: If we mix wealth, knowledge and effort judiciously, we will get desired result which will affect the society favourably. Unequal mixture is dangerous to both man and society.

Sale of Property – Wealth – Business

Conducting business of land or building or landed property is generally profitable in the present day. Reputed businessmen and business organizations have jumped into this business. It is very clear now that man and money are deeply entwined. The land which was available for hundred rupees thirty years before is worth more than a lakh. The inflation rate of gold is not as much as this and in the same comparison there is not much inflation in food commodities. One rupee wheat costs ten rupees now.

Chanakya had instituted punishment for people who cheated on sale, auction, demarcation of fields or exemption on taxes.

During an auction, an auctioneer hits three times with his hammer saying 'once, twice, thrice and only then is the lot deemed to be sold. There is a misconception among people that the system of auctioning came to our country from Europe. But it is not so. It has been prevalent since Chanakya's time. Because it is mentioned in Arthashastra 3:65:9 *Trih aaghoshitam vyaahatam kreta kretum labhet.*

It was the usual custom for the prospective seller of a field or land to inform his neighbour, his village headman or the resident royal emissary. Only upon their refusal could he ask others. Gnaati saamant dhanikaah. *Kramena bhoomi parigrahaana kretumbhya. Bhaageyah tatho anye brayeh.*

But the situation has changed so much now, people sell their properties or buy properties furtively. There are various rules to be followed even today but nobody follows it. Chanakya's orders were that if a person dug a well, deepened a well, or cleaned a well, one should not have any business with that person for five, four or three years. *Tadag- santhubandhaanam nava paravartane-pancham varshikaha parihaarah!*

Chanakya had excellent planning for streets, villages, meadows, land, social work, loan and tax and the style of living. He had clearly given the mode of taxation – ordinary people had to pay 1.25 percent, businessmen 5 percent, people living in forest and conducting business 10 percent and people conducting business through seas 20 percent as taxes.

Sappada panaa dharmya masavruddhi pana shatasya.
Panchapanaa vyaavahaariki.
Dasha panaa kaantharangaanam.
Vimshati panaa samudraanam.

2

Life, Thoughts and Knowledge

Chanakya was both a spiritual as well as modern thinker, thoughtful, creative and extremely hardworking yet detached minister, was a revolutionary being, a director who could complete a work or get the work completed, controlled economist, judicial advisor, could secretly control the spreading or gathering of communication, an experienced and influential statesman. He was on the whole a complete organization by himself. He was unparalleled in all the fields and for many centuries a rival equalling his calibre has not been born. His inner strength and external achievements have been a great source of inspiration even to this date.

Chanakya was the first victorious administrator who assimilated politics from past statesmen, philosophy from the past philosophers and he both straightened and twisted the administration, developed the existing process so well that the question of failure never arose because it had the complete description of every progress, downfall, slips, spiral growth, steps for development and growth and there is a detailed explanation of how to make use of these concepts and administer the country correctly and perfectly. Hence he belonged to everyone and every age.

Hence he became the greatest and strongest thinker, minister, writer, director. His greatest achievement was to abdicate the post of the most powerful minister and gifting it to his sworn enemy. That too at such a time when he was in complete zenith of glory, fame and was venerated by all. At a time when he had entwined the entire country under one rule and had made it a strong and powerful country. No one can even imagine for a second giving up the perks of glory even before enjoying it. It can never happen, more so when people are bent on grabbing other's rightful place and enjoying it. This kind of rivalry is taking place in all countries everywhere with killings, bombings and bloodshed.

Search for Administrator

Chanakya was aware that he was not a warrior, could not fight any battle, he could hold books and not a sword. He could author many plots but not chop someone's head. But he had sworn to annihilate the race of Nanda. He was in search of a warrior who could support him in destroying the race of Nanda and after the victory become an able ruler of the country and rule judiciously because Chanakya could direct from behind scenes but not lead the army from front.

Hence he needed a warrior who was brave yet humble, disciplined disciple, intelligent, strong having a good vision and who would be remembered forever in the minds of people. Only such a person could help chanakya in fulfilment of his vow, could help in fructification of his plans, could help in the realisation of his vow, could help in implementing of his plans, could help in realisation of his ideas and rise to the pinnacle. Chanakya was in search of such a person. Luck was on his side.

One day Chanakya was walking on the banks of River Ganga in Pippilikaanan in the Champaran area of Bihar, which is called as Pipara in the present Bihar, a place always green and fertile. He saw the grazing cattle and cattleheads. His attention zeroed on a tall well built youngster. This youngster sat straight on a tall rock. On one hand he had kept a watchful eye on his cattle and on the other, he was ordering the boys.

He was acting like a king then. Chanakya watched the play with enjoyment. The boy sat on the stone as if it was a throne. He sent many boys here and there on duty either as soldiers or emissaries. When he saw Chanakya, he beckoned him towards him. When Chanakya came near, he asked, "Honourable Brahmin! What do you want?"

The lad was aware as to how to show respect to a learned Brahmin. Chanakya replied very politely, "I need cows as I need milk for my disciples."

The lad was aware of the importance of charity. He replied without any hesitation, "Let this honourable Brahmin be given 101 cows."

Chanakya questioned him in the same humble tone, "Have you taken permission from your guardians?"

A king does not require permission from anyone. The lad was clearly aware of the power of a king. He was also aware that he was doing something good. A man should be charitable by nature. Chanakya asked him in the same tone, "Where are your parents?"

The lad pointed in the direction of his village with his forefinger looking highly excited. Chanakya had already read the lad's forehead and now he had the opportunity of reading his palm. He was able to see what he was in search of. The lad said, "I don't have my father. My mother lives there."

"What is your mother's name?" Chanakya wanted further details. Mother's name is Mura was the thoughtful reply. Chanakya blessed the child and said, "Glory to the King! I shall come again to collect the cows." He went towards the village then.

Chanakya met the lad's mother. The boy also reached there. He requested the permission of the mother to make her son, the king. The mother was not entirely ready to let go of her only son. The boy was also on his mother's side. Chanakya spent not only the entire evening but also the night in trying to make them understand.

The next morning was very bright. Chanakya brought the lad to his hermitage so that he could begin his education. All the disciples living in his hermitage were the harbingers of future glory.

The lad was given a new name called Chandrgupta Maurya and he is considered to be the founder of Maurya Empire. The surname Maurya was given to him in the memory and honour of his mother Mura.

Explanation: Tension and burden can be reduced by industry and intelligence. If the human processes are not strong and action oriented then much needs to be done but if it is strong and industrious, then a lot of time and effort can be saved.

Effect: If you elect the eminent one, you can be content, but if you elect an ordinary one, then always you will live in confusion.

Master of Administration

After achieving everything in a favourable manner, Chanakya dedicated himself to social service and in writing a book. But his spies ran the organization in a very organized manner and kept an eye on everything from there itself. In addition, he used to teach the administrators. He himself was a great administrator, yet spent time in collecting the framing rules and regulations and based on these, made stricter rules which had rules right from simple things such as weights and measures to the most complex and successful plans like attcaks and safety. Thus he made the king, the kingdom and the administration very strong.

Chanakya is revered as the world's foremost master of administration in the name of Kautilya even though there has been a long tradition of earlier kings and princes getting education in administration. His speciality was that his teaching was a complete cleansing of both inside and outside and treating unethical practices as sin.

Chanakya gathered all the practices followed till then and responded in the same kind. They were loudly derided. Before making a rule to be followed by the society, Chanakya used to follow it himself, test it out, only after that did he include it in the book-Kautilya Arthashastra. Using the same weapons and arms in a systematic manner, he established the Mauryan empire and extended it so much so that not only the neighbouring small kingdoms joined this empire, but also the kingdoms which were far away either joined voluntarily or were forced to accede to this empire. Neighbouring countries were also united and once again re-established India to its former glory and height.

There were the administrative methods and ideologies of Chanakya behind this, in addition to this was the training given by Chanakya to his disciples which they spread all round and elevated him as the teacher of administration. These administrative ideologies were not limited to just India but spread to the villages and got included and improvised in the panchayat and co-operative societies. It is a fact that after Tulasidas, the oft quoted personality is Chanakya. The students are specifically taught his ideologies. It is another story that in the last ten years, the lesson on Chanakya has been removed from all the text books. We are getting the profit of his thoughts in a different way as all the national and international college of management are teaching his ideologies as a subject and the day is not far away when the text books will once again include his teachings. Nobody could stop Chanakya from spreading is ideologies when there were no books, how can he be stopped now that there are innumerable books, when they are instilled in the hearts of people?

Chanakya's simple, yet lucid language is enough to keep him alive in people eternally. If one can simplify his complex Sanskrit sandhis, then chanakya will become the world greatest writer who has written the treatise in simple yet lucid language. No one has ever given such complex thoughts in such simple language. It is indeed a wonder that such deep and complex ideologies have been explained in a simple, clear manner.

Chanakya's Education

We do not have enough information about Chanakya's early education like we have of other sages, saints or teachers. The reason is that Indians do not give more importance for a man's life because body is mortal and importance is given to the good deeds done during his life time. It said that *Kirthihi yasya sa jeeviti* meaning the one who does good deed is the one who lives. The mortal body perishes but the fame lives eternally.

Regarding Chanakya's life one fact which is accepted widely is that he completed his education at Taxila and lived there as a teacher and soon rose to the position of a head teacher. While being in that position he had a thought of touring the country and left for it.

It was the tradition in Taxila that all the students had to be completely educated in literature and religion. Only after achieving mastery over these, would the students be taught other subjects. Combing these two resulted in the learning of literature and philosophy. This was the biggest university in the whole world. Students used to be educated in all basic subjects which are listed below.

The subjects taught in Taxila

Literature	Philosophy
Different languages	Grammar
History	Mathematics
Economics	Astrology
Geography	Universe – Past and Future
Science	Medical Science
Ayurveda	Surgery
Agricultural Science	Ancient Science
Archery	War Science

Only after learning all these subjects could a student choose another subject and the subjects that had a lot of demand were legal studies, surgery, planning a strategy, an argument and counter argument along with Upanishads and Puranas, courses were given in eighteen kinds of art like music, painting etc. Though there were no special courses like veterinary science, botony, venom science etc., Chanakya was knowledgeable in these too! Either the information available is incomplete or Chanakya must have mastered these from someone else.

Omniscient

As a lot of research used to be conducted on various subjects in the university, Chanakya could have gained the knowledge from there or learnt it from the duty conscious teachers living in Nalanda. Even though he learnt a lot later by himself, the major part of his learning was at Taxila itself.

These observation are mentioned here because the books on Chanakya prove his versatility that he used to comprehend each topic very deeply and his comprehension ability is so unique that it is proved beyond any doubt that not only was he intelligent knowing only about the present or wise knowing about the future, but also he was an intellectual who knew about past, present and future. Chanakya was an omniscient scholar.

Dependence on Modernity

Since that time kings like Ashoka have been ruling the country following the philosophies of political science. It has to be noticed that at a time when the philosophy of Chanakya has achieved fame and is followed everywhere, taught everywhere, how the modern administrators are going to govern the country and remove from men the fear and the dependence on machines, on electricity, on computers and safeguard everyone.

Till fifty years before, Indians were self confident. Villages were grouped into 22 to 42 quarters so that different families could unite and become self sufficient. Just like all other systems, this system also has undergone changes and somehow or the other machines have become part and parcel of life. The machine requires a lot many other things, which cannot be got from villages but which come out of factories. Now self sufficiency is no longer prevalent.

It is a known fact that machines can only perform those tasks for which they have been created- if raw material is given, they give out the finished goods. Machines can never become a human nor can it acquire power of doing a variety of work. The more security is given to those, the less secure the human life is becoming. Despite spending unlimited amount of money, man hasn't been able to eradicate even mosquitoes. Since machines manufacture quickly, we have a glut of unnecessary things and weapons. The worldwide problem of garbage disposal has reached such a level to keep even a small town clean, to dispose garbage, cleaning of drainage, no contactor is agreeable even after offering crores of rupees. This work has not been possible even though many machines are used.

The annual budgets of city corporations are only an eye wash. The people's minds are filled with garbage while trying to overcome the problem of garbage. Either the stench is being filled in the mind or is being generated by the mind. The garbage earlier could be converted into manure, the garbage of present day do not turn into manure and are eating away the fertility of earth.

This is a major challenge faced by the administrators. The major challenges are lying unsolved. In spite of doctors and medicines, ancient or modern implements, hospitals, most of the human beings except a few, are suffering from either physical or mental ailment.

It has to be seen as to which policy of Chanakya can be used in the present day. It is the system in the business administration that professions which deal with physical health and entertainment are not categorised as 'professions'. The players are being charged as unprofessional and have indeed turned so. Match fixing has become very common. When there is a talk of any profession, automatically there is a tyalk of gambling and speculation and a talk of income and expenditure. For example is there anyone on this earth today who is able to live in a healthy, safe, comfortable, happy and contented manner? Animals, birds, fish, trees, plants, medicines, roots and plants and healthy food have become scarce and synthetic packed food is the mode of the day. Water is contaminated, cities are polluted and so congested that there is no space for even the polluted air to flow. Half of the ozone layer has disappeared from the sky, multiplication of buildings, plastics, chemical manures, etc has led to the depletion of fertility of soil. How can human life be safe? If we have to question succinctly will there be life on earth?

Chanakya's Commentary

Chanakya's detailed commentary can be got from Kautilya's Arthashastra which are available in 15 cantos and 180 chapters. It has broadly been divided into 4 volumes. He has described each and every path, treaty, relation in such a detailed manner that one can develop and progress in the administrative affairs as well as in one self. He has also described in detail those things which will result in turmoil, result in murders, or safeguard oneself, family and wealth. There is description of severe punishment and method of punishment which doesn't even spare the heir apparent, the prince, son, friend or relative. The punishment depends on the crime committed and the punishment is more a corrective one rather than a cruel one.

Chanakya's political philosophy and rules which are given here in detail help us in becoming self developed, self controlled and self disciplined. If a man is disciplined then he can keep others also disciplined and make good use of them. The stipulated wealth will come only after stipulated time. And man can safeguard his wealth and family and inturn safeguard the society and the country.

The Enemy of an Enemy is a Friend

Chanakya's one principle was that the enemy of an enemy is a friend. But what happens from this? One has to instil complete confidence in him that he will receive unconditional support and it is possible. Only then will he agree to do anything or give anything. One such memorable and quotable incident is given below.

Dhananand, the king of Magadh was neither intelligent nor strong but was filled with lust and debauchery. His forefathers too had the same traits. They were tyrannical.

Some of his courtiers and majority of people were against the king but feared to openly rebel against him. No one had the guts to speak fearlessly. In his arrogance, Dhananand forgot his duty towards the safety of his subjects. He had also forgotten that the crown is given to him by people and it can also be snatched away by them. Chanakya had watched all these, had understood everything, but when people came to know of his vow and the talk of the ruin of Dhananand, hope blossomed in them that if he succeeds then there will be peace. This hope strengthened when Chanakya was able to create an army out of nothing and was annexing kingdoms all around. People started praising him in muted tones. They supported him but could not do it openly. This incident took place then.

It was a matter of co-incidence that the priests, businessmen and a few rich men of three different places- Gaya, Mithilanchal and Vaishali- came to meet Chanakya. The spies had already passed on this information to him. Chanakya created such a situation that the people from all the three places reached on the same day. Arrangements were made for their stay and the time for meeting was fixed.

Chanakya being aware of their arrival, was also aware of the purpose of their visit and their problems. Though his secret network was small, it was at work since many months. Wherever he used to go, he used to select a few men, speak to them individually and give them secret work. He was even aware of the complete details of his visitors. The fact that they arrived together made it evident that people from various areas were discontented with Dhananand and were keen on seeking Chanakya's help.

Chanakya decided to meet the people of Gaya first because it was closest to the capital city. The people were influential and had keen interest in the administration. Though Vaishali was also close, the people there were not affected by the administration and Mithilanchal was a bit far and Dhananand was not bothered about it.

Instead of calling them to his quarters, he himself went to place where they were staying. He welcomed everyone with folded hands. The leader of the group came forward and introduced himself as Abhay Shroff, from a family of gold merchants since generations. The names of others were not told but Chanakya was aware of each one of them.

Abhay Shroff narrated everybody's problems ans said thus. "We are suffering instead of living. Hence we are ready to do anything for security, progress and peace."

Chanakya replied, "This is not the right time for any kind of treaty. But I promise that when Chandragupta Maurya ascends the throne, then we shall have the greatest treaty with you. There will be innumerable benefits in your agriculture and business. You will benefit from the forests and rivers will help in better irrigation. People will be safe and satisfied."

Chanakya's explanation was believable. Chanakya added, "The meaning of administration is security and progress. That will be given to all. This is the truth and not just words of assurance. From tomorrow neither Magadh's soldiers nor officers will come to your place."

This was Chanakya's second announcement. The leader responded, "Based on this assurance, we shall manufacture arms and weapons for you and complete it on time. But how will this happen?"

"Last night four cruel officers of your area were killed. Both the roads leading to your area are secure now. We have the control over it and the Magadh army can't go from there. Your own people are planning to take the place of those officers."

Chanakya explained what a handful of his soldiers had done the previous night so that the strangers could form any treaty without seeking any conditions. Their faces brightened with admiration. Joy blossomed inside waiting to break out. The leader agreed. "You do the work very swiftly. Those four were not only cruel, but also tyrannical because they were close to the king."

Chanakya revealed a few more facts, "It is just not only I but everyone is firm on performing one's duty. The country cannot be safe if its people are not safe."

The leader said, "We have a few vehicles filled with wealth which we request you to accept as initial payment. Kindly permit us to leave now. We are eager to know the detailed information of the events."

They took leave of him. Chanakya met the representatives of the other two kingdoms. More or less he had the same kind of conversation with them too. Thus Chanakya did not face any dearth of wealth, implements or youth power. He collected them very comfortably and used them very specially.

It was Chanakya's good fortune that people were getting rebellious quietly. Thus the movements of Mauryan army used to reach Dhananand very late. Not just the common people but even the administrative officials were eager to desert Dhananand and join Chanakya. Chanakya was aware of the value of new places, dispersed hands and industrious people.

Explanation: If the workers feel, safety, security, happiness and freedom in their work place, it will be truly beneficial to the administration. There will be fourfold development in hard work and skill.

Effect: The progress of wealth, implements and workers will in all circumatances help in the progress of development.

3

Chanakya –
Accomplishment with Multifaceted Talent

Whoever knows something about Chanakya, has read something about Chanakya will undoubtedly vouch that he is a veritable storehouse of multifaceted talents and genius. It is useless to use any other word other than 'formidable' for him. Whoever knows something about him cannot remain uninfluenced by his ideals.

Safeguarding Duty

The most commonly used meaning of duty is in the context of business. The word duty is usually correlated with either physical or moral work, like the duty of fire is to burn, it won't forego its duty. If it is fire, it has to burn. Duty comes foremost when we speak of four powers, wealth only later. Western philosophers have equated wealth with only money. But that which brings us virtue is also wealth. It does not just teach us about proper administration or following of rules or getting others to follow the rules but it teaches us self control and self discipline which will help us in safeguarding both our body and our soul but also in following the law of nature.

Safety of Women in Pataliputra

The brilliant and enthusiastic master and his disciples of Taxila reached Pataliputra, known as the most beautiful capital of Magadh Empire. Chanakya went to the market place to discover more about the city. It was a very neat city with beautiful buildings and decorated shops.

When he was immersed in admiration of the city's architect's town planning, he heard a feminine voice screaming for help. He turned towards the direction of that voice. A woman was being dragged against her will by two strong men. She was resisting with all her might, all the while crying for help. Chanakya was surprised to see no one go forward to help that poor woman. He walked quickly towards them and asked, "What is your problem? Why are you dragging her like a goat towards the slaughter house? Has she cheated you or looted you?"

One of the retorted, "This is not your responsibility. Continue to go where you were initially headed. Allow us to do our work."

"And your work is to drag a shivering and screaming woman. Are you sure that you have been appointed for this immoral and antisocial work?" Chanakya displayed the courage of a teacher.

The same man repeated, "Go away! Don't waste our time and don't teach us any morals."

"You require education as well as lashings. It is completely immoral to drag a woman who is resisting. Is she related to you? Is she your wife? Has she taken a loan from you? Are you the court officials?" Chanakya was firm in wanting to know the truth.

The man lost his temper. "Go away or you will be killed."

Chanakya displayed deeper anger. "For the second time I tell you, release the woman or else you will be imprisoned."

Till then the passers by had never interfered whenever they saw women being dragged like this. Nobody used to oppose such acts. But it was different that day. Some people stood there watching the exchange and paying attention to the words like 'morality', 'anti social' etc which they had not heard before. They had forgotten these words.

Brandishing a stick/club smeared with oil, the man threatened. "Go away or else you'll get thrashed!"

Chanakya retorted in an even more severe tone, "You must not have learnt how to use the club/stick properly but I teach the young and strong students the art of using the clubs/sticks. The moment you lift the club/stick for using, you'll find that your head would have split into two."

Saying this, Chanakya quickly wrapped the books he had in his hand with his shawl and tied the shawl around his waist and stood ready to fight. He assumed the posture of an attacking mode pushing his right leg forward.

The moment those men saw his posture, they realised that grabbing the club/stick from them and using it on them will be a child's play for him. They looked at each other and quickly released the woman. They didn't want to be thrashed in the market. Amorous men have not much of physical strength and absolutely no mental strength. They cannot face a moral man fearlessly.

Explanation: The escapist attitude in people is very ruinous. All everyone thinks of is escaping from danger or harm. We must not turn a blind eye when a man or a woman is in danger. Never think of escaping to save yourself. Face the danger courageously and confidently. Your fearless facing of danger will reduce its dreadful impact. Then it will be very easy to overpower it.

Effect: Trembling limbs denote weakness whereas steady and firm tread surprisingly weakens the enemy.

Multifaceted Personality

Chanakya's personality is endowed with eight to ten facets having knowledge which is varied, deep, wide and high, has dedication making his personality an admirable one. It is usually felt and said that a knowledgeable man cannot be a good administrator. He will spend his time in self improvement of knowledge, accumulation and dispersal of knowledge. It that is true, then Chanakya is one digression to that thought. All his life, he went on giving ideas on practical principles and converting principles into practice.

It is also co-incidental that Chanakya has many titles. It won't be surprising if he has many more than he already does. Prolific writer, poet, eminent administrator, venerable teacher, knowledgeable saint, deep patriot, patriotic countryman, truthful speaker, successful fulfiller of vows, moral thinker, architect of a kingdom, king maker, fearless, sober, valiant, patient, an epitome of good behaviour, etc., etc. and completely successful in every aspect and sphere. With all these virtues, Chanakya doesn't remain a mere personality. He has become a symbol, a thought, an ascertainment, a visionary with the collection of various visions.

Chanakya has to be studied with complete faith and interest and his teachings have to be followed staunchly, minutely, fearlessly so that there can be no doubt in the achievement and success and there is internal as well as external progress with the changed thought process and ideas which can only result in our progress and not in regress.

If anyone needs the proof of this, he should read the 19th chapter – *Nishanth Praneedhihi* and the 20th chapter – *Aatma Rakshitam* from the 15th canto of the forst volume of Kautilya Arthashastra. What should be the ordinary and extraordinary measures to be deployed for safeguarding the king's palace. How many schemes should be made for it. There should be armed soldiers both outside and inside. The ways of identifying dangerous people is so clearly described. What a fantastic way of warning! After a detailed explanation of all these, Chanakya has further said just as a king is ready to attack others, he should be ready to face any attack anytime from his enemies.

Yatha cha yaga purushaihi anya raja apratishtati
Tatha yayam anya badhebhyo rakshed aatmaanam aatmavaan.

It is indeed a wonder that an ordinary, feeble man can keep in his tiny brain all these thoughts, lessons, secrets, rewards, punishments, treaties, dedications so well! Whether an ordinary man or an erudite scholar, if he sees Chanakya, reads Chanakya and understands Chanakya, he becomes illuminated by it.

Good Health First

As Chanakya used to give greatest importance to physical well being of people, the one thing that worried him most, was the ill health of the people of all castes, sects in Pataliputra. Nothing substantial can be achieved if one is unwell. And if there is no life then there is no meaning of father-mother, wife-children, kith-kin. These either burn or inter us in the graveyard.

Anarchy was rampant in Magadh then. No one was ready to respect and follow social, religious or moral values. Tyranny, malpractices and corruption were rife. Peace was totally absent from the city.

Lust was at its zenith. The lustful behaviour of the king had also spread amongst his subjects. At such time the health of the people is affected. As the feeling of lust was rampant, there were many cases of venereal diseases.

Chanakya had one such experience in an area which had very rich and well to do residents. He saw a youth twisting and writhing in pain near the entrance arch. It was clear that the youth was sick but there wasn't anybody near him. Chanakya's attention was drawn towards the youth due to his groaning. Chanakya went towards the youth to know the extent of the pain wondering at the reason for his suffering. He had an inkling of it but wasn't very sure. Going towards the man, he asked kindly, "What has happened to you? Why are you writhing in pain? Why don't you take some medicine?"

The youth looked at Chanakya and turned his face away but the pain in his body cannot just reduce or vanish just because he turned his face away. Chanakya spoke in a soothing and sympathetic manner which also sounded supportive and assuring. "Don't worry! Speak clearly! I can help you!"

In a trembling voice the youth replied, "There is no cure for this. I suffer from venereal disease. I'm facing the consequences of my arrogance." The man spoke with great difficulty, writhing with pain.

Chanakya had specialised in Ayurveda too. He identified the man's ailment the moment he saw him, but felt that it would be improper to mention it aloud. He knew the reason for this too- excessive, unprotected sexual relations with many women and prostitutes. Now that the disease was revealed, remedy had to be done.

"If nature has given diseases, it also has given us cure. It is our fault that we don't know, don't recognise or don't use it. The punishment meted out for immorality has to be borne no doubt. And the bitterness of Chiraitha is milder than the bitterness of the pain. Boil Chiraitha in the water thrice a day and drink it. It cleanses your polluted blood. Wash your private parts with water many times a day. It will make it better and with the stipulated treatment, you will regain your health within a month. Eat food with khadiraisht to remove the disease you're your body and to safeguard yourself from the recurrence of the disease. Every year eat khadirarisht for one month continuously."

The man was sceptical. "Is it possible?"

Chanakya replied confidently, "Surely, believe me"

Chanakya then continued on his way thinking about this incident.

Explanation: Self control and balance are the requisite weapons for success in life. Nothing can be achieved unless we have control over self, circumstances, wealth, commodities and workers. A man can grow, become wealthy and lead a peaceful life if he is able to have self control right from his food habits to work and work place, right from his speech to action.

Effect: There is very slight difference between progress and destruction. Steady and dedicated steps leads to progress and unsteady and tottering steps lead to destruction.

Reformation and Progress of a Society

Chanakya immersed himself in bringing about a reformation in the society the moment he came to Pataliputra. This work did not allow him even a moment of idleness or rest. This reformation work continued during the times of strife as well as after victory. He started these reforms in a specific manner and in small units. There were so many such small units that wor continued smoothly even in the areas where there were no workers. Only knowledgeable and moral were given prominent posts and whose instructions were followed implicitly. Thus the immorality in the society was removed. Moral destruction was stopped and rather than taking medicines, good thoughts, good food and healthy life style were inculcated in people so that they lead a healthy life.

This work gained momentum after the establishment of Mauryan Empire. People were advised monogamy and to have relation ship with only their spouse. The people who had suffered for venereal diseases welcomed this move gratefully. People wouldn't have followed the sanctity of marriage if there weren't so many diseases.

This is one of the reasons for Chanakya to discuss monogamy in Kautilya's Arthashastra. It is appropriate to discuss it here.

Accepted ways of Marriage

1. **Brahma Vivaah :** *Kanya daanam, Kanya mangalam Krutya Brahmo vivaha.* When a courteous, healthy, well mannered, intelligent, hard working and ideal groom is given a bride through kanya daana [gifting of the girl], then it is called Brahma vivaah [marriage]. No prior conditions are set but if the bride's father wants, he can give gifts befitting his status and desire.

2. **Daivya Vivaah:** *Anthah veda amruthabeeje daanad daivyaha.* When a father selects a knowledgeable saint and gifts his daughter to him in marriage along with wealth and ornaments, then it is called daivya vivaah. It coincidentally takes place during another yagna.

3. **Aarsh Vivaah:** *Gomithunaad naad aartshah.* If a marriage takes place in accordance with custom and tradition but without gifting any material wealth or goods, then it is called aarsh viivaah.

4. **Prajapatya Vivaah:** *Saha dharmacharya prajapatya.* When a groom seeks the hand of a marriageable girl and weds her promising that both will lead a moral life. Such a marriage is called prajapatya vivaah.

5. **Aasur Vivaah:** *Shulka-daanaad aasuraha.* When the groom's parents and relatives are gifted with a lot of wealth during the wedding, it is called aasur vivaah.

6. **Gandharva Vivaah:** *Mithah samvaayaad gandharvaha.* When the girl and the boy meet each other, like each other and marry secretly in a temple or some other place by exchanging garlands, it is called gandharva vivaah.

7. **Rakshas Vivaah**: *Prasayaad aanaad rakshasaha*. If the girl is forcibly taken away after beating up her relatives and married off to the boy, it is called rakshas vivaah. There will be a dearth of compassion here.

8. **Paishach Vivaah**: *Supta aadanaad paisachaha*. If a physical relationship is forced on a girl who is sleeping or mentally unwell or unconscious, such a marriage is called paisach vivaah. It is thus named as such a behaviour is usually found only in demons.[paishach].

No one is getting any enlightenment even despite blind run under the name of modernity, man has abandoned the institution of marriage and has become a sex maniac. He has become immune to morality and has fallen to such a level of spreading homosexuality in all which will only result in utter destruction. People are not only suffering from venereal diseases but also from a terrible disease called AIDS. Now only aasura and paishach marriages are in vogue. As a result wives are being burnt alive, murdered, divorced and men want to be out of this relationship some way or the other. In spite of all these nobody is getting enlightened, despite the opening of hospitals for venereal diseases, continuous increase of handicapped people and increase of mental hospitals. It is difficult to even think how man can get back on track after falling into the pit of disgrace. It is an utter waste to live without good health.

4

Chanakya's Firmness

Conscious Mind and Deep Insight

With concentration and deep insight, the statesman Chanakya saw the nature, society and life. He had such an innate ability that he could find similarity in things that were completely unalike to the normal eye and find a commonality to it. He used to take decisions intelligently and usefully. With this the inner eyes of the others also opened and they were able to get proper comprehension of policies and business. With such a talent people will be able to see a different route and comprehend new resources. To understand this thought there needs a discussion on a lifesaving method from a seemingly useless idea.

Once, the Mauryan army was surrounded and they had to hide in a cave. The entire Mauryan army was hungry as there was no food. They couldn't go out of the cave as the cave was surrounded by the army of Magadh.

One day Chanakya saw an ant carrying a grain of rice, though there was no way grains could be available there. He saw that the grain was cooked. He took it and examined. It was freshly cooked and was still warm. Chanakya asked the soldiers to search all around.

The news reached very soon that the army of Magadh were stationed behind the cave too and were preparing food there for the army to eat. The Magadh army went there in batches, ate food and went back to their places. Most of them were having their food then. He also got a vital piece of information that the soldiers would not be ready for an attack while eating because all the weapons would be piled up in two or three places.

Chanakya divided his army into three units and ordered one unit to attack the enemies. The Magadh soldiers saw the Mauryan soldiers and as they were aware of their valour, they ran away to safe guard themselves. Instead of running towards their weapons, they ran away to save themselves. There was no need for any battle at all, they left behind horses, chariots and weapons in their flight. Mauryan army was able to get the much needed weapons and food and they were safe too.

Explanation: If we are very conscious of each and everything in our surrounding we will develop an indescribable insight. One has to be very attentive in order to develop this matchless ability, should not allow mind to wander but must centralize it in one place and practise it. Even then it takes time to acquire this quality. Such a person pays attention to each and everything, doesn't neglect anything thinking it is worthless. As a result he never gets duped. This method is called as the flow of insight in psychology.

Effect: Whatever happens, cannot be termed as worthless. It has some meaning or worth to it. This is so because every incident has a beginning and a reason behind it.

Weakening the Foe

One way of weakening the enemy force is to plant our people in the enemy's organization using subterfuge and an even easier way is to entice people from the enemy's side to our side. This system has been in vogue since ages and is very rampant today. Right from army to education, from profession to administration, people are bribing the government officials or workers in every department either by paying or by receiving money. Each tries to weaken the other. This selfishness will destroy people, society and Chanakya was very brilliant in doing this.

Once Chanakya met Maatang, a minister at the court of Magadh on a bridge. The meeting seemed as if they met by chance. But it was a very cleverly orchestrated one. It was afternoon and the traffic was sparse on the bridge. There weren't people nearby.

Maatang was a very experienced and powerful minister but he was always disregarded because he wasn't a flatterer. Chanakya was very proficient in measuring up such people and enticing them to his side. This meeting was also a part of it. There was a great possibility of getting a lot of help from Maatang which was sure to contain a lot of information. Chanakya wanted to divide Dhananand's forces and take a large part of his forces thereby weakening him.

Chanakya: Salutations to the powerful one!

Maatang: Salutations Master! The slighted don't have strength.

Chanakya: Each thought of yours is as worthy as gems

Maatang: I have collected these gems but haven't got any respect.

Chanakya: Honour is the brightest glittering gem in a man's necklace. My hands are impatiently waiting to garland this glittering gem on a worthy person.

Maatang: One who has fallen on dirt cannot be called worthy.

Chanakya: Revolutionaries adorn their forehead with the dirt of their motherland. The true mother of all likes this a lot

Maatang: Mother will receive my head the moment she wants.

Chanakya: But mother will safeguard her precious sons in her lap.

Maatang: I shall wait for the sunrise.

Chanakya: Such sons should not get lost in sunset.

Maatang: You are right master! Salutations!

Chanakya: Salutations to a patriot!

Explanation: Success depends on the idea or plan of action. This strength is greatly found in sensitive, patriotic and spiritual people. They do not have ideas that fulfil only physical desires. When it comes to a do or die situation, one doesn't bother with hunger, but will be worried about the welfare of self, others and the safety of the country.

Effect: People aspiring for success, should not omit even one plan, must strive sincerely because failure could also mean that we have not worked sincerely.

Knowledge Tested through Experience

⇨ City dwellers cannot have an identity without rural system, the work of villagers and their production. The path of development begins only from the villages.

⇨ A balanced planning of work brings balance in life. When only 1/8th part of produce is given to the producer, can't we understand the value given to the producer? When there is no fixed labour today, labourers are employed depending on demand and supply. Hence there in an increase in strikes or there is increase in disenchantment. As labour is equated with money, this inflation effect is shown on goods too.

⇨ There are workers today who are paid from two thousand rupees to two crore rupees every month.

⇨ Workers have to be appointed according to the work. They should have complete knowledge of their work and responsibilities.

⇨ Workers should be given correct information at the right time. They should not be waiting for information. The biggest reason for the defeat of Indians in 1962 Indo-China war was because the Indian army was waiting for the declaration of war.

⇨ One should have the right and clear vision to wrestle down the enemies and opponents.

⇨ Internal communication should be so complete and clear that no one can point fingers at any of its contents.

⇨ A person who is bent on forming a new union, should not have any confusion. He should be fully aware of the work and be completely trained before starting work. He should also provide the arrangement and have it under control so that he can scale heights and retain his place there.

⇨ Workers should be so skilful and hard working that the administrators themselves should feel that they are not paid their worth. But the workers should not demand for more.

- Taxes have to be paid on time so that there are no problems to be faced.
- Working on different things at the same time should be avoided.
- The administrator or the manager should be learning new things always.
- One can go to a different organisation if one has gained knowledge in one's field. But changing organizations for mere monetary gains is not recommended.
- In case a worker dies while on duty, the organization should take care of his family.
- Apt opportunities should be identified and grabbed.
- Make wealth so that there is no burden. Be a saviour so that there is no fear.
- Never besmirch a pure heart.
- To be secretive and to safeguard that secret is a weapon for success.
- Never think of harming anyone, keep doubling the profits.
- Build a strong pillar not a weak beam.
- Keep yourself busy so that you can keep others busy.

Directions for work and Attack

"In small groups, march forward among the people in the manner of a soldier and not like a puffed up arrogant one. Don't fight like as if in a battle field. Attack when the enemy is not prepared. Attack from five directions so that the opponent gets confused . One unit should wait patiently and replace the unit which gets tired.

Wherever one is, one should have control of one's senses. Listen to all the sounds and watch every movement carefully and read everyone's face clearly. Never lose concentration and safeguard the power of comprehension. Retaliate violently when necessary but bide the ideas and surprises. Attack the opponents when they have no time to even retaliate.

Stay close to central places but be conscious of other places apart from the central ones. Direct your anger on your weapons while attacking and wound deeply and heavily. Channelize it on your feet when you have to run, but never let it out of your head.

Destroy the king and opponents, but safeguard the public. Destroy the organizations and palaces but never trample on the plants. Destroy the forts but not the markets."

This is how Chanakya used to advise his trained and enthusiastic army, workers in armed forces. This exercise was very effective. He learnt his lessons from his initial failure received from the army of Magadh empire. Initially he tried attacking the central capital so that the palace could be besieged. But the palace was heavily guarded.

Comprehending that such an attack is useless and dangerous, he changed his planning and accordingly gave instructions to his people.

Explanation: An enlightened mind keeps all senses in vigilance. It has to be clear as to who has to do it, who has to do it first, who later and how to do it. One can only find one's way out of the dense, dark worldly jungle through caution.

Effect: Safety of life is very important in every aspect because it is necessary to have a busy life in order to have an existence.

Acquisition of Knowledge from the Elders

Though Chanakya tried his level best to keep calm, to keep his anger and feelings under control, he would surprisingly find himself in one of the either extremes. He was not able to balance his emotions. On one hand he was in search of achieving his equilibrium and on the other he brought about a balance even in that extreme. He never tottered or fell. This was possible because he always kept his external as well as internal eyes wide open and this helped him acquire an unnatural vision because if a person loses his steadiness while at an extreme end, his destruction is imminent.

The advantage of keeping the eyes open was that the path was very clearly seen. There was even a time when Chanakya faced defeat from all directions. He used to attack, but never succeeded. This incident belongs to those days.

Following the instructions of Chanakya, the Mauryan army under the stewardship of Chandrgupts Maurya attacked Magadh from three directions but had to retreat unsuccessfully from all the three directions. They were not in the position of undergoing great loss, but whatever loss they faced was itself back breaking. Chanakya was worried. He was unable to understand where the fault lay. He was perplexed and left for his regular nightly rounds with restless mind.

There were a lot of advantages in these nightly rounds. It gave him time to ponder on things away from the comfort of his home, gain information on the external affairs, get news from the spies employed specially by him, understand people's problems, their worries. He used to give instant orders when required. Hence he never used to follow a routine route.

One night he was passing through a villagre when he saw light glowing in a hut. Why was someone awake at this hour? He went to investigate. The canvas of the hut was in tatters. Hence it was easy to see what was happening inside. He looked in as he wanted to know wht was happening inside.

He saw an old woman and a young man inside. It was evident from their conversation that they were mother and son and that the woman was a widow. She was able to get some wheat late in the evening. Therefore there was delay in the preparation of dinner. She powdered the wheat and made rotis and gravy and gave it to her son. The son started breaking the roti from the middle, but the steam from inside escaped and he pulled back his hand in haste. The lady berated him in anger. "Have you also become like Chanakya that you are tearing the rotis from middle? Food should always be eaten from the edges and not from the centre."

Chanakya was stunned when he heard this. What a simple solution for his complex problem! And that too from an old village woman! This was blessing indeed! He stood there for a long time lost in thought and returned to his house taking sure steps.

It is unnecessary to even mention that from then on Chanakya started his attack from the periphery of the kingdom. He delayed the attack on the capital. Though the victories seemed small and insignificant, they raised the morale of the Mauryan army. This paved way for the final victory.

The Final Assault

A worldly wise man will not face any scarcity of processes or come across troubles due to lack of processes. He will have the ability of getting the work completed with his limited means. He would use his limited means in such a manner that work gets completed and makes the organization he has created more powerful.

One has to view the method used by Chanakya in destroying the race of Nanda in this manner. Chanakya was aware that he couldn't overpower the strong army of Dhananand. Whatever he wanted to do, he had to do with his small ary and limited weapons. He could not bear any loss of his army because he would then have no army, nor could he bear any loss of Dhananand's army because he wanted to get the work done in future by them. He could also not bear the destruction of the subjects because then there would be no meaning in changing the rule of the country. He would not only lose the people and their wealth but also lose their belief.

His success depended on Dhananand's army becoming defunct. Chanakya planned a final attack on Dhananand keeping all these things in his mind. How did this happen? Its imperative for us to know.

It is evident that Chanakya planned his final assault on Dhananand right from the night he took his vow. He planned an attack which would be safe and successful. He collected information, processed it and took each step based on it. He placed his men or spies in specific places according to his plans. Initially he attacked the capital but changed his plans and began attacking those places which couldn't be easily reached by the Magadh forces. He gained easy victories in those and the Magadh army could not retaliate even if it wanted to. The reason was that the news reached them in a delayed manner and they were not quick in retaliating the sharp attacks of the enemy.

Chanakya was not satisfied with his victory over the border areas. He had taken a vow of complete annihilation of Nandas. *Poorna vinaasham Vadaami*.

Chanakya had planted his spies in pataliputra and in Dhananand's palace. He not only used the four forms or techniques – sama, bheda, daana and danda, but added three more of his own and used them. He did this to make the palace, people living in palaces, citizens useless before the final assault.

Chanakya went on methodically separating from Dhananand all those people who had been hurt by the king at some time or the other and who were still smarting from that hurt. Dhananand did not have even an inkling of what was happening in his palace and capital. Whenever necessity arose, he sent a message or himself went. Thus Chanakya appointed many people to do work for him, the majority of them privy to the internal affairs of the administration. He not only brought the soldiers to his side, but also along with the officers, ministers, merchants he also brought the prostitutes and their people to his side.

The reason for bringing the prostitutes to his side was because the soldiers and the civilians used to regularly visit these women. During the final assault, these women laced the alcohol with poison and gave to Magadh making Chanakya's work easy. All these activities were hidden behind the veil of secrecy and there wasn't anyone to inform these acts.

His spies went on methodically demolishing the strong pillars one by one that Nanda's race collapsed like a pack of cards in the final assault. Everything took place in a systematic manner.

After all arrangements were made, Chanakya and Chandragupta reached Pataliputra one fine day with their entire force. They spread in such a way that the important people were captured and important places besieged. The people implicitly obeyed all the orders.

The ready Mauryan army attacked Pataliputra after midnight. They entered the palace, even before the Magadh army could react or the inhabitants could get some information. Many of the officers were caught in the state of stupor or sleep. Dhananand was caught while he was making merry with a bevy of women. He was captured in a near nude state. Within a few hours all the royals were captured without much bloodshed. Some were killed then and there and the rest after getting necessary information from them. Thus the race of Nanda was completely annihilated. By the dawn of the next day, people could find a lot of changes. Chanakya bathed, completed his worship and in a festive atmosphere reknotted his lock of hair. He did this at the same spot where he had taken his vow. The final assault was completely successful and the seemingly impossible vow of Chanakya was fulfilled.

The sun shone brightly and happily that day.

Explanation: The joy that we get, when we succeed in our secret work whether it is small or huge, is indescribable. A successful man will enjoy such successful moments repeatedly. They keep him focussed and dedicated and also inspire him to work with renewed effort. Let us work hard consciously, enthusiastically and with concentration so that we achieve success each time and enjoy the pleasure, joy and happiness of success. Let success be a cause for our living.

Effect: The greatness lies in complete achievement of work rather than a part achievement. There is no doubt about this. If an effort is made with complete patience and dedication, the result becomes even more precious because every achievement is after all the fruit of an effort.

Niti and Kautilya's Arthashastra

Kautilya's Arthashastra is not based on the subject 'economics' which is taught in schools and universities. The treatise does not deal with the theory of economics or characteristics of a country, of place or race. It is not about accumulation or dispersal of wealth. It is not like any western book dealing with theories or businesses.

Kautilya's Arthashastra ia both extensive and widespread in structure, in context and in the profound publication of the content. The most significant point is that it acts as a guideline for good administration, it decides on the policies of politics and political science and frames rules and law. It contains topics right from weights and measurements to discussions on turmoils, punishments, treaties etc. It is not an euphonic combination of grammar but a union of politics.

It is two sided. On one side it explains the ethics of administration and on the other explains very clearly the rights and duties of the ruler and his subjects. There is discussion on various modes of income, discussion on safety, assessment of tax, collection of taxes in this book.

Chanakya explains the meaning of economics in the last two or three verses of the book. Manushyanam vruthihi Arthaha. The process of man's life is called 'wealth'. *Manushyavati bhoomihi ithi arthaha*. The earth which is made productive by man is called 'wealth'. It is even presumed that the English word 'earth' is also taken from this though there is no proof anywhere in English lexicon to substantiate it. *Tasya pruthvyaha laabha paalana upaayana shastram arthashastram.*

The science that explains the usefulness of earth and the ways and means of safeguarding it, is called Economics. This science is given a vast scope in India. It also gives moral education. *Dharma artha virodhenakaam sevet na nih sukhah syaat.* One should follow the rules of righteousness and wealth and anyone going against it will not achieve any comfort.

Three Meanings of Wealth

1. Expressible, Predictable
2. Goal, Metaphor
3. Irony

The word 'wealth' [arth] is punned a lot in Sanskrit.

↪ If we have to request someone in a polite manner – ***Tvami mam artha arthayati***

↪ When we try to get something – ***Priya prabruti nimittam abhyarthaye***

↪ Meaning, intention, desire – ***gnana athognaana sambandham stotrum srotaha***

↪ Cause, things which are known through shape, essence, odour, touch and voice –***Indriyabhyaha parahye artha-arthebyah cha param manah.***

↪ Business, work, proceedings, proposal, solution – ***Artho ayam athantar bhavya eva***

↪ Money, wealth, earned wealth, one strength out of four – ***Apya artha-kaaman tasyaastaam dharmeva manishinaha***

↪ Usage, virtuous action, profit and bonus – ***Tatha hi sarve tasya aasan pararthe phalaagunaaha.***

Arthagam – any kind of earning is called as income and it brings joy. ***Arthoparjan-*** It is necessary to earn wealth through good deeds. Through that we will acquire artha gowravam [economic respect] and our prestige increases. ***Artha tatvam*** – wealth is the truth and essence. One is ***Artha dooshanam*** if one is a spend thrift and misuses the wealth. Some people search for ***Arth vikalp***. They realise that the most distinct alternative of wealth is internal dedication, perfection in work and proficiency in work because only from them we get ***Arthotpati, arthoparjan, arthosanchay and arth raksha***.

Chanakya has given almost 32 meanings to the word 'wealth' [arth] and used them in appropriate places while writing Arthashastra. It is a joy to read and comprehend all that. He has also given us 32 ways and short cuts for accumulation and safeguarding of wealth.

When 'wealth' is accepted as one of the sources of power of mankind, we cannot understand it in limited sense. Mere accumulation of money does not mean wealth. If it is used profitably, spent usefully and the joy and prestige is received by self and others,then it will be called wealth. Chanakya make it clear that while wealth has to be earned and enjoyed, it cannot be done through illegal and immoral ways.

Dharmam artham cha kaamam cha pravartayati paati cha.
Argham anartham vidweshan idam shastram idam nihanti cha.

Wealth should have three qualities through which it has to be earned. It should be '*Aanandadayakam*', '*Dharma Dhaara Kam*', and '*Moksha Kaarakam*'. What is the use of wealth if it can't give joy? If one cannot safeguard righteousness then what is the use of wealth? If it is not a means of salvation and if it hinders salvation then what is the use of wealth? If the wealth is used only for food, clothing, shelter and luxury, it is an expenditure and is of no use at all.

Infliction of Arthshastra

Although this immortal classic gained fame much later, it had got its form, shape etc much before because such a systematic work cannot be done just like that.

Co-incidentally Chanakya, the systematic and enterprising teacher got all the gratuity very naturally as he kept everyone's thoughts awake and continuously flowing. There were so many kingdoms and territories then but he used to identify their weakness very clearly while working with them. He thought of various ways of removing them too. It is difficult to know when his book was published and how its numbers increased but India is a country having a rich tradition of literary works with sharpness of knowledge and memory. Therefore one cannot deny that changes would have been incorporated from time to time.

This book clearly describes the destruction, reconstruction and long lasting ways for success. Therefore it is clear that the vow that he took in the court of Nanda would have made him vigilant which helped him in weeding out Nanda's weaknesses and overseeing that weakness did not trouble the newly established kingdom. That is why this work is immortal. Whether people are aware or not, whether they agree or not, immortal works are very rare and that which is indeed immortal will be due to its author's long term effort and dedication.

That is why he announced that the king who strives for the welfare of his subjects and all living things – *Sarvabhuta hite raha*, one who administers his kingdom justly and nobly, keeps his attention on education, will be able to reign for a very long time.

Vidya vineeto raja hi prajaanam vinaye rataha
anyanam pruthivim bhunkvathe sarvabhut hite rataha.

One who has gained control over six enemies called lust, anger, greed, dignity, arrogance and jealousy can gain victory of any kingdom.

The king requires many supportive hands. He cannot do anything alone just as a cart cannot run on one wheel. – *Sahaya asaadhyam chakram ekam na vaitate*. Hence it is necessary to employ different types of people in the royal courts or organizations.

Arthashastra formulated punishments after dividing the crimes as social and criminal and gave instructions for good administration. While accepting that the severity of punishment should depend on the severity of crime, Chanakya was firm that every crime deserved punishment. No one pays any heed to that king who doesn't punish when needed or punishes unfairly. The one who gives punishment only is revered.

Teekshana dando hi bhutaanam udejaniya
Mrudu dandaha paribhuyate, yathartha dandaha poojyaha.

If we look at the complete work of Kautilya Arthashastra, we find that there more than 6,000 words, 380 verses which are divided into three volumes and 15 chapters which in turn have 150 sections and 180 topics. There are a lot of other information apart from the given ones.

Work and accomplishment of work	*Advice and acting upon advice*
1. Political Practice	1. Work, Organization, organizer
2. Politics	2. Virtue of the Period, Public Policy
3. Courage, Enterprise, Action	3. Treaty
4. Practice	4. Wealth and Work
5. Source of Income	5. Punishment
6. Crime	6. Character
7. Permeation of Work	7. Excitement, Decision, Completion of Work
8. Morality, Worship of Virtue	8. Kinsmen.

Important Foundations

Chanakya instituted so many things but it isn't useful or necessary to put them all in one place. They have to be understood in various contexts. But there are some which require special and separate mention. They are given below.

↪ An organization work can begin only after one manages himself properly.

↪ Organization cannot be separated from the administrator.

↪ The meaning of self control is – along with the senses of sight[eyes], hearing [ear], smell [nose], speech [lips] and feel [skin], one should also control lust, anger, arrogance, ignorance, greed and gluttony.

↪ Humility is the core of self control- *Indrasya mulam vinayam*

↪ Through morality, discipline and humility one can control oneself.

↪ *Viroopa sevanam vignaanam*- one can gain knowledge through service to the elderly.

↪ Science, art, knowledge of human behaviour together forms 'wisdom'.

↪ Knowledge of literature, philosophy, spirituality is acquisition of knowledge- *Vignanena aatmanam sampaadayet.*

One should strengthen oneself by consolidating worldly knowledge. One should use related speech in a restrained language while conducting daily business as this will help in the smooth completion of work undertaken.

- ➥ ***Sampadita –Aatma jeetatma bhavati-***He who acquires knowledge wins over himself. He then becomes capable of doing any work because he has gained equilibrium in thought, word and action. He will not consider his welfare more important than the welfare of the organization. He will not take any decision based on external influences and will not let go of his duty towards society for the sake of his organization.

- ➥ ***Jeetalma sarvartha sanyujyate-*** One who has self control will stay away from all vices and will be endowed with virtues.

- ➥ ***Sarvarteh*** – He will have everything: wealth, workers, implements, plans and will be able to accomplish all his responsibilities successfully.

6

Chanakya's Commentary on Women

Chanakya's commentary on women requires a separate mention as he has given a lot of commentary supporting women as well as deriding them. He has written very beautifully on womanhood and all that he has written is absolutely true. The verses he has written on womanhood is innumerable.

Woman – An Oxymoron

Woman is an oxymoron. A woman who loses her strength quite soon, regains it by drinking milk. In order to maintain balance of nature sometimes massive and minute are created topsy- turvy. One can find extreme and opposite characters in the same place. One finds a lot of opposing work when it comes to describing woman hood.

⤏ Woman is source of strength, yet weak, woman is faith, trust, ambrosia but having an aversion to it. An overdose of ambrosia makes it venomous and when she takes revenge, she is called cobra both as a praise and as a curse.

Woman you are a faith on the silver path of trust
Flow as a source of ambrosia in the life's barren planes.

And also

Life of a woman alas is your story
Milk in your veil and tears in your eyes.

Woman is trust, belief and source of ambrosia. She is helpless yet strong. Her tears are heart wrenching while her smiles are uplifting. She changes herself and becomes ordinary, she changes others and they become extraordinary.

Woman is different and wonderful. 'Saw your unique creation and kept it in my heart.' But Chanakya never kept his thoughts suppressed in himself. He had the strength of speech, strength of explanation, which he used for explaining everything.

Woman – A Balance

Woman is Sita, Radha, Rukmini, Lalitha. Woman is Parvati, Durga, Kali, Savitri, Savita. She is Kausalya, Urmila. She is Gayatri, Saraswathi, Lakshmi.

While on one hand she is an Apsara, Menaka, Rambha, she is both Damayanti and Mandodari, she is Shaivya, Shabari, Ahalya and Anasuya and on the other hand she is Kaikeyi and Manthara. If she is Kunti, Panchali, Gandhari, she is also a prostitute and also the saintly Gargi and Maitreyi. She is both finite and infinite. She is love and repose – *Sa bhasya yatra nivruthi.* She is thirst as well as the satiation – *Truptihi sadhyaha shaktihara nari sadhyaka shakti karam payam.* A woman quickly destroys the mighty and by drinking her milk, one gets instantaneous strength.

A woman is a toy in man's hands and yet makes the man dance like a puppet in her hands. The role of a woman is very dominant in all the schemes made by man and the woman herself makes many a schemes. Man holds the strings in which women are puppets, women are the centres and men the boundaries. Man is a provider, supporter, woman runs the family and man is dependent on her. Woman is charitable, whereas, man rarely praises and accepts charity grudgingly. Man is strong while woman is weak. But she is a source of strength and weak man is always suppliant. These are contradictory, yet true thoughts. Woman can never be perceived in one particular form because she is a mine of forms and a treasury of faults.

All women are one, yet varied, one donning different roles during different times with different behaviour, actions and effects. She will be visible in the form you want her to be as she has many forms and many characteristics. She is beyond comprehension – *Daivo na jaanati kuto manushyaha.* She has similar and varied feeling, different thoughts, independent views, capacity to destroy and better the existence. Hence Chanakya was of the opinion that there wasn't any work that a woman was incapable of doing –*Kim na kurvanti yoshitaha.*

Chanakya studied women minutely. He tested them on the criteria of humanitarianism in society, examined their variety of work compassionately, thought deeply about the troubles they faced due to all the above and provided easy ways of solving them.

Chanakya was able to clearly and openly opine on a woman's utter ruin, eminent progress and all the conditions in between. He did not try to explain everything related to woman at one place or time but only wrote whenever needed and how much ever was required.

Views

Chanakya has praised woman in the form of a child, a young girl, a faithful wife, a competent housewife and a mother. Chanakya gave woman an enviable status in the role of a mother. He said that there was no greater verse than Gayatri verse and no greater God than a mother.

Na gayatriyaha paro mantro na matuhu param daivam.

There are five kinds of mothers – king's wife, teacher's wife, friend's wife, wife's mother and the mother who bears her child – not only in the opinion of Chanakya but also in the opinion of Indians.

Raja patni, guru patni mitra patni thathaiva cha.
Patni maata swamaata cha panchaita maatarah smruta.

He considered mother to be the most excellent teacher – one teacher is equal to ten tutors, one father is equal to hundred teachers and one mother is equal to thousand fathers in imparting knowledge.

Chanakya's opinion was that food women safe guarded the house completely – *Satsriya Rakshayati Griham*. Such women are friends – *Bharya mitram griheshu cha*. Just as love and business has to take place among equals, governing is an apt thing for a king and agriculture is the best profession, in the same manner a virtuous woman is an invaluable gem to her family.

Samane shobhate preetihi, raagni sevacha shobhate
Vaanijyam vyavahaareshu diya stru shobhate graham.

He has thus given an exalted place for fidelity.

Kokila swaro rupam, strinaam rupam pativratam
Vidya rupam kurupaanaam kshama rupam tapasvinaam.

The beauty of a cuckoo lies in its voice, a woman's beauty is in fidelity, the beauty of deformed and ugly in their education and the beauty of hermits in their forgiveness. *Patihi eve guru strinaam-* A husband is the master to his wife.

According to Chanakya a good wife is one who satisfies her husband through thoughts, speech and action. She should be adept in work, love her husband and tell the truth.

Sa bharyaha shuchiti, daksha sa bharya ya pativrata
Sa bharya pativrata sa bharya satyavadini.

A man's life becomes heavenly if his wife works according to his desires, if his son is obedient, if he is satisfied monetarily.

Yasya putro vshibhuto bharya chandaanugaamini
Vibhave yashena santhusthastasya swarga ihaiva hi.

Maybe that is why it is said that a woman cannot become pure by giving charity, by undertaking pilgrimage. She can attain purity only by serving her husband.

Na daane shuddayate naari na upavaasa shatche api.
Na teertha seva tadvad bharthaha paadow vakaihi yatha.

Chanakya said that for a wife, her husband is most important. He felt that joyful feelings in women occur when their husbands are enthusiastic. *Pati –utsaah yuta naaryaha.*

A woman who commences her work only after taking her husband's permnission with his approval is a true wife. If her husband stops her from performing some work, then she should stop it. When a woman is unwell, but fasts despite her husband's disapproval. She will undergo terrible troubles and her life span will reduce if her husband gets tensed up.

Prathyuhu aagya binaa naari uposhya vratcharini.
Aayushayam harate bhartuhu sa naari naraka vrajet.

One who doesn't respect these virtues will live instress. Her husband's condition will also be similar. As a result their life will be full of strife. The problem with the present generation is that no one controls one's passions nor does anyone lead disciplined life. Women suffer if they do not have husbands- *Striyo nashtaa hyabhartikaha*. A wife's quality is severely tested only when there is loss of wealth. *—Bharya cha vibhavakshaye.*

A prostitude who is shameless suffers. If a housewife becomes shameless, she also suffers. *—Stri bhramanti vinashyati.* If a woman goes along with someone else, she too suffers- *Nashyati parahasta gataa striyaha.* Women should not stay in some one's house those who live in someone else's house also undergo suffering

Naditeere cha ye vruksha paragruheshu kaamini.
Mantriheenaha-cha rajaanah sheeghra nasyanya samshayan.

Chanakya has praised the attraction in women. According to him there cannot be anyone who hasn't fallen under the charm of a beautiful woman. *Stribhihi kasya na khanditam bhuvi manaa ko naama ragnaampriyah.* He has even described to such an extent that a man who doesn't dream of hugging a woman's breasts or hips in his dreams is like an axe which chops a young tree.

Naari peena payodharoru yugalam swaplano api na aalingat.
Maatu kevalam eva yaowvvana vanachhedo kutaira vayam.

A king's strength lies in his shoulders, a brahmin's strength in his knowledge and a woman's strength in her looks, youthfulness and sweet behaviour.

Bahu veerya balam ragno brahmano brahma vidbali.
Roopa Yaowvvan madhurya strinam balam uttamam.

Youthfulness is the greatest wealth to a woman which she doesn't like to lose. Someone asked an old lady who was walking with his bent head, what she ws searching and if she had lost anything. The lady replied, "O foolish man! Don't you know? I have lost my pearl of youth."

Atah pasyasi kim vruddhe patitam tava kim bhoovi.
Re re murkha. Na jaanaasigatam taarunyam-mauktikam.

The more you massage and twist sugarcane, sesame plant, an inferior person, women, gold, earth, sandal wood, curd and betal leaves, the more their qualities improve.

Iskhu daudah tilah kshudrah kaautaa hemacha medina.
Chandana dadhi tambula mardanam gunavardhanaam.

The more the superior wealth is one which is useful for the welfare of others and the most superior woman is a virtuous woman. Virtuous women are like the wealth safeguarded in a chest and used for only one where as prostitutes are like tha wealth which is used everywhere by travellers.

Kim taya kriyati lakshya ya vadhuhu iva levalam.
Ya tu veshyeva saa maanya pathikeh api bhujyati.

Chanakya calls the people having relationships with other women as low born wretches. *Paradasybhi marshanam chandaalam uchyate.* He asks all to treat other's wife as mothers. *Maatruvat paradaareshu.* He calls those who love prostitutes and dance to their tunes as fools..

Yo mahanmanyate moodo srakteyam mayi kaamini.
Sa tasya vashago bhutvaa nrutyetu krida shakunta vat.

This is because a prostitute does not belong to one. While she talks to one, she leers at someone else and thinks of someone else in her mind.

Jalapanti saadharmanyena pasyantrayanya savibhrama.
Hridaye chintyantyanya na strijaame kato rathih.

Nirdhanam purusham veshya tyajet – Prostitute discard the men who lose their wealth. Therefore while calling such men as fools, Chanakya also says that for a man who has absolute self control a woman is like straw – *Jitha asya trinaam naari.*

Only after contemplating for a long time, has he said that a girl should be married into a good family- *Sukule yojayayet kanya* because a girl is given only once –*Sakut kanya pradiyante.* Chanakya respected girls as an embodiment of Goddess Lakshmi and said that they should never be touched with feet – *Paadabhyam na sprushyedam kumari.*

Contrast – Dishonourable

When there is a talk of ruin of women, it was prevalent in those days too. It is difficult to say the time of origin of prostitutes. The number of balanced women was common in ancient ages. It was so during middle ages. But it has reduced a lot in the modern age and if we compare according to the percentage of population then it is common. There has been unnatural increase in the young girls becoming lustful the moment they reach adolescence and the middle-aged women revelling in sexual activity without any shame or restraint – everywhere, at all places. There doesn't seem to be even an iota of self control between boys and girls and men and women.

Chanakya was very frank in his opinions on women. He said that women eat twice the amount men do, their intelligence is four fold, courage is six fold and desire is eight fold.

Strinaam dwigunam aahaaro buddhistaasam chaturgunaa
Saahasam shadgunam kaamo ashta gunam ucchyate.

The discussions on women are done in a variety of places. The woman, however she may be in her youth, becomes honourable as she ages – ***Vruddha naari pativrataa*** because she no longer is sharp at that age.

Chanakya counted the faults of women very openly. Uttering lies, commencing work without forethought, behaving rashly, conspire cunningly, being impure and having no feeling of pity are some of the general faults in women. But now a days men are competing with women in these characteristics and it is impossible to say who is leading in this. Except for a few, most of the men and women have become the way Chanakya found women during his age.

Anrutam saahasam maaya murkhatvam atilubhitata
Ashowchavyam nirdayatvam strinaam dosha swabhaavajaa.

Deception is a woman's inherent quality. If one wants to learn the art of deception, one can learn it from a woman. ***Stribhyaha sikshet kaitavam.*** The worst cheats are the characterless women. ***Streenam dhurtaa cha maalini.***

Such women should not be trusted. Chanakya included women in the list of those who should not be trusted. They are animals with big claws, rivers, animals with horns, armed men, people working in the palaces.

Nakheenaam cha nadeenaam va shrungeenaam shastra paaninaam.
Vishwaaso naiva kartavyaam strishu rajakuloshu cha.

What we consider as faults are the natural traits in women. Onlya woman with firm determination and who is filled with purity of thoughts can be rid of these faults. Generally woman is filled with jealousy and hatred. The feeling is generally targeted on women and known ones. No woman can bear or accept if another woman is praised or if she hears complaints of her parents' house. One woman is another woman's enemy. An old woman cannot bear a young one and vice versa. Characterless women cannot stand virtuous women and virtuous women don't even want to look at characterless women. Similarly widows abhor married women and married women consider widows as bad omen.

Murkhanaam pandita dweshya agnanaam mahadhanaah
Varaanganaa kula striyam shubhaanganaan cha durbhagaa.

Women spend most of their time enjoying worldly pleasures like food, adornments and physical joys. Many of them become eager for spontaneous physical relationships. This is the natural behaviour women without self control. This has been in vogue since ancient times. Modernity is not a cause for this. It is not the fault of a young girl that she is a poison to old men. –***Vriddhasya Taruni Visham.*** That is the weakness of the old man and the man who marries a young girl is a fool. Chanakya said that it is wrong to take care of a prostitute.

Murkha shisya upadeshena dushta stri bharaneena cha.
Dukhite samprayogena pandito api avasidati.

Death is inevitable to one who has relation with woman of evil qualities, with one who speaks rudely, with one who had disgraceful character, with an evil friend, who has a retorting servant and whose house is infested with snakes.

Dushta bhaarya shatam mitram bhrutyah cha uttaradaayikah
Sarpecha grihe vaaso mrutyu evana samsayaha.

Hence a ruler should neither have proximity nor distance from fire, water, master and woman. He has to use a via media between the extremes.

Atyaasanna vinaashaya durastha na phalaprada.
Samvitam madhyabhaagena raja-vahni-guruh-striyah.

A short tempered wife is wretched. Such wives and unloving relations should be abandoned. *Tyajet krodhamukhi bhaarya nisnehaan baandhavya tyajeet.* It is better to be without a wife rather than being with a wicked wife. *Varam na daara na kudaaradaara.* There won't be peace at home if the wife is a wicked woman – *Kudaara-daareh-cha kutho gruhe ratih.* Not just a characterless wife, but also a characterless mother is an enemy. *Jaraa Strinaam Pati Shatru.* A father who is always in debt and a mother who is characterless are one's enemies. A beautiful wife and a foolish son are also one's enemies.

Runakarta pita shatru, maatacha vyabhichaarini
Bharya roopavathi shatru, putrah shatru apanditaa.

Characterless women do not get respect anywhere. *Sabhamadhye na shobaante jaara-garbhaiva striyah.*

Chanakya has given a detailed description of women for those who are curious and interested in knowing about women. Chanakya's thoughts are relevant in all places and at all times as all that he has said are found in our scriptures. He has not deviated from scriptures at all and had its approval.

Woman as Axis, a Person

It is common yet a very significant question as to why Chanakya wrote such a detailed commentary on women and gifted to public. One far-fetched question is that why he did not write anything on venomous women [vish kanya] when it is a well known fact that in order to protect Chandragupta from these venomous women, Chanakya himself gave poison to Chandragupta in small doses. Chanakya himself created these women and used them against his enemies. May be the information on these venomous women doesn't have any significance in the commentary when compared to other women.

He wrote this commentary to warn the public and the posterity to have self control and to lead a safe life. But the people of present age – children, adults, men, women, old – are not careful or safe. The attacks on men-women are so frequent in 20th century. This number is so huge that it outnumbers all the fights, murders, separations of all twenty centuries put together. Maybe it wrong to call this life. We can say that we are spending years either nobly or ignobly.

Then the question arises why such a lengthy discussion on women.

Though Chanakya thought very deeply he wrote only 1/100 th part of his thoughts. He has penned his thoughts in the form of maxims, verses. Thought he verses are very brief, they are laden with meaning. The meaning gets deeper and maxim spreads wider when it is used in right context.

It is very evident from his writings that Chanakya acknowledged the importance of women in life. It is a fact that there is life and the female beings give birth to other beings and women give birth to other human beings. The fact that the woman is the pivot of life, giver and destroyer of strength, could not be hidden from Chanakya. Women form the central part of a life cycle and pervades to the entire life. She is an indispensable part of life. There are many reasons for death but for the birth only one reason – Woman! The one who conceives and procreates!

The one who does not have a mother does not enjoy the child hood. And the one without a wife in old age doesn't lead a contented life. It goes without saying that everyone needs her during their adult hood. Chanakya announced that the lives of those people are worth less if they have not been able to embrace a woman.

All the above descriptions hold true when a woman can make or mar a man's life. Woman is the starting point of not only life but also of comfort. A good life is responsible for the welfare of her family, hence she is the medicine. But if her posture changes, she could become the cause of death too. Chanakya's commentary on women not only speaks of his greatness but also the greatness of women hood.

SECTION-2

METHODICAL MAN AND SOCIETY
COMPLETE POLICY OF CHANAKYA

Chapter-1

Chapter-2

Chapter-3

Chapter-4

Chapter-5

Chapter-6

Chapter-7

Chapter-8

Chapter-9

Chapter-10

Chapter-11

Chapter-12

Chapter-13

Chapter-14

Chapter-15

Chapter-16

Chapter-17

Chapter – 1

1. Pranamya shirasa vishnum trailokyadhipathim prabhum
Naana Shaastra ukta uddhrutam vakshye rajaneeeti samucchayam.

Bowing to the Omnipotent, Omniscient Lord Vishnu, the Lord of three worlds – the Earth, the Heaven and the Hell- I wish to describe the knowledge of administration which are compiled from various shaastras.

2 Adhityedam yathasaastram naro jaanaati sattama
Dharma upadesha vikhyatam karya-akarya shubha-ashubham.

Virtuous men should learn it dutifully and understand the practices of scriptures which are possible or not possible to be performed and the practices which are lucky or unlucky to us.

3. Tad aham sam pravakshyami lokaanaam hita kaamyayaa
Yasya vignaan maatrena sarvagnatvam prapadyate.

Hence praying for the welfare of the humanity I describe this knowledge, gaining which man become all-wise.

4. Murkha shishya upadeshena dushta stri bharanenacha
Dukhitai samprayogena pandito api avasidati.

A wise man also faces trouble if he advises a fool, if he protects an evil woman, if he wastres wealth and has dealings with depressed man.

5. Dushta bhaarya shatam mitram bhrujyah cha uttaradayaka
Sasarpecha gruhe vaaso mrutureva na samshayaha.

Death is inevitable for one having an evil character wife, evil minded friend, a servant who retorts or living in a house infested with snakes.

6. Aapadaarthe dhanam rakshed daariah api dhanai api.
Aatmaan satat rakshed daaraiah api dhanai api.

One should save wealth for saving oneself during misfortunes.

7. Aapadaarthe dhanam rakshed – imataam kuta aapadah.
Kadachid chalita lakshmih sanchito api vinashyati.

One has to save wealth for use during the times of misfortunes because one who does that can easily save oneself during times of distress. But one has to also remember that frivolous unsafe of wealth will result in the loss of wealth.

8. Yasmin desho na sammano na vruthihi cha bandhava
Nacha vidya aagamah kaschit tam desham parivarjayet.

One has to forsake a country in which one does not get respect, a country which doesn't provide one means of livelihood, where there are no kith and kin.

9. Dhanikah srotriyo raja nadi vaidyastu panchama.
Pancha yatra na vidhyante na tatra divas am vaset.

One should not live for even a day in places where one doesn't find the following five – the rich, Brahmins well versed in vedas, the king, the rivers and the physicians

10. Lokayatra bhayam lajja daakshinyam tyaagasheelata.
Pancha yatra na vidyate na kuryat tatra samsthitham,

A person should not live where there are no means of livelihood, where there is no fear of punishment for a crime, where there is no public modesty, where people are not adept in their profession, where there is no habit of charity.

11. Jaaniyaat preshane bhrutyaan baandhavaan vyasana aagame.
Mitram cha aapathi – kaleshu bharyaam na vibhavakshaye.

The quality of servants is tested while at work, kith and kin are tested while we face problems, the friend is tested at the time of danger and the wife is tested when there is loss of wealth.

12. Aature vyasane praapte durbhikshe shatru sankate
Rajadwaare smashaane cha yah tishtati sa baandhavah.

One who supports us during our time of sickness, our time of misery, during famine, during problems faced from enemies, during the court and during the final journey, is the actual friend.

13. Yo dhruvaani parityaja adhruvam parishevate.
Dhruvaani tasya nasyanti adhruvam nashta mevacha.

A person who hankers after uncertainty ignoring the certainty, undergoes a loss of certainty as well as uncertainty.

14. Varayet kulajaam praagno virupaam api kanyakaam.
Roopasheelam na neechasya vivaaham sadrushe kute.

An intelligent man should know that he should marry a beautiful woman from a respectable family and not someone from a disrespectable family. The alliance should be formed between people of the same caste.

15. Nakheenaam va nadeenaam va srunginaam sastra paaninaam.
Viswaaso na eva kartavyah strishu raja kuleshu cha.

One should not believe those with big nails, with big horns, with weapons, women and people of royal birth.

16. Vishaad api amrutham graham etyaad api kaanchanam.
Neechad api uttama vidya striratnam dushkulaad api.

If there is ambrosia in venom, if there is gold in unclean thing, if there is good education in a fool, if there is a gem of a girl in a disreputable family, then one should take them.

17. Strinaam dwigunaah aahaaro lajja chaapi chaturguna.
Saahasaa shadgunaam chaiva kamoh ashtaguna ucchyate.

Women eat twice more than men, their knowledge is four times sharper, courage six times more, and work eight times more than men.

Chapter – 2

1. Amrutham saahasam maaya murkhatvam ati lubdate.
Ashowchatvam nirdayatvam strinaam doshaah swabhaavacha.

It is the common fault in women to tell lies, to begin work without a prior thought, to try something daring, to plot and scheme, to be greedy and to be impure.

2. Bhojyam bhojana shaktih cha rati shaktih varaanganaa.
Vibhavo daana shaktih cha na alpasya tapas phalam.

To have good items in food, to have the ability of digesting that food, to meet a beautiful woman, to have the ability of having a physical relation with her, to be able to have wealth and also the ability of charity – all these become possible only as a result of good penance and not otherwise.

3. Yasya putra vashibhutaa bhaarya chanda anugaamini.
Vibhave yah cha santushtah tasya swarga ihaiva hi.

For a man his life on earth becomes a heaven when his son is obedient, his wife is faithful and dutiful, and when he is satisfied with his wealth.

4. Te putra ye pitrubhaktaah sa pita yastu poshakah.
Tanmitram yasya vishwasah sa bhaarya yatra nivruttih.

An ideal son is one who is devoted to his father, an ideal father is one who brings up his son correctly, an ideal friend is one on whom one can repose trust and an ideal wife is one from whom one gets complete satisfaction.

5. Parokshe karya hantaaram pratyakshe priyavaadinam.
Tyajate taadrusham mitram vishakumbham payomukham.

One should discard a friend who back stabs but speaks sweetly in front because he is like a pot filled with venom but covered with milk on the brim.

6. Na viswaset kumitre cha mitre cha- api na viswayet.
Kadachit kupitam mitram sarva guhya prakashayet.

Never trust both true friend and false friend. Who knows they might blurt out your secrets when in anger.

7. Maanasa vichintanam karya vachasa na prakashayet.
Mantrena rakshayed gudam karye cha api niyojet.

One should not reveal one's thoughts, should safeguard it stringently and constantly thinking about it, should convert these thoughts into action.

8. Kastam cha kalu murkhatvam kastam cha khalu yowvvanam.
Kasta ati kastakaram cha eva para geha nivaasanam.

Foolishness is painful, youth sorrowful. But the most painful one is to be beholden by someone and to live in their house.

9. Shaile shaile na maanikyam mowktim na gaje gaje.
Saadhavo na hi sarvatra chandanam na vane vane.

One can't get gems in all mountains, all elephants don't have pearls, one doesn't find saints in all places and every forest will not have sandal wood trees.

10. Putracha vividhaih sheelaih niyojyaah satatam

Naatigna sheela sampanna bhavanti kula poojithaah.acha vividhaih

Intelligent people should endow their sons with great qualities because only those who know morality and are virtuous are respected in their caste.

11. Maataa shatruh pitaa bairi bhaaryaam baala na patitaah.
Na shobhante sabhamadhye hamsa madhye baka yatha.

The parents who don't give noble education to their children are like enemies. The ignorants don't get respect in the court and are like herons amidst swans.

12. Laalnaad Bahavo doshaah taadanaad bahavo gunaah.
Tasmaat putramcha shishyam cha kaadayena tu laalayet.

A lot of faults creep in when children are pampered. Punishment helps in blossoming of good qualities. Hence children and students should not be always pampered but punished now and then.

13. Shlokena ya tadarthena tadardhardhaksharena va.
Avandhyam divas am kuryaad daana adhyayano karmabhih.

It is the duty of every man to spend his time in giving charity and in learning and should not waste his time. He should learn and revise one lesson every day. If that is not possible then he has to learn at least half a lesson or a part of a lesson daily.

14. Kanthiviyogah swajan apamaanah runasya sheshah krunupasya seva.
Daridra bhaavo vishama sabha cha vinaagnima ethe pradahanti kayam.

Separation from wife, digrace from the relations, burdened with debts, working under a bad employer, being penniless, living in a society of selfish people burns our body even without fire.

15. Naditeerecha ye vrukshah para geheshu kaamini.
Mantriheenah cha raajanah sheegram nashyanti asamshayam.

A tree on a river bank, a woman in someone else's house, a king without a wise minister, without doubt, will perish soon.

16. Baalam vidya cha vipraanaam ragman sainyam balam thatha.
Balam vittam cha vaisyaanaam shudrenaam paricharyakam.

A Brahmin's strength lies in his wisdom, a king's strength lies in his soldiers, a merchant's strength lies in his wealth, a worker's strength lies in his work and a shudra's strength lies in his physical strength.

17. Nirdhanam purusham veshya praja bhagnam nrupam tyajet.
Khagaa veeta phalam vruksham bhuktva cha abhyagata graham.

A prostitute forsakes a penniless man, people the defeated king, birds forsake a fruitless tree and the guests the house after feast.

18. Gruhitva dakshinaan vipraah tyajanti yajamaanakam.
Praapta vidya gurum shishya daghda aranyam mrugah thathe.

A Brahmin forsakes a master's house after getting money, the student leaves the hermitage of his teacher after acquiring education and beasts forsake the forest when it becomes arid without water.

19. Durachaarini duraa drushtih dura aavaasi cha durjanaah.
Yanmaitri kriyate pumbhi: sat u sheegra vinashyati.

One who befriends a characterless person, a person who harms others, a person who lives in squalor is destroyed soon.

20. Samaane shobate preetih raagnih sevacha shobate.
Vaanijyam vyavahaaresha stri divya stri shobate graham.

Relation among same caste brings glory, the work of a king brings glory, the business of a trader brings glory and the presence of a virtuous and adept woman brings glory to the home.

Chapter – 3

1. Kasya doshah kule naasti vyadhina kona peeditha.
Vyasan kena praptam kasya soukhyam nirantaram.

Every cast has some faults, every life has some disease, one drowned in bad habits has to undergo troubles and nobody leads a contented life always.

2. Aachaarah kulam aakhyati desham aakhyati bhaasanaa,
Sambhramah-sneham-aakhyaati vapuraa khyaati bhojanam.

A man's caste is known through his actions, his status through his speech, his love through respect he shows and his health through the food he eats.

3. Satkule bhojayet kanyam putram vidhyaasa yojayet.
Vyaasane yojayet shatrum mitram dharma niyojayet.

It is the right for a girl to be married into a good caste, for a son to be given good education, for the enemy to be shown the wrong habits and for the friend to be directed towards right path.

4. Durjanasya cha sarpasya varam sarpo na durjanah
Sarpo damshti kale tu durjanaah pade pade.

If one has to save either a bad man or a snake, then let the snake be saved because snake bites only in defence whereas an evil man bites us in every step.

5. Etadartham kuleenaanaam nrupaah kurvanti sangraham
Aadi-madhya avasaaneshu na tyajanti cha te nrupam.

The king keeps only virtuous people with him because they do not forsake him at the time of his rise, fall or danger.

6. Pralaye bhinna maryaada bhavanti kita saagaraah.
Saagara bhedam icchanti pralaye api na saadhavah.

The ocean also crosses its limits and drowns everything during the storm or pralaya. But the virtuous do not cross their limit even when they face stormy situations.

7. Murkhastu parihartavyah pratyaksho dwipadah pashuh.
Bhinnatti vaakya shalyena adrushtah kashtaka yatha.

Foolish man should be forsaken because a foolish man is like a two legged animal. He brings much misery to the virtuous like a thorn piercing a body.

8. Roopa- yowvvana- sampanna vishaala kula sambhavaah.
Vidyaheenaa na shobhatte nirgandha iva kimshukaah.

An uneducated man, though handsome, young and born in a high caste, is like the artificial flowers which are never respected.

9. Kokilanaam swaro rupam strinaam roopam pativratam.
Vidya roopam kuroopaanam, kshama roopam tapasvinaam.

The beauty of the cuckoo lies in its voice, the beauty of a woman in her fidelity, the beauty of ugly looking person is in his knowledge and the beauty of the sage is in his forgiveness.

10. Tyajet ekam kulasyarthe gramaasyaarthe kulam tyajet.
Graamam janapadasyaarthe aatmarthe prithvi tyajet.

In order to save the caste, an individual has to be sacrificed, in order to save the village, a caste has to be sacrificed, in order to save the population, a village has to be sacrificed and in order to save the soul, the earth itself has to be sacrificed.

11. Udhyoge naasti daaridrayam japate naasti paatakam.
Mowneeha kalaho naasti, naasti jaagarto bhayam.

A hardworking person is never a destitute, the sins of a devout man are washed away, silence will never lead to any fights and there is no fear in one who is enlightened.

12. Ati roopena vai seta, ati garveena raavanaah
Ati daanaad balih –rbaddho ati sarvatra varjayet.

Sita was abducted because of her extreme beauty, Ravana was killed because of his extreme arrogance, Bali was killed because of his extreme generosity. Hence one should beware of extremity.

13. Ko hi bharah samarthaanaam kim dooram vyavasaayinaam
Ko videshah savidhaanaam ko priyah priyavaadinaam.

Nothing is burdensome to capable people, no place is too far for a merchant, no place is foreign for a learned man and for a soft spoken no one is a stranger.

14. Ekena api suvrukshena pushpitena sugandhinaa
Vaasitam tad vanam sarvam suputrena kulam thathaa.

Just like a single tree with aromatic flowers spreads aroma throughout the entire forest, the birth of a noble son increases the glory of his family.

15. Ekena shuska vrukshena dahyamaanena vahnina
Dahyati tad vanam sarvam kuputrena kulam yathaa.

Just like if one dry tree catches fire, it spreads through the entire forest, the birth of an ignoble son destroys the glory or respect of his family/caste.

16. Ekena api suputrena vidya yuktena sadhuna
Aahlaaditam kulam sarvam yatha chanduna sharvari.

If a son is both knowledgeable and noble, his entire caste becomes happy, just like the arrival of moon dispels the darkness with its moon light.

17. Kim jaatih bahubhih putraih shoka-santaapa kaarakaih.
Varamekah kulaalambi yatra visramyate kulam.

What is the use of having many sons who only cause sorrow and heart burn? Just one virtupous son who brings glory to his family is enough.

18. Laalayet panesha varshaani darsh varshaani taadayet.
Praapte tu shodashe varsha putram mitra mivaacharet.

One should love one's son till his five years, punish him till ten years, but become his friend once he reaches seventeen years.

19. Upasarge anya chakra cha durbhikshe cha bhayaavahi.
Asaadhujana sansarge yah palayati sah jeevati.

One who escapes natural dangers, pestilences, attack by the enemies, loneliness or the friendship with evil men gets saved.

20. Dharma-artha-kama-moksheshu yasyaiko apina vidhyate.
Janma najmani matyenshu maranam tasya kevalam.

One who doesn't have at least one of the following - virtues , wealth, desire, salvation, will have repeated births and deaths.

21. Moorkhah yatra na pujyante dhaanyam yatra susamchitam.
Daampatye kalaho naasti tatra srih swayam aagataa.

Goddess Lakshmi lives in such a place where the fools are not venerated, where food is always available in one place and where there are no fights between husband and wife.

Chapter – 4

1. Ayah karma cha vittam cha vidya nidhanam eva cha.
Panchaitaani hi srujyante garbhasysteva dehinah.

The moment life is formed in the womb of the mother, God decides its life span, fate, wealth, education and death.

2. Saadhubhyaste nivartante putraa mitraani baandhavaah.
Ye cha taih saha gantaarah – tad dharmaat – sukrutam kulam.

One who treats his kith and kin, hermits and noble people equally, his entire clan gets salvation.

3. Darshan – dhyaan – samspashaih matsi kurmi cha pakshini
Shishum paalayate nityam thathaa sajjana sangati.

Just the way a fish takes care of its young by just keeping an eye on them, the tortoise by taking care of its young through nurturing and the birds by caressing, a man's upbringing becomes good in the company of virtuous people.

4. Yaavat swasthe hyayam deho yaavan mrutah cha durateh
Taavat – aatmahitam kuryaat praanaante kim karishyati.

One can go on cleansing the soul as long as the body is healthy and death is far away. What can be done after death?

5. Kaamadhenugunaa vidya hyakaale phaladaayim.
Pravaase maatru sadrushi vidya guptam dhanam smrutham.

Vidya has the quality of Kaamadhenu. One gets instant result from it. Learning is correlated to mother in foreign countries. It is considered as a secret stash.

6. Ekopi guni putro nigunaah cha shatari api.
Ekah chandrah tamo hanti na cha tara sahasrashah.

One virtuous son is better than innumerable vicious sons because only one moon and not thousand stars dispel the darkness.

7. Murkhah chiraayuh jaato api tasmaat jaata mruto varah
Mruta cha alpa dukhaya yavat jeevam jado dahet.

A son who dies the moment he is born is far better than a fool with a long life. The suffering will only be there for a few days. But a foolish son who lives for a long time gives only sorrow all the life.

8. Kugraama vaasah kulaheena seva kubhyanam krodha mukhi cha bhaarya.
Putrascha murkho vidava cha kanya vinaa agninaa shat pradahati kaayam.

Living in a bad village, serving a cruel man, eating bad food, a quarrelsome woman, a foolish son and a widowed daughter – these will burn us even without fire.

9. Kim tajaa kriyate dhenva yaa na dogdhri na garbhini.
Ko-arthah putrena jaatena yon a vidwaan na bhaktimaan.

Just as a cow which cannot conceive or give milk is of no use, the son who is neither learned nor spirited is of any use.

10. Sansaara taapadagdhaanaam triyo vishrantihetavah.
Apatyan cha kalatram cha sataam sangati evacha.

The sad people get peace from three things in this world. Good progeny, faithful wife and company of good people.

11. Satrut jalpanti rajaanah sukrut jalpanti panditaah
Sakrut kanyaah pradesyanti trinyetaani sakrutsakrut.

The king gives orders only once. The learned men give out only one opinion after a deep thought, a girl gets married only once and the person who gives his word once should follow it faithfully.

12. Ekakinaa tapo dwabyaam pathanam gaayaanam tribhihi.
Chaturbhirgamanam kshetra panchabhi barhubhi ranam.

Penance is performed alone, learning is done with another, music with three people, travel will be enjoyable with four, five are needed for agriculture but a lot of people are required during a war.

13. Saa bhaaryaa yaa shuchirdakshaa sa bhaaryaa ya pativrata
Sa bharyaa yaa patiprita sa bharya satyavaadini.

A wife is excellent if she is adept in her work, a faithful wife is excellent, the wife who loves her husband and tells only the truth is excellent.

14. Apatrasya graham shunyam dishah shunyaastva baandhavaah
Murkhasya hrudaya shunyam sarvashunyaa daridrataa.

A home is empty without a son, all directions are empty without a son, all directions are empty without kith and kin, a fool's heart is empty and for the wretched everything is empty.

15. Anabhyaase visham sastram jeerne bhojanam visham
Daridrasya visham goshti vruddhasya taruni visham.

If scriptures are not practised and followed they become poison, if the food is inedible it becomes poison, a wretched living among people is poison and for old men, young girls are poison.

16. Tyajet dharma dayaheenam vidyaheenam gurum tyajet.
Tyajet krodhamukhi bhaaryaa nisnehaam baandhavaah tyajet.

Where there is no compassion in a religion, forsake it, forsake a guru who has no knowledge, forsake a short tempered woman and forsake those kith and kin who have no feeling of love.

> *17. Adhvaa jaraa manushyaanaam vaajinaam bandhanam jaraa.*
> *Amaithunam jaraa strinaam vastraanaam aatapo jaraa.*

One who walks a lot grows old faster, the horses which are kept tethered for long grow old faster, women grow old faster when they over work and the clothes fade quickly if left in sun.

> *18. Kah kaalah kaani mitraani ko deshah kau vyaya aagaman.*
> *Kasyaaham ka cha me shaktih iti chintyam muhurmuhuh.*

One should keep on contemplating on the following questions – How is the current time? How many friends are there? How is the country? What is the expenditure and income? Who am I? What is my strength?

> *19. Janitaa chopneta cha yastu vidyaam prayacchate*
> *Annadaata bhayatraata panch ete pitarah smrutaa.*

There are five kinds of fathers – one who provides us life, one who performs thread ceremony, one who gives knowledge, one who provides food and one who dispels fear.

> *20. Rajapatni guropatni mitrapatni tathaiva cha.*
> *Patni maata swamaata cha pancha-etaa maatarah.*

There are five kinds of mothers – king's wife, master's wife, friend's wife, mother of one's wife and one's birth mother.

> *21. Agnih devo dwi jaatinaam muneenam hrudi daivatam.*
> *Pratimaa swalpa buddhinaam sarvatra samadarshinah.*

Brahmins, vysyas and Kshatriyas are called dwijaati and yagna is their God. The Gods of hermits reside in their heart. Idols become Gods for the fools. But to an enlightened soul, God is everywhere.

Chapter – 5

*1. Guruh-agnih dwijaateenam varnanaam brahmano guruh
Patih evam guruh strinaam sarvasya abhyagato guruh.*

Agni or fire is the master for Brahmin, Vysya and Kshatriya., the Brahmin is the guru for four castes, a husband is the master of his wife and a guest is the guru for all.

*2. Yatha chaturbhih kanakam parikshyate nidharshana
Tatha chaturbhih purushah parikshyate tyaagena sheelena guneena karmena.*

Gold is examined in four ways viz – by rubbing, by cutting, by heating and by pounding. In the same way a man should be examined in four ways – sacrifice, honour, character and deed.

*3. Taavad bhayena bhetavyam yaavada bhayam anaagatam
Aagatam tu bhayam drushtva prahartavyam ashankaya.*

The fear of difficulty remains till it happens. But when faced with difficulty, we should tru to remove it with all our might.

*4. Ek udara sam udbhoota eka nakshatra jaatakaah.
Na bhavanti samaah sheele yatha badarikantaka.*

The children born to the same mother and having the same birth star are not similar in their deed or traits just as berries of the same tree are not identical nor are the thorns alike.

*5. Nispruho na adhikaari syaana akaami mandana priyah.
Na avidaghdah priyam bruyaat spashtavaktaa na vanchakah.*

No officer should be greedy, the feeling of lust is more in romantic people, the foolish people cannot speak sweetly and the one who speaks frankly will never cheat.

*6. Moorkhaanaam panditaa deshya adhananaam kulaangana.
Durbhagaanaam cha subhagaah kulataanaam kulaangana.*

The foolish abhor the learned, the poor abhor the rich, prostitutes abhor virtuous women and unlucky abhor the lucky.

7. Aalasya upahataa vidyaa parahasta gataah striyah
Alpabeejam hatam kshetram hatam sainyam anaayaham.

Learning gets spoilt due to laziness, a woman who is under some one else's hand gets spoilt, crops get spoilt due to deficiency of seeds and the army becomes useless without a commander.

8. Abhayasaad dhaaryate vidya kulam sheelena dhaaryathe
Gunena gnaayate twaaryah kapo netrena gamyate.

Learning improves with practice, the honour of clan remains safe with exalted learning, the eminent are recognised by their good qualities and the anger is revealed through the eyes itself.

9. Vittena rakshayate dharmo vidya yogena rakshyate
Mrudunaa rakshyate bhoopah satstriyaa rakshyate graham.

Virtue is safeguarded by wealth, learning by plans, a king can be safe guarded by sweetness and virtuous women safe guard their homes.

10. Anyatha veda paandityam shastram aacharanamanyathae
Anyatha kuvachah shaantam lokaah klishyanticha anyatham.

Those who speak ill of a learned men and their learning, who say that scriptures are useless, who call the dignified brave men as tricksters, always remain sorrowful.

11. Daaridrya naashan daan sheela durgati naashanam.
Agnaana-naashini pragnaa bhaavapa bhaya naashini.

Poverty ends by charity, difficulties end by good practices, ignorance ends through learning and fear vanishes due to devotion to God.

12. Naasti kaamasamo vyaadhirnaasti mohasamo ripah.
Naasti kopasamo vahnih naasti gnaanaat param sukham.

There is no worse disease than lust, no enemy worse than desire, no fire worse than anger and no contentment better than knowledge.

13. Janmmrutyu hi yaatyako bhunakteyek shubha ashubham.
Narake se patatyeka, eko yaati paraam gatim.

Man is born alone, bears alone the fruits of both sins and cirtues, bears the pains of hell alone and attains salvation too alone.

14. Trunam brahmavidah swargah trunam shurasya jeevitam.
Jivakshasya trunaa naari nispruhasya trunaam jagat.

Heaven is like a blade of grass for an enlightened soul, life is like a blade of grass to the courageous, woman is like a blade of grass for a person with self control and for a man who is selfish the entire world is a blade of grass.

15. Vidya mitram pravaaseshu bhaarya mitram gruheshu cha
Vyaadhitasya aushadam mitram dharmo mitram mrutasya cha.

Learning is a friend during travel, wife is a friend at home, medicine is a friend for the sick and virtue is a friend to the dead.

16. Vrutha vrushtih samudreshu vrutha trupteshu bhojanam.
Vrutha daan dhanaadyeshu vrutha deepo diva apicha.

Raons do not matter to an ocean, it is useless to feed a satiated person, it is useless to give alms to a rich man and it is useless to light a lamp during the day.

17. Naasti meghasam toyam cha aatmasambalam
Naasti chakshusam tejo naasti dhaanyasam priyam.

There cannot be any water like a cloud, there cannot be strength like mental strength, there cannot be sharpness like eyes, there cannot be anything as dear as food.

18 Adhanaa dhan icchanti vaach chaiva chatushpadaah
Maanavaah swarga icchanti moksham icchanti devataah.

The poor desire wealth, the cattle wish to speak, man desires heaven and Gods desire only salvation.

19. Satyena dhaaryate pruthvi satyena tapate ravih
Satyena vaati vaayah cha sarva satye pratishtitam.

The earth is steady due to truth, the sun shines due to truth, the sun shines due to truth, the wind blows due to truth, everything is based on truth.

20. Chala lakshmih achalah praanah achalam jeevit yowvvanam
Chala-achala cha samsaare dharma eko hi nischalam.

Wealth is unstable, life is perishable, life and youth are lost one day. In this ever changing world, only virtue is constant.

21. Naraan naapito dhoortah pakshin chaiva vaaryasah
Chatushpadaam srugaalastu strinaam dhurtaa cha maalini.

Barber is the cleverest in men, crow in birds, jackal in animals, a gardener's wife is the cleverest among women.

Chapter – 6

1. Śrutvā dharmam vijānāti śrutvā tyajati durmatim.
Śrutvā jñānam vāpnōti śrutvā mōksam vāpnuyāt.

Man understands the secret of dharma by listening to vedas and scriptures. Afteer listening to the words of scholars, the evil will let go of evilness, upon receiving knowledge from teacher, man gains salvation.

2. Paksinām kākah cāndalah paśūnā caiva kukkurah.
Munīnām kōpī cāndālah sarvēsām caiva nindakah.

The crow is the most barbaric among birds, the dog among animals. A short tempered sage is barbaric among sages and among men, the calumniators are barbaric.

3. Bhasmanā śudhyatē kānsyam tāmram amlēna śudhyati.
Rajasā śudhyatē nārī nadī vēgēna śudhyati.

When polished with ash, the bronze shines, copper with acid, woman attains [purity with puberty and the river cleanses itself by flowing.

4. Bhraman sampūjyatē rājā bhraman sampūjyatē dvijah.
Bhramana sampūjyatē yōgī strī bhramantī vinaśyati.

The king who keeps travelling, gets respected, the Brahmin who keeps travelling gets venerated, the yogi who keeps travelling gets revered but a woman who keeps travelling gets destroyed.

5. Tādrśī jāyētē buddhih vyavasāyō ani tādrśah.
Sahāyāh tādrśā ēva yādrśī bhavitavyatā.

A man's thought process is dependent on the fate with which he is born. He selects his work accordingly and his helpers are also of the same ilk.

6. Kālah vacati bhūtāni kālah sanharatē prajāh.
Kālah suptēsu jāgarti kālō hi duratikramah.

Time destroys everything, time is the reason for death, Time remains awake even when we are asleep and it is impossible to overcome time.

7. Na ca paśyati ca janmāndhah kāmāndhō naiva paśyati.
Na paśyati madōnmattō hyarthī dōsām na paśyati.

One who is blind since birth cannot see anything, one who is blind of work cannot see anything, one who is blinded by arrogance cannot see anything and one who is blinded by selfishness also cannot see anything.

8. Svayam karma karōtya ātmā svayam tat phalam aśnutē.
Svayam bhramati sansārē svayam tasmād avamucyatē.

A man who labours himself enjoys the fruits of labour himself, keeps travelling to various zones and attains salvation by himself.

9. Rājā rāstrakrtam pāpam rājñah pāpam purōhitah.
Bhartā ca strīkrtam pāpam śisyapāpam guruh - tathā.

A king has to bear the sins of his kingdom, a priest bears the sins of the king, a husband bears the sins of his wife and a teacher, the sins of his disciple.

10. Rnakartā pitā śatruh mātā ca vyabhicārinī.
Bhāryā rūpavatī śatruh putrah śatruh apanditah.

A father who leaves debts on his son is an enemy, a prostitute mother is an enemy, a beautiful wife is an enemy and a foolish son is an enemy.

11. Lubdham arthēna grhanīyāt stabdham anjali - Karmanā.
Mūrkha chandānurōdhēna yathārtha tvēna panditam.

By giving money to a greedy person, by respecting a self-respecting person, by doing the work the way a fool wishes and by telling the truth to an educated person, we can bring them under our control.

12. Varam na rājyam na kurājarājyam varam na mitram na kumitra - mitram.
Varam na śisyō na kuśisya śisyō varam na dārā na kudāradārāh.

It is better to have no rule instead of a bad one, it is better to be friendless instead of having a bad one, it is better to have no wife instead of a bad wife and it is better to remain without disciples in stead of having bad ones.

13. Kurājarājyēna kutah prajāsukham kumitramitrēna kutō asti nivrtih.
Kudāra dārāh ca kutō grhē ratih kuśisyam adhyāpatah kutō yaśah.

One never gets any comfort under a bad king's rule, from cheating friend, one doesn't get any fame if he has evil disciples, and one doesn't get any peace if he has an evil wife.

14. Sinhād ēkam bakād ēkam śiksē catvāri kukkutāt.
Vāyasāt panca śiksēta ca sat śunah trīni gardabhāt.

Man should lesrn one quality each from a lion and a heron, four from hens, five from a cow, six from a dog and three from a donkey.

15. Prabhūtam kāryam alpam vā yannarah kartum icchati.
Sarva ārambhēna tatkāryam sinhāda ēkam pracaksatē.

Whether the work is small or big, one has to begin work with dedication. We have to learn this lesson from the lion.

16. Indriyāni ca sanyamya bakavat panditō narah.
Dēśa-kāla-balam jñātvā sarvakāryāni sādhayēt.

An intelligent man has to keep his senses under control like a heron and complete his work according to the situation.

17. Pratyuthānam ca yuddham ca sanvibhāgam ca bandhusu.
Svayam ākramya bhuktam ca śikse catvāri kukkutāt.

From a hen he should learn to get up on time, be ready for the war always, giving adequate share to all his kin and eat whatever he has hunted.

18. Gūdha maithunacāritvam kālē kālē ca sangraham.
Apramattam aviśvāsam panca śiksēta vāyasāt.

From the crow he has to learn to hide and observe, being haughty, collecting things from time to time, always being careful and not believing others completely.

19. Bahvāsī svalpasantustah sunidrō laghu cētanah.
Svāmibhaktah ca śūrah ca sad aitē śvānatō gunāh.

From the dog he has to learn to eat voraciously when food is available, being calm when not available, sleep unperturbed, but wake up at the slightest noise, have self-respect and be prepared to fight.

20 Suśrāntō hī vahēd bhāram śīta - usna na ca paśyati.
Santustah - caratē nityam trīni śiksēcca gardabhāt.

Man has to learn the following qualities from a donkey- carrying loads for his master even though he is tired, not affected by either warmth or cold and move about in a self satisfied manner.

21. Ya ētāna vinśati gunāna ācarisyati mānavah.
Kārya avasthāsu sarvāsu ajēyah sa bhavisyati.

A man who assimilates all these qualities will be highly successful in all the work he undertakes.

![Chanakya illustration]

Chapter – 7

1. Arthanāśam manah tāpam grhē duścaritāni ca.
Vancanam ca apamānam ca matimān na prakāśayēt.

One should not reveal to others, the loss of his wealth, his heartache, the faults at home, being cheated by someone or his disgrace.

2 Dhana - Dhānya prayōgēsu vidyā sangrahanēsu ca.
Āhārē vyavahārē ca tyakta lajjah sukhī bhavēt.

A man will be contented if he is not ashamed of his monetary dealings, his education, improvement in his work, or while eating or conducting business.

3. Santōsa amrta trptānām yatsukham śāntacētasām.
Na ca tad dhana lubdhānām itah cētah ca dhāvatām.

A man who is satisfied with the nectar of happiness, who is calm in mind, gets so much of comfort which is not got by one who is greedy for money and keeps running behind it.

4. Santōsastrisu kartavyah svadārē bhōjanē dhanē.
Trisu caiva na kartavyō adhyayanē tapa - dānayō.

A man should be satisfied with the kind of wife he gets, food that he eats but should never be satisfied with the way he practises whatever he has learnt and of meditation and donations he makes.

5. Viprayōh vipra vahnayōh ca dampatayōhsvāmi bhrtyayōh.
Antarēna na gantavyam halasya vrsabhasya ca.

One should not walk between two Brahmins, between fire, between a husband and wife, between employer and employee and between the plough and bulls.

6. Pādābhyām na sprśēda agnim gurum brāhmanēva ca.
Naiva gām na kumārī ca na vrddham na śiśum tathā.

One should not stamp fire, teacher, Brahmin, cow, unmarried girl, aged people and infants with foot.

7. Śakatam panca hastēna daśahastēna vājinam.
Gajam hasta sahasrēna dēśa tyāgēna durjanam.

One should stay away by 5ft from a bullock cart, 10ft from a horse, 100ft from an elephant and should escape from the place where there is an evil man.

8. Hastī ankuśamātrēna bājī hastēna tādyatē.
Śrrngī lagudahastēna khangahastēna durjanah.

An elephant has to be controlled with a goad, horses with a whip, animals having horns with sticks and the evil man with a sword.

9. Tusyanti bhōjanē viprā mayūrā ghanagarjitē.
Sādhavah parasampattau khalah para vipattisu.

A Brahmin is satisfied with food, a peacock when it becomes cloudy and starts to thunder a saint with the well being of the others and an evil man with others' difficulties.

10. Anulōmēna balinam pratilōmēna durjanam.
Ātmatulyabalam śatrum vinayēna balēna vā.

A strong man can be subdued with polite behaviour, an evil one by opposing him and an equally strong man with politeness.

11. Bāhuvīryam balō rājñō brāhmanō brahmavid balī.
Rūpa - yauvanam - mādhuryam strīnām balam - uttamam.

A king is strong because of his army, a Brahmin is strong because of his knowledge, woman's strength is her beauty, youth and pleasantness.

12 Nātyantam saralai - bhāvyam gatvā paśya vanasthalīm.
Chidyantē saralāh tatra kubjāh tisthanti pādapāh.

Man should not be very simple and straight forward. One sees in the forest that straight trees are chopped off while the crooked ones are left alone.

13. Yatrōdakam tatra vasanti hansāh tathaiva śuskam parivarjayanti.
Na hansatulyēna narēna bhāvyam punah tyajantē punah āśrayantē.

Where there is water, you find swans and they vacate the place the moment water dries up. A man cannot be like the swans because sometimes he has to become dependent on someone he had previously discarded.

14. Upārjitānām vittānām tyāga ēva hi raksanam.
Tadāga udara sansthānām parīvāha ivā ambhasām.

The safety of wealth is in letting it go, in spending it wisely and in trying to earn profit from it. It is similar to the fact that water in the pond gets cleaner when we keep removing water from the pond.

15. Yasya arthāh tasya mitrāni yasya arthāh tasya bāndhavāh.
Yasya arthāh sa pumāmllōkē yasya arthāh sa ca jīvati.

One who has wealth, has friends, has kith and kin, is great and that one alone lives.

16. Svarga sthitānām iha jīvalōkē catvāri cihnāni vasanti dēhē.
Dāna - prasangō madhurā ca vānī dēva arcanam brāhmanatarpanam ca.

There are four main traits in every life which comes from heaven to earth – to give charity, to speak sweetly, service to Brahmin and devotion to God.

17. Atyanta kōpah katukā ca vānī daridratā ca svajanēsu vairam.
Nīcaprasangah kulahīna sēvā cihnāni dēhē narakasthitānām.

There are four traits in every life which come from hell to earth – intense anger, rude speech, poverty, hatred against people, friendship with evil and service to evil.

18. Gamyatē yadi mrgēndra mandiram labhyatē karikapōlamauktikam.
Jambukālayagatē ca prāpyatē vatsapucchakharacarmakhandanam.

Upon entering a lion's den one may get the pearl found on the head of an elephant, but when one enters the den of a jackal, all one gets is only bits of flesh.

19. Śunah puccham iva vyartham jīvita Vidyayā vinā.
Na guhya gōpanē śaktam na ca danśanivāranē.

Without education, a man's life is like a dog's tail, which cannot cover the private parts or can swat away mosquitoes.

20. Vācām śaucam ca manasah śaucam indriya nigrahah.
Sarvabhūtē dayā śaucam ētah śaucam parā arthinām.

Purity of speech, purity in heart, control of senses, compassion towards creatures, purity of wealth are the signs of one going on the path of salvation.

21. Puspē gandham tilē tailam kāsthē agnih payō ghrtam.
Iksau gudam tathā dēhē paśyātmānam vivēkatah.

Just like the fragrance is in flower, oil in sesame, clarified butter in milk, jaggery and sweetness in sugarcane, in the same manner both individual soul and the supreme soul are present in a society.

Chapter – 8

1. Adhamā dhanam icchanti dhanam mānam ca madhyamāh.
Uttamā mānam icchanti mānō hi mahatām dhanam.

Mean people crave for wealth, average people crave for both self respect and wealth, whereas superior people crave only for self respect, because self respect is the greatest wealth.

2. Iksu āpah payō mūlam tāmbūlam phalam ausadham.
Bhaksayitvā api kartavyāh snāna - dānādikāh kriyāh.

Even after consuming sugarcane, water, milk, tuber root, fruit juice and medicines, one can take bath, give charity, do virtuous work etc.

3. Dīpō bhaksayatē dhvāntam kajjalam ca prasūyatē.
Yadannam bhaksyēnnityam jāyatē tādrśī prajā.

Light eats darkness and makes collyrium, in the same manner a man's progeny will be like their parents and behave like them.

4. Vittam dēhi gunānvitēsu matimannānyatra dēhi kvacit.
Prāptam vārinidhih jalam ghanamukhē mādhuryayuktam sadā.
Jīvānsthāvara jangamānśca sakalān sanjīvya bhūmandalam.
Bhūyah paśya tadēva kōti gunitam gacchantam ambhōnidhim.

Give wealth to only an intelligent or good charactered man, never give wealth to a characterless man. The salt water from the ocean mixes with the sweet water from the cloud and becomes sweet and after giving life to all the living creatures and things, once again goes and joins the ocean.

5. Cāndālānām sahasrē ca sūribhih tattva darśibhih.
Ēkō hi yavanah prōktō na nīcō yavanāt parah.

The scholars who understand the logic have said that one Greek is equivalent to thousands of cannibals. There is none more evil than him.

6. Tailābhyangē citādhūmē maithunē ksaurakarmani.
Tāvad bhavati cāndālō yāvat snānam na ca ācarēt.

If a man doesn't bathe after an oil massage, after a touch of pyre, after having pleasure and after having a haircut, he remains a chandaal until he bathes.

7. Arjīnē bhēsajam vāri jīrnē vāri balapradam.
Bhōjanē ca amrtam vāri bhōjanāntē visapradam.

Water is a cure for indigestion. Water gives strength after the digestion of food. It is ambrosia if drunk during the meal but becomes poison if drunk at the end of a meal.

8. Hatam jñānam kriyāhīnam hatah ca ajñānatō narah.
Hatam anāyakam sainyam striyō nastā hyabhartrkāh.

Knowledge remains useless unless it is put into practise; man gets destroyed due to ignorance. An army gets destroyed without a commander. Women get destroyed when they lose their husbands.

9. Vrddhakālē mrtā bhāryā bandhuhastē gatam dhanam.
Bhōjanam ca parādhīnam tisrah punsām vidambanāh.

A wife's death during one's old age, losing wealth to a relative, eating food donated by others is as sorrowful as death.

10. Agnihōtram vinā vēdā na ca dānam vinā kriyā.
Na bhāvēna vinā siddhih tasmād bhāvō hi kāranam.

Learning without a fire ceremony is useless, a sacrifice is useless without a donation and knowledge cannot be gained without dedication and hard work. The feeling of dedication helps us in achieving our knowledge.

11. Kāsthapāsānadhātunām krtvā bhāvēna sēvanam.
Śraddhayā ca tayā siddhah tasya visnuh prasīdati.

One has to work with concentration while working on wood, stone or metal. Such dedicated people are loved by Lord Vishnu and they acquire knowledge.

12. Na dēvō vidyatē kāsthē na pāsānē na mrnmayē.
Bhāvē hī vidyatē dēvah tasmād bhāvō hī kāranam.

There is no God in mud, wood or stone. God is present in the feeling of dedication, devotion, hence He is venerated.

13. Śāntitulyam tapō nāsti na santōsa param sukham.
Na trsnāyā parō vyādhih na ca dharmō dayāparah.

There is no penance greater than peace, comfort greater than happiness, disease greater than greed and religion greater than the feeling of pity.

14. Krōdhō vaivasvatō rājā trsnā vaitaranī nadī.
Vidyā kāmadudhā dhēnuh santōsō nandanam vanam.

Anger is like Lord Yama, avarice is like Vytarini river, education is Kamadhenu and happiness is nanadanavana.

15. Gunō bhūsayatē rūpam śīlam bhūsayatē kulam.
Siddhih bhūsayatē vidyām bhōgō bhūsayatē dhanam.

Character increases beauty, honour increases the value of race, success increases the value of education and the rightful usage of wealth helps in the veneration of wealth.

16. Nigurnasya hatam rūpam duhśīlasya hatam kulam.
Asiddhasya hatā vidyā yabhōgēna hatam dhanam.

The beauty in a characterless person is useless, a race loses its name because of a characterless person, failure stops education and wealth gets wasted it it is not used properly.

17. Śucih bhūmigatam tōyam śuddhā nārī pativratā.
Śucih ksēmakarō rājā santustō brāhmanah śucih.

Water inside the earth is very pure, an honourable lady is pure, a forgiving king is pure and a contented Brahmin is pure.

18. Asantustā dvijā nastāh santustāh ca mahībhrtah.
Salajjā ganikā nastā nirlajjāh ca kulānganā.

A discontented Brahmin gets destroyed, a satisfied king gets destroyed, a prostitute who has feeling of shame and a shameless girl of honourable family get destroyed.

19. Kim kulēna viśālēna vidyāhīnēna dēhinām.
Duskulam ca api vidusō dēvaih api supūjyatē.

There is nothing great about any race if there is no education. If a man of an evil race is educated, even Gods will respect him.

20. Vidvān praśasyatē lōkē vidvān gacchati gauravam.
Vidyayā labhatē sarvam vidyā sarvatra pūjyatē.

A knowledgeable person gets praised in the world, gets respect and reverence and almost everything. Education is revered everywhere.

21. Mānsabhaksaih surāpānaih mūrkhaih ca aksara varjitaih.
Paśubhih purusa ākāraih bhāra ākrāntā ca mēdinī.

The world is bogged down by meat eating, alcohol drinking, foolish and illiterate animal like people.

22 Annahīnō dahēd rāstram mantrahīnah - ca rtvijah.
Yajamānam dānahīnō nāsti yajñasamō ripuh.

A sacrifice is like an enemy which has participants as people who make the country become food less; Brahmins not knowing hymns performing sacrifice and one who doesn't have the feeling of donating.

Chapter – 9

1. Muktim icchasi cēttāta visayāna visavat tyaja.
Ksamā ārjava dayā śaucam satyam pīyūsavad piba.

One who deserves salvation should let go of bad habits treating them as poison and accept forgiveness, compassion and tolerance as nectar.

2. Parasparasya marmāni yē bhāsantē narādhamāh.
Ta ēva vilayam yānīta valmīkōdara sarpavat.

Those who find faults with others, use harsh words on them, get destroyed like how a snake gets destroyed when it fall into an anthill.

3. Gandhah suvarnē phalam icchu dandē na ākāri puspam khalu candanasya.
VidvānM dhanādhyah ca nrpah cirāyuh dhātuh purā kōpi na buddhidōbhūt.

Lord Brahma did not add aroma to gold or fruits to sugarcane plant. Admittedly the sandalwood tree does not have flowers and the knowledgeable people do not have wealth. A king does not live a long life. At such a time one feels that there is none to give good advice.

4. Sarva ausadhīnāma amrtā pradhānā sarvēsu saukhyēsvaśanam pradhānam.
Sarvē indriyānām nayanam pradhānam sarvēsu gātrēsu śirah pradhānam.

Ambrosia is the most important of all the medicines, food gives the maximum contentment. The sense of sight is the most important among all the senses in the humans and the head is very important among all parts of the body.

5. Dūtō na sancarati khē na calēcca vārtā
Pūrvam na jalpitam idam na ca sangamō asti.
Vyōmni sthitam raviśaśigrahanam praśastam
Janāti yō dvijavarah sa katham na vidvān .

Messengers do not move in skies, there is no conversation from there, then why can't the learned people follow the thoughts told by learned Brahmins about the soilar and lunar eclipse?

6. Vidyārthī sēvakah pānthah ksudhārtō bhayakātarah.
Bhāndārī pratihārī ca sapta suptān prabōdhayēt.

If a student, a servant, a traveller, a tourist, someone suffering hunger pangs, one who is scared, a treasurer, or a security person sleeps at 7, then we have to wake them up.

7. Ahim nrpah ca śārdūlam kitim ca bālakam tathā.
Para śvānam ca mūrkham ca sapta suptāna na bōdhayēt.

If a snake, a king, a tiger, a wasp, a child, other's dog and a fool sleep at 7, we should not wake them up.

8. Artha ādhītāh yē vēdāstathā śūdra anna bhōjināh.
Tē dvijāh kim karisyanti nivisā iva pannagāh.

One who learns vedas for the sake of earning wealth, one who eats the food given by evil people, becomes like a snake without any venom incapable of doing anything.

9. Yasmin rustē bhayam nāsti tustē naiva dhana āgamah.
Nigrahō anugrahō nāsti sa rustam kim karisyati.

One who is not afraid of getting angry and doesn't expect something to remain calm and happy, one who doesn't either punish or pardon, doesn't spoil anything for anyone.

10. Nirviśēsana api sarpēna kartavyā mahatī phanā.
Visamastu na cāpyastu phanātōpō bhayankarah.

The poisonless snake should also spread its hood because no one knows whether it is poisonous or not.. But people will get afraid at such display.

11. Prātah dyūta prasangēna madhyāhnē strīprasangatah.
Rātrau cairya prasangēna kālō gacchatya - dhīmatām.

Foolish men spend their morning gambling, their day in the company of women and at night in thieving.

12. Svahastagrathitā mālā svahastāda ghrstacandanam.
Svahastalikhitam stōtram śakrasyāpi śriyam harēt.

Through the garland woven by oneself, the sandal paste rubbed by oneself and the praise written by oneself, one gets the control over the wealth of Indra.

13. Iksudandāh tilāh ksudrāh kāntā hēma ca mēdanī.
Candana dadhi tāmbūlu mardanam gunavarddhanam.

The more you press the sugarcane, gingelly, small man, woman, gold, land, sandalwood, curd and betal leaf, the brighter their character shines.

14. Daridratā dhīratayā virājatē kuvastrā śubhratayā virājatē.
Kudannatā cōsnatayā virājatē kurūpatā śīlatayā virājatē.

Lack of wealth will not make us lose patience during poverty, it will be fine when we keep our ordinary clothes clean, the old and cold food will become healthy when reheated. With qualities like gentleness, even an ugly person will look good.

Chapter – 10

1. Dhanahīnō na hīnaśca dhanikah sa suniścayah.
Vidyāratnēna yō hīnah sa hīnah sarvavastusu.

A person without wealth cannot be called poor whilst a wealthy person without education is worthless. The one who has wealth in the form of education is always happy. But when a man doesn't have the jewel of education, he is wretched in all forms.

2. Drstipūtam nyasēt pādam vastrapūtam pibējjalam.
Śāstrapūtam vadēd vākyam manah pūtam samācarēt.

One should set one's foot forward only after checking everything, should drink water only after filtering it with a cloth, should speak according to scriptures and should perform a task whole heartedly only after thinking and comprehending it.

3 Sukhārthī cēt tyajēt vidyā vidyārthī cēt tyajēta-Sukham.
Sukhārthinah kutō vidyā kutō vidyārthinah sukham.

If a man is only interested in seeking comfort, he should sacrifice the desire to learn. If a man desires to acquire knowledge, he should sacrifice comfort. Knowledge does not come to people seeking the comfort, comfort does not happen to people seeking knowledge.

4. Kavayah kim na paśyanti kim na kurvanti yōsitah.
Madyapāh kim na jalpanti kim na khādānti vāyasāh.

Poets can see everything through their imagination and women can do anything. A man can utter anything under intoxication and a crow can eat anything.

5. Rankam karōti rājānam rājanam rankamēva ca.
Dhaninam nirdhanam caiva nirdhanam dhaninam vidhih.

Luck can change a penniless man to king and vice versa. A wealthy person turns poor and a poor person wealthy.

6. Lubdhānām yācakah śatruh mūrkhānām bōdhakah ripuh.
Jārastrīnām patih śatruh cōrānām candramā ripuh.

A person who asks is an enemy to a greedy man, one who tries to give knowledge is an enemy to a fool. A husband is the enemy to a characterless woman and the moon is the enemy to the thieves.

7. Yēsām na vidyā na tapō na dānam cāpi śīlam na gunō na dharmah.
Tē matryalōkē bhuvi bhārabhūtā manusyarūpēna mrgāh caranti.
Dharatī para bōjha haim. Vē manusya rūpa mēm mrga paśu kē samāna haim.

One who doesn't have education, hasn't done any penance, doesn't have the habit of donating, doesn't have knowledge, doesn't have the feeling of pity or humility, doesn't have good qualities or right behaviour becomes a useless weight on the earth. He is an animal in the garb of a human being.

8. Antahsāravihīnānāmupadēśō na jāyētē.
Malayācalasansargāt na vēnuh candanāyatē.

One who doesn not have inherent capability, it is useless to advise him in any matter. Even if a bamboo has relation with a mountain it cannot get any fragrance from it.

9. Yasya nāsti svayam prajñā śāstram tasya karōti kim.
Lōcanābhyām vihīnasya darpanah kim karisyati.

One having no common sense cannot be safeguarded by the scriptures. All scriptures are useless to him like how scenery is useless to a blind person.

10. Durjanam sajjanam kartumapāyō na hi bhūtalē.
Apānam śatadhā dhautam na śrēstham indriyam bhavēt.

There is no means in this world through which a bad person can be turned into good just like how many ever times we wash the rectum, cannot become a superior organ.

11. Ātmadvēsād bhavēt mrtyuh paradvēsād dhanaksayah.
Rājadvēsād bhavēt nāśō brahmadvēsāt kulaksayah.

One who hates himself dies. One who hates others loses his wealth. One who hates the king gets destroyed. And the entire race of one gets destroyed if one hates a Brahmin.

12 Varam vanam vyāghra-Gajēndra-sēvitam drumālayamē patraphalāmbu-sēvanam.
Trnēsu śaiyā śatajīrnavalkalam na bandhumadhyē dhanahīna jīvanam.

Let a man live in the forest amid lions and tigers, eat fruits and leaves, sleep on grass, wear torn and old clothes, but let him not live as a destitute among his kith and kin.

13. Viprō vrksah tasya mūlam ca sandhyā vēdāh śākhā dharmakarmāni patram.
Tasmānmūlam yatnatō raksanīyam chinnē mūlē naiva śākhā na patram.

A Brahmin is like a tree and prayer and adoration are his roots. Virtue and deeds are his leaves. Hence the root has to be safeguarded dedicatedly because the destruction of roots will result in the lack of branches or leaves.

14. Mātā ca kamalā dēvī pitā dēvō jarnādanah.
Bāndhavā visnubhaktāh ca svadēśō bhuvanatrayam.

A man acquires the blessings of the three worlds if his mother is Goddess Lakshmi, father is the Almighty God and the devotees of God – his relatives.

15. Ēkavrksāsamārūrhā nānāvarnā vihangamāh.
Prabhātē diksu daśasu kā tatra parivēdanā.

Many hues of birds come to roost on a tree at night. They fly away in different directions during the day. There is no need to feel sad about this fact.

16. Buddhih yasya balam tasya nirbuddhēh tu kutō balam.
Vanē sinhē madōnmatō śaśakēna nipātitah.

One having knowledge has strength. What strength can an ignorant person have? A lion which was moving about arrogantly in the forest was pushed down into a well by a rabbit.

17. Kā cintā mama jīvanē yadi harih viśvambharō gīyatē nō
cēdarbhakajīvanāya jananīstanyam katham nihsarēt.
Ityālōcya muhurmuhuryadupatē laksmīpatē kēvalam tvatpādāmbuja sēvanēna
satatam kālō mayā nīyatē.

Why should I worry about my life when there is Lord Vishnu? Without his help how can a mother get milk in her breasts even before her child is born? We have to keep remembering such miracles and prostrate before Lakshmipathi.

18. Gīrvānavānīsu viśistabuddhih tathāpi bhāsāntaralōlupōham.
Yathā surānām amrtē sthitē api svarga ānganānām adharāsavē rucih.

I am greedy for other languages apart from Sanskrit, just like how the Gods desire to drink the nectar of the apsaras lips inspite of drinking the heavenly nectar.

19 Annād - Daśagunam pistam pistād daśagunam payah.
Dugdhād - astagunam māsam mānsād daśagunam ghrtam.

Wheat has ten times more strength than rice, milk ten times more than wheat. Meat has eight times more strength than milk and ghee has ten times more strength than meat.

20. Śākēna rōgā varddhantē payasā varddhatē tanuh.
Ghrtēna varddhatē vīryam māmsānmāmsam pravarddhatē.

Eating too much of greens will increase the diseases. Body grows when we have milk, semen increases when we have ghee and flesh increases when we eat meat.

Chapter – 11

1. Dātrtvam priyavaktrtvam dhīratvam ucitajñatā.
Abhyāsēna na labhyantē catvārah sahajā gunāh.

There are four inherent things in man the desire to donate, the desire to speak well, the feeling of patience and knowledge of the right and wrong. These cannot be acquired through practice.

2. Ātmavargam parityajya paravargam samāśrayēt.
Svayamēva layam yāti yathā rājā anya dharmatah.

One who quits his society and takes the help of other society, comes to an end just like a king who gets destroyed when he takes the shelter of another rreligion.

3. Hastī sthūla - tanuh sa ca ankuśavaśah kim hastimātrō ankuśō
Dīpē prajvalitē pranaśyati tamah kim dīpamātram tamah.
Vajrēnāpi hatāh patanti girayah kim vajramātrō girim
Tējō yasya virājatē sa balavān sthūlēsu kah pratyayah.

A huge bodied elephant can be controlled with just a spear. A small lamp can dispel the darkness. A small hammer can break the mountain. A thing becomes strong due to its sharpness not due to its size.

4. Kalau daśasahasrāni harih tyajati mēdinīm.
Tadarddha jāhnavītōyam tadarddha grāmadēvatāh.

The omnipotent God will leave this world after 10,000 years of Kaliyug. River Ganga will dry up in half of that time. The village Gods will leave their villages in half of that time.

5. Grhāsaktasya nō vidyā na dayā māmsabhōjinah.
Dravyalubdhasya nō satyam strainasya na pavitratā.

One who is attached to his house does not get education; one who eats meat doesn't have a feeling of mercy. One who is greedy for money will not have truth in the one. And one who is surrounded with pleasure won't have purity.

6. Na durjanah sādhudaśāmmupaiti bahuprakārērēpi śiksyamānah.
Āmūlasiktah payasā ghrtēna na nimbavrksō madhuratvamēti.

Even if a neem tree is tended with milk and ghee, it cannot become sweet. In the same manner a bad man will never turn into good even if taught in a variety of manner.

7. Antargatamalō dustahtīrthasnānaśatairapi.
Na śudhyatē yathā bhāndam surayā dāhitam ca yat.

A pot of alcohol doesn't become pure despite heating it. In the same manner, an evil man who is filled with filth cannot pourify himself even if he takes bath in thousands of pilgrim centres.

8. Na vētti yō yasya gunaprakarsam sa tam sadā nindati nātra citram.
Yathā kirātī karikumbhalavdhām muktāh parityajya bibharti gunjām.

A man who does not have the knowledge of the greatness of some one's character, will always keep cursing him. But none get surprised with such behaviour, because neglecting the pearls got from the forehead of an elephant, wishes to wear the garland made of clod of earth.

9. Yē tu sanvatsaram pūrnam nityam maunēna bhunjatē.
Yugakōtisahasram tu pūjyantē svargavistapē.

A man who remains quiet for a year, eats food quietly, gets respect and regard for crores of years in heaven.

10. Kāmam krōdham tathā lōbham svādu śrngārakautukē.
Atinidrā atisēvē ca vidyārthī hyasta varjayēt.

The students should give away the lust, the anger, greed, tasty foody, game, comedy and insincere praise.

11. Akrstaphalamūlāni vanavāsarati sadā.
Kurutē aharahah śrāddham rsi viprah sa ucyatē.

One who eats the fruits and roots which are not grown from the crops, remains happy even in a forest and one who performs the timely death ceremony is a rishi.

12. Ēka āhārēna santustah satkarmaniratah sadā.
Rtukāla abhigāmī sa ca vipra dvija ucyatē.

One who is satisfied with one kind of food, who completes his daily work, has relationship with a woman only for the sake of progeny, is called a dwij.

13. Laukikē karmani ratah paśūnām paripālakah.
Vānijyakrsikartā yah sa viprō vaiśya ucyatē.

One who is drowned in the worldly affairs, tends to animals, does agriculture and farming is usually called a vysya.

14. Lāksāditailanīlānām kusumbhamadhusarpisām.
Vikrētā madyamānsānām sa vipra śūdra ucyatē.

One who trades in lac, oil, blue, dyes, ghee, alcohol, meat etc is called a shudra.

15. Parakāryavihantā ca dāmbhikah svārthasādhakah.
Chalī dvēsī mrduh krūrō viprō mārjāra ucyatē.

One who spoils the work of others, is a cheat, always tries to fulfil his selfish needs, cheats others, finds fault in others, is cruel though acting humble, is called a cat.

16. Vāpīkūpatadāgānāma ārāmasuravēśmanām.
Ucchēdanē nirāśankah sa vipra mlēksa ucyatē.

One who is not afraid of spoiling water bodies, wells, ponds, gardens or temples is called a menial or low born.

17. Dēvadravyam gurudravyam paradārā abhimarsana.
Nirvāhah sarvabhūtēsu vipra cāndāla ucyatē.

One who steals the wealth of Gods, who has relationship with other women, who lives with all kinds of animals, is called a Chandaal.

18. Dēyam bhōjyadhanam sadā sukrtibhirnō sancayastasya vai śrīkarnasya
balēh ca vikramapatēh adyāpi kīrtih sthitā.
Asmākam madhudānabhōgarahitam nastam cirāt sancitam nirvānāditi
naijapādayugalam gharsantyāhō maksikāh.

Even the bees repent while gathering honey that it may get spoilt if it is not donated. Some people do not donate and when the wealth gets depleted they repent. But people can make good use of wealth by donating it. It is only due to the quality of donating that Karna, Bali and Vikramaditya are remembered in the society even today.

Chapter-12

1. Sānandam sadanam sutāstu sudhiyah kāntā priyālāpinī icchāpūrtidhanam
svayōsiti ratih svāājñāparāh sēvakāh.
Ātithyam śivapūjanam pratidinam mistānnapānam grhē sādhōh sangama
upāsatē ca satatam dhanyō grhasthāśramah.

A man's house is blessed when his sons and daughters have good knowledge, when his wife is soft spoken, when he has wealth earned through hard work and honesty, when his friends are good, when he has affection towards all when his servants are obedient, where his guests are well taken care of, where the Lord is venerated everyday, where good food is cooked and relished, when he is always in the company of good men. Then this becomes laudable and comfortable household.

2. Ārtēsu viprēsu dayānīvatah ca yat śraddhayā svalpam upaiti dānam.
Anantapāram samupaiti rājan yaddīyatē tanna labhēd dvijēbhyah.

O'King, if a man donates something to a needy brahmin with the feeling of pity and generosity the man does not merely gewt back what he has donated but he gets back much more due to God's benevolence.

3. Dāksinyam svajanē dayā parajanē śāthyam sadā durjanē
prītih sādhujanē smayah khalajanē vidvajjanē ca ārjavam.
Śauryam śatrujanē ksamā gurujanē nārījanē dhūrtatā
ittham yē purusāh kalāsu kuśalāh tēh ēva lōkasthitih.

The world is still in progress only because of people having good behaviour with kith and kin, pity towards others, a careful behaviour with evil people, love towards good people, cruelty towards evil people, simplicity with men and patience and cleverness in dealing with women.

4. Hastau dānavivarjitau śrutiputau sārasvatadrōhinau.
Nētrē sādhuvilōkanēna rahitē pādau na tīrtham gatau.
Anyāya arjita vittapūrnam udaram garvēna tungam śirō.
Rē rē jambuka munca munca sahasā nicam sunindyam vapuh.

A man has to give up his life early if both his hands have never donated anything, his ears have never listened to the chanting of vedas, his eyes haven't seen great people, his feet haven't gone on pilgrimage, he hasn't served his parents his parents and teacher, he has earned wealth unethically and enjoyed it, he walks around arrogantly, he is meaner than mean men.

5. Patram naiva yadā karīravitapē dēdō vasantasya kim
Nōlūkōpya avalōkatē yadi divā sūryasya kim dūsanam.
Varsā naiva patanti cātakamukhē mēghasya kim dūsanam
Yatpūrvam vidhinā lalātalikhitam tanmārjitum kah ksamah.

What is the fault of spring if a new plant doesn't have leaves? Can sun be faulted if an owl can't see during the day? Can the clouds be faulted if the rain drops don't fall on the cuckoo? The creator of the universe will only give each what he deserves, his fate cannot be erased, he has to bear it.

6. Satsangāta bhavati hi sādhutā khalānām
sādhūnām na hi khalasangamātē khalatvam.
Āmōdam kusumabhavam mrdēva dhattē
mrdgandham na hi kusumāni dhārayanti.

An evil person can also become good in the company of good people but not vice versa just like the fragrance of flowers can be got on the mud, but the smell of mud on any flower.

7. Sādhūnām darśanam punyam tīrthabhūtā hi sādhavah.
Kālē phalanti tīrthāni sadyah sādhusamāgamah.

One gets virtue just by seeing good people as the good people are themselves holy. Holy places give fruits at specific time but instant gain can be achieved in the company of good people.

8. Viprāsminnagarē mahānM kathaya kastāladrumānām
ganah kō dātā rajakō dadāti vasanam prātargrhitvā niśi.
Kō daksah paradāra vitta haranē sarvē api daksō janah
kasmāt jīvasi hē sakhē visakrminyāyēna jīvāmyaham.

One traveller asked a Brahmin when he reached a city.

"Hey Brahmin! Who is the greatest in this city?"

The Brahmin replied, "The Palmyra grove."

The traveller then asked, "Who is the generous person in this city?"

The Brahmin replied, "The dhobi who takes the clothes in the morning and returns them in the evening."

The traveller asked, "Who is the cleverest person in this city?"

The Brahmin replied "Everyone is clever in stealing other's wife and wealth. The traveller said, "How are you living in this state?" The Brahmin replied, "I am like the insect born out of poison, live in it and die in it."

9. Vipra pāda ōdaka kardamāni na vēdaśāstradhvanigarjitāni.
Svāhāsvadhākāravivirjitāni śmaśānatulyānī grhāni tāni.

A house is like a grave yard where Brahmin's feet have not been washed, where vedas and scriptures haven't been recited, where the echoes of swaaha and swadha are not heard.

10. Satyam mātā pitā jñānam dharmō bhrātā dayā svasā.
Śāntih patnī ksamā putrah sadtē mama bāndhavāh.

Truth is my mother, knowledge is my father, righteousness is my brother, pity is my sister, peace is my wife and patience is my son. These six qualities are my relatives.

11. Anityānī śarīrāni vibhavō naiva śāśvatah.
Nityam sannihitō mrtyuh kartavyōh dharmasangrahah.

This body is perishable, wealth is not permanent, death is closeby. Hence every man should spend his time in following the dharma.

12. Āmantrana utsavā viprā gāvō navatrnōtsavāh.
Pati utsāha yutā bhāyī aham krsna! Ranōtsukah.

Being invited for a feast is a festival for a Brahmin, getting green grass for grazing is a festival for cattle, the enthusiasm in their husbands is a festival for the women and a place near the feet of Lord Krishna is festival for the saints.

13. Mātrvat paradārēsu paradravyēsu lōsthavat.
Ātmavat sarvabhūtēsu yah paśyati sa pandita.

A man is called a pandit if he respects others' wives as mothers, treats others' wealth as dust, and looks at all creatures as a part of himself.

14 Dharmē tatparatā mukhē madhuratā dānē sama utsāhatā
mitrē-avancakatā gurau vinayatā cittē ati gambhīratā.
Ācārē śucitā gunē rasikatā śāstrēsu vijñātrtā
rūpē sundaratā śivē bhajanatā satyēva sandrśyatē.

One can find the following qualities in good human beings – always busy doing righteous things, sweet in speech, always ready to donate, not treating his friends differently, humility towards his teacher, purity in action, good looks and devotion to God.

15. Kāstham kalpataruh sumēruh acalah cintāmanih prastarah
sūryah tīvrakarah śaśī ksayakarah ksārō hi vārānnidhih.
Kāmō nastatanuhbali - aditisutō nityam paśuh kāma
gaurjāstē tulayāmi bhō raghupatē kasyaupamā dīyatē.

The Kalpataru which fulfils every desire is a wood, the steady Sumeru is a mountain, the gem which removes worries is only a stone. Sun has powerful rays, the moon keeps waxing and waning, the ocean is salty, Lord Kamadeva has no body, King bali was a demon, Kamadhenu is a cow. Tell me O' Lord! Wth whom can I equate you? You are peerless.

16. Vinayam rājaputrēbhyah panditēbhyah subhāsitam.
Anrtam dyūtakārēbhyah strībhyah śiksēt kaitavam.

Man should learn to behave humbly with kings, to speak knowledgeably with learned men and not to cheat women.

17. Anālōkya vyayam kartā hyanāthah kalahapriyah.
Āturah sarvaksētrēsu narah śīghamMra vinaśyati.

One who spends a lot without thinking or seeing, fights with all despite being physically weak, as always eager for pleasures, gets destroyed very early.

18 Na-Āhāram cintayēt prājñō dharmam ēkam hi cintayēt.
Āhārō hi manusyānām janmanā saha jāyētē.

An intelligent man should not worry about food. He should be preoccupied with only virtue or duty because his food has already been decided at the time of his birth.

19 Jalabindu - Nipātēna kramaśah pūryatē ghatah.
Sa hētuh sarvavidyānām dharmasya ca dhanasya ca.

Just like how a pot gets filled by drops of water, the continuous consolidation of wealth, education or virtue also occurs.

20. Vayasah parināmē api yah khalah ēva sah.
Supakvam api mādhuryam na upayāti indra vārunam.

An evil man continuous to be evil even after he matures, just like the fruit of Indrayan never becomes sweet even when it ripens, it remains only bitter.

Chapter-13

1. Muhūrtam api jīvēcca narah śuklēna karmanā.
Na kalpam api kastēna lōkadvayavirōdhinā.

If we get a life of just a muhurth [just 48 minutes], we should spend it doing virtuous work. It is useless living for hundred years both on the earth and the heaven doing vicious work.

2. Gatē śōkō na kartavyō bhavisyam naiva cintayēt.
Vartamānēna kālēna pravartantē vicaksanāh.

Never feel sad on things which are already over, never worry about future too. Intelligent people work according to the present.

3. Svabhāvēna hi tusyanti pitarah sajjanāh surāh.
Jñātayō mānpānābhyām vākyadānēna panditā.

Gods, good people and ancestors are satisfied by nature. Kith and kin get satisfied with good hospitality and learned men become happy with sweet conversation.

4. Ahō bāta vicitrāni caritāni mahā ātmānam.
Laksmīm trnāya manyantē tad bhārēna namanti ca.

It is a matter pf great wonder that great people consider wealth as grass but remain bent due to its weight.

5. Yasya snēhō bhayam tasya snēhō dukhasya bhājanam.
Snēha mūlāni duhkhāni tattat tyaktvā vasēt sukham.

One who likes another, will be worried for that someone/ Liking someone os a cause for sorrow. Hence one has to give up friendship and live comfortably.

6. Anāgata vidhātā ca pratyutpannamatistathā.
Dvāvētau sukhamēdhētē yadbhavisyō vinaśyati.

One who is prepared beforehand to overcome the future obstacles and when danger befalls him, plans on removing them, gains a lot of comfort. But one who believes that whatever happens is due to destiny gets destroyed.

7. Rājñi dharmini dharmisthāh pāpē pāpāh samē samāh.
Rājānam anuvartantē yathā rājā tathā prajā.

If a king is righteous, his subjects will be righteous, if a king is vicious, his subjects will also be vicious. If the king is careless, his subjects will also be careless because the way a king behaves, his subjects also will behave.

**8. Jīvantam mrtavanmanyē dēhinam dharmavarjitam.
Mrtō dharmēna sanyuktō dīrghajīvī na sanśayah.**

One who does not follow virtuous path is equivalent to dead despite being alive but a man following a virtuous path will remain alive for a long time even after his death.

**9. Dharma artha kāma mōksānām yasyai ēkō api na vidyatē.
Ajāgalastanah ēva tasya janma nirrathakam.**

A man's life is useless like the breasts hanging on the neck of goats which are useless if he doesn't have virtue, wealth and salvation.

**10. Dahyamānāh sutīvrēna nīcāh para yaśa agninā.
Aśaktāh tatpadam gantum tatō nindām prakurvatē.**

An evil man burns with jealousy seeing the fame of others and when he becomes unsuccessful of gaining that post, he starts bad mouthing the other person.

**11 Bandhāya visayā - āsakta sangō muktē nirvisayam manah.
Mana ēvam manusyānām kāranam bandha mōksayōh.**

Man is shackled in relationships only due to his thoughts but can get free from relationships through thoughts. Desiring things is shackles and release from it is salvation.

**12 Dēha-Abhimānē galitē jñānēna parama ātmanah.
Yatra tatra manō yāti tatra tatra samādhayah.**

When one lets go of ego and becomes one with God, he will attain salvation wherever he goes.

**13. Īpsitam manasah sarvam kasya sampadyatē sukham.
Daiva āyattam yatah sarvam tasmāt santōsam āśrayēt.**

All desires of man cannot be fulfilled. Hence man should learn to be happy in his life.

**14. Yathā dhēnusahasrēsu vatsō gacchati mātaram.
Tathā yacca krtam karma kartāramanugacchati.**

Even if ther are thousands of cows, a calf will run only towards its mother, in the same manner, one who needs to get something done will run behind the doer.

**15. Anavasthitakāryasya na janē na vanē sukham.
Janē dahati sansargāda vanam sangavivarjanāta.**

A man who is clumsy in work never enjoys comfort in the society or in the forest. The company of people in the society makes him sorrowful while in the forest he feels lonely.

**16. Yathā khātvā khanitrēna bhūtalē vāri vindati.
Tathā gurugatām vidyā śuśrūsamh adhigacchati.**

Just as we get water when we dig the earth, we get the knowledge when we serve our teachers.

**17. Karmāyattam phalam punsām buddhih karma anusārinī.
Tathāpi sudhiyah ca āryāh sanvicāra ēva kurvatē.**

Man gets the fruits according to his fate and man's mind also works according to fate. Inspite of this, the intelligent people and good people work after thinking deeply and a lot.

18. Ēka aksara pradātāram yō gurum na abhivandati.
Śvānayōniśatam bhuktvā cāndālēsvabhijāyētē.

One who does not chant'Om' is born 100 times from the womb of a dog and is born again in the womb of a chandaal.

19. Yugāntē pracalatē mēruh kalpāntē sapta sāgarāh.
Sādhavah pratipannārthān na calanti kadācan.

Even the Sumeru mountain does not remain in its place at the end of a Yug or epoch, the ocean will also cross its borders but the great men will complete the work they have pledged to do.

Chapter-14

1. Prthivyām trīni ratnāni jalam-annam subhāsitam.
Mūrhai pāsāna khandēsu ratnasanjñā vidhiyatē.

There are only three jewels on this earth – water, food and words that bring well-being. But the fools think the broken stones to be jewels.

2 Dāridraya - Rōga - dukhāni bandhana - vyasanāni ca.
Ātmā aparādha vrksasya phalānya ēti dēhinām.

Poverty, disease, despair and attachment are the fruits of man's non-virtuous tree.

3. Punah vittam punah mitram punah bhāryā punah mahī.
Ētad sarvam punah labhyam na śarīram punah punah.

Health, friends, wife can be acquired repeatedly on the earth, but a human life/body cannot be acquired repeatedly.

4. Bahūnām caiva sattvānām samavāyō ripunjayah.
Varsādhārādharō mēghah trnaih api nivāryatē.

The enemy can be definitely defeated with unity just like a thick bunch of reeds can stop the flow of stream.

5. Jalē tailam khalē guhyam pātrē dānē manāgapi.
Prājñē śāstram svayam yāti vistāram vastuśaktitah.

Just as oil spreads on water, secret spreads from a bad person, donation spreads when given to deserving, the knowledge of scripture spreads everywhere when given to a knowledgeable person.

6. Dharma ākhyānē śmaśānē ca rōginām yā matih - Bhavēt.
Sa sarvadaiva tisthēccēt kō na mucyatē bandhanāt.

People get unshackled from attachments if they have the feeling that they get while listening to holy stories or while in the cemetery or while sitting beside a sick person permanently.

7. Paścāttāpōpajātasya buddhirbhavati yādrśī.
Tādrśī yadi pūrvam syāt kasya na syān - mahōdayah.

The mindset during the remorse a man gets after committing an evil deed is present in him even before doing it, then a man can attain salvation.

8. Dānē tapasi śauryam vā vijñānē vinayē nayē.
Vismayō na hi kartavyō bahuratnā vasundharā.

One need not admire a man who has the habit of donating, penance, valour, scientific temper, humility and obedience to law because there are one better than the other jewels on the earth.

9. Dūrasthō api na dūrasthō yō yasya manasi sthitah.
Yō asya hrdayē nāsti samīpasyō api dūratah.

Even if a person is physically far, but lives in someone's mind, he is still nrae. But if he is not in the mind, then even though he is near will stiff be far.

10. Yasya ca apriyam icchēta tasya brūyāt sadā priyam.
Vyādhō mrgavadham kartum gītam gāyati susvaram.

One who desires evil always speaks sweetly just like in order to trap a deer a fowler sings in a very sweet voice.

11. Atyāsannā vināśāya dūrasthā na phalapradāh.
Sēvyatām madhyabhāvēna rājā vahnih guruh striyah.

One should neither be too far or too near a king, a teacher, fire and a woman. One should be in the middle.

12. Agnih āpah striyōm mūrkhah sarpō rājakulāni ca.
Nityam yatnēna sēvyānī sadyah prāna harāni sat.

One should be careful of fire, water, women, fools, snake and royal members because these six can take life anytime.

13. Sa jīvati gunā yasya yasya dharmah sa jīvati.
Gunadharma - vihīnasya jīvitam nisprayōjanam.

The person is considered alive when he has good character and virtue, The life of one who doesn't have these is useless.

14. Yadi icchasi vaśī kartum jagata ēkēna karmanā.
Purā pancadaśāsyēbhyō gām carantīm nivāraya.

If one wants to control the world with just one act then he has to have the control of demeaning others in fifteen ways. [5 organs of action, 5 senses of knowledge and five things – appearance, essence, odour, touch and word are the 15 ways]

15. Prastāvasadrśam vākyam prabhāvaih sadrśam priyam.
Ātmaśaktisamam kōpam yō jānāti sa panditah.

One who knows how to talk according to the situation, speaks sweetyly according to his fame and becomes angry according to his strength is actually a learned person.

16. Ēka ēvam padārthah stu tridhā bhavati vīksitah.
Kunapah kāminī māmsam yōgibhih kāmibhih śvabhih.

People see the same thing in three ways. Sages look at meat as the cursed corpse. Lustful people look at it as a beautiful woman and the dogs look at it as a lump of flesh to be eaten.

17. Susiddham ausadham dharmam grhacchidram ca maithunam.
Kubhuktam kumrtam caiva matimān na prakāśayēt.

Intelligent people will not reveal before others the medicines they take, the virtuous path they follow, their relationship with women, bad food and the curses they have heard.

18. Tāvanmaunēna nīyantē kōkilaiścaiva vāsarāh.
Yāvat sarvajana ānandadāyinī vākpravartatē.

The cuckoo remains silent until the onset of spring season which brings cheer to everyone.

19. Dharmam dhanam ca dhānyam ca gurōh vacanam ausadham.
Sugrhītam ca kartavyam anyathā tu na jīvati.

Following the right path, generating food, collecting wealth, teachings of a guru are the medicines to be acquired with dedication. The life will cannot be spent well otherwise.

20. Tyaja durjana sansargam bhaja sādhusamāgamam.
Kuru punyamahōrātram smara nityam - anityatām.

We have to leave the bad company, be in the company of good people, keep doing good deeds and meditating God day in and day out.

15

Chapter-15

1. Yasya cittam dravībhūtam krpayā sarvajantusu.
Tasya jñānēna mōksēna kim jatābhasmalēpanaih.

If a man's heart weeps with pity towards all living beings then why should he want tp pursue knowledge, ways of salvation, apply sacred ash on forehead?

2. Ēkam ēva aksaram yastu guruh śisyam prabōdhayēt.
Prthivyām nāsti taddravyam yaddatvā ca ānrnī bhavēt.

If a teacher can give his disciple one letter of 'OM' in his education, that disciple can never repay the debt of his master.

3. Khalānām kantakānām ca dvividhaiva ca pratikriyā.
Upāna - na - mukha - bhangō yā dūratō vā visarjanam.

There are only two ways of escaping evil people and thorns, either stamp their face with booted legs or remain afar from them.

4. Kucailinam dantam alōpadhārinam bra" vāsinam nisthura bhāsinam ca.
Sūryōdayē ca astam itē śayānam vimuncati śrīh yadi cakrapāni.

People wearing soiled clothes, having dirty teeth, eating too much, speaking harsh words, sleeping during the day time or the evening, do not enjoy wealth, health, beauty and glory.

5. Tyajanti mitrāni dhanaih vihīnam dārāh ca bhrtyāh ca suhrd janāh ca.
Tam ca arthavantam punah āśrayantē arthō hi lōkē purusasya bandhuh.

When a man doesn't have wealth, his friends, wife, servants and relatives desert him. If he regains his wealth, then people return to him. Wealth is the only relative of man.

6. Anyāya upārjitam dravyam daśavarsāni tisthati.
Prāptē ca ēkādaśē varsē samūlam tasya vinaśyati.

Wealth acquired through immoral means lasts only for ten years. It will be lost along with the principal amount on the 11th year.

7. Ayuktam svāminō yuktam yuktam nīcasya dūsanam.
Amrtam rāhavē mrtyuh visam śankarabhūsanam.

An improper work if performed capable and intelligently can nbe considered proper. If an evil man does good deeds it will still be considered evil. Ambrosia became poison for Rahu while the venom became an ornament adorning the throat of Lord Shiva.

8 Tad- Bhōjanam yaddvijabhuktaśēsam tatsauhrdam yatkriyatē parasmin.
Sa baddhimāna yō na karōti pāpam dambham vinā yah kriyatē sa dharmah.

The actual food is that remains after all the Brahmins are fed. One can call an emotion a love or affection only when it is shown on others, a sign of intelligence is for a man to stay away from doing evil deeds and a man should ideally not have the quality of cheating.

9. Manih lunthita pādāgrē kācah śirasi dhāryatē.
Krayavikrayavēlāyām kācah kācō manih manih.

Even if at certain times our feet trip on diamonds, while buying, a glass remains a glass and a diamond remains a diamond.

10. Anantaśāstram bahulāh - ca vidyāh alpah ca kālō bahu vighnatā ca.
Yatsārabhūtam tad - upāsanīyam hansō yathā ksīram iva ambum dhyāt.

Scriptures are vast, education is vast, but we have very less time and there are various obstacles. In such case we should comprehend the gist of things like how a swan drinks only milk and leaves out the water.

11. Dūrāgatam pathi śrāntam vrthā ca grham āgatam.
Anah cayitvā yō bhungaktē sa vai cāndāla ucyatē.

A man will be called a chaandaal if he eats his food without offering it to a hungry wayfarer who has come from afar.

12. Pathanti caturō vēdān dharma śāstrāna anēkaśah.
Ātmānam naiva jānanti darvī pākarasam yathā.

One who doesn't comprehend the individual soul and the supreme soul despite learning scriptures are equivalent to which the maggots which keep moving on plants and vegetables but never realise the taste of them.

13. Dhanyā dvijamayī naukā viparītā bhavārnavē.
Tarantya adhōgatāh sarvē uparisthāh patantayadhah.

The boat named Brahmin is very blessed in this ocean of world and it moves in the obverse direction. Those who are beneath this boat reach the other shore but nothing can be said of those above it.

14 Ayam amrta nidhānam nāyakō api - ausadhinām
amrtamaya śarīrah kāntiyuktō api candrah.
Bhavati vigata - raśmih mandalam prāpya bhānōh
parasadananivistah kō laghutvam na yāti.

A person's prestige reduces when he goes to another's house just like how the attribute of the ambrosiaic quality of the moon which is the master of a variety of medicines, reduces if it goes into the sun.

15. Alirayam nalinīdalamadhyagah kamalinīmakarandamadālasah.
Vidhivaśāt - paradēśam upāgatah kutajapusparasam bahu manyatē.

The bee sits on the petal of the lotus flower, but if it goes to a plant with thorns, it will no doubt get the nectar but it has to undergo a lot of troubles.

16. Pītah kruddhēna tātah caranatalahatō vallabhō yēna rōsād
ābālyād vipravaryaih svavadanavivarē dhāryatē vairinī yā.
Gēham mē chēdayanti pratidivasam - umākāntapūjānimittam
tasmāt khinnā sadāham dvijakulanilayam nāthayuktam tyajāmi.

Lord Vishnu asked Goddess Lakshmi why she hated the Brahmins. The goddess replied that Sage Agasthya drank the ocean in a fit of anger. Sage Bhrigu kicked on the heart of her beloved husband. These people are bent on pleasing Goddess Saraswathy right from their childhood. They pluck lotus flowers daily for performing pooja to Lord Shiva. Hence she remains afar from the Brahmins.

17. Bandhanāni khalu santi bahūni prēmarajju drrhabandhanam anyat.
Dārubhēdanipunā api sadaghrih niskriyō bhavati pankajakōśē.

There are a lot of shackes in this world, but the shackle of love is wonderful. The wasp can split the wood but gets destroyed when trapped inside the lotus flower.

18. Chinnō api candana tarurna jahāti gandham
vrddhō api vāranapatirna jahāti līlām.
Yantra arpitō madhuratām na jahāti cēksuh
ksīnō api na tyajati śīlagunān kulīnah.

The sandalwood retains its fragrance even after it is cut. An elephant does not stop frolicking even after becoming old. The sugarcane does not lose its sweetness despite being in the bog. In the same manner, a moral man does not become immoral despite becoming penniless.

Chapter-16

1. Na dhyātam padam īśvarasya vidhivat sansāravicchittayē
svargadvārakapātapātana patuhdharmō api na upārjitah.
Nārī-pīna-payōdharōru yugalam svapnē api na ālingitam mātuh kēvalam ēva
yauvana vanah chēdē kuthārā vayam.

One who hasn't taken the name of Lord for cutting the net like world and has not followed the righteous path for the entry into the heaven's gates and has not embraced a woman, destroys the youth of his mother and wastes his life.

2. Jalpanti sārdhamanyēna paśyantyanyam savibhramāh.
Hrdayē cintayantyanyam na strīnām ēkatō ratih.

A prostitute doesn't love anyone. She talks to someone while her amorous glances are directed at another and the thoughts are centred on yet another.

3. Yō mōhānmanyatē mūrhō raktēyam mayi kāminī.
Sa tasya vaśagō bhūtvā nrtyēt krīrāśakuntavat.

A fool who is under the impression that a prostitute loves him dances to her tunes like a puppet.

4. Kō arthān prāpya na gavirtō visayinah kasyāpadō astam gatah
Strībhih kasya na khanditam bhuvi manah kō nāma rājñām priyah.
Kah kālasya na gōcaratvam kō arthī gatō gauravam
Kō vā durjana durgunēsu patitah ksēmēna yātah pathi.

There hasn't been any man in this world who hasn't felt proud after acquiring wealth. There has been no man who hasn't had to face troubles. There hasn't been anyone who hasn't fallen under the spell of a beautiful woman and there hasn't been anyone who hasn't fallen prey to evil people and has been unable to live righteously.

5. Na nirmitah kēna drstappūrvōh na śrūyatē hēmamayah kurangah.
Tathā api trsnā raghunandanasya vināśakālē viparīta buddhih.

No golden animal has been created till date, nor has anyone seen it. Yet Lord Rama was anxious to snare a golden deer. The truth behind this is that everyone loses his sensibility at the time of danger.

6. Gunaih uttamatā yānīta na nicaih āsana sansthitaih.
Prāsādaśikharasthō api kākah kim garudāyatē.

Man achieves greatness due to his good qualities. No one will be called great just becauseone holds a high post. Just because a crow perches on the top floor of a palace, it cannot become an eagle.

7. Gunāh sarvatra pūjyantē na mahatyō api sampadah.
Pūrnēnduh kim tathā vandyō niskalankō yathā krśah.

One gets respect only due to one's qualities not due to wealth. The moon filled with so many spots is venerated more than on the second day of lunar month than it is venerated on a full moon.

8. Paraprōktagunō yastu nirgunō api gunī bhavēt.
Indrōapi laghutām yāti svayam prakhyāpitaihgunaih.

If a man is praised for certain qualities he doesn't possess, it will still be accepted, but even Indra becomes worthless if he sings his own praises.

9. Vivēkinam anuprāptā gunā yānīta manōjñatām.
Sutarām ratnam ābhāti ca āmīkara niyōjitam.

Just as a jewel encrusted in an ornament looks very beautiful, a man by bettering his character through common sense makes his personality more resplendent.

10. Gunaih sarvajña tulyō api sīdatyēkō nirāśrayah.
Anargha api mānikyam hēmāśrayam apēksatē.

A wretched man, though endowed with great qualities still remains wretched. The most precious diamond also likes to be embedded with gold. Man longs for support in this manner.

11. Atiklēśēm ca yē arthā dharma syātikramēna tu.
Śatrūnām pranipātēna tē hya arthā mā bhavantu mē.

The wealth acquired by harming others, doing immoral deeds or forcibly being taken from the shivering enemies is useless.

12. Kim tayā kriyatē laksmyā yā vadhūrita kēvalā.
Yā tu vēśyēva sāmānyā pathikaih api bhujyatē.

Just like a daughter-in-law, the wealth which is useful only for one is useless. Wealth has to be like a prostitute which can be enjoyed by the wayfarers.

13. Dhanēsu jīvitavyēsu strīsu ca āhāra karmasu.
Atrptāh prāninah sarvē yātā yāsyanti yānīta ca.

There is none on this earth who is satisfied with the consumption of wealth. The consumption of wealth is in life's work, service of women, food and after doing all these still feels dissatisfied.

14. Ksīyantē sarvadānāni yajñahōmabalikriyāh.
Na ksīyatē pātradānamabhayam sarvadēhinām.

Food, water, clothes, penances, homas, sacrifices get destroyed, but the donation given by a worthy person and the blessing given by a sincere friend never gets destroyed.

15. Trnam laghu trna ātulam tūlādapi ca yācakah.
Vāyunā kim na nītō asau māmayam yācayisyati.

Straw is very light, the thread is lighter than the straw, the air is lighter than a thread but a beggar is lighter than all these.

16. Varam prānaparityāgō mānabhangēna jīvanāt.
Prānatyāgē ksanam duhkham mānabhangē dinē - dinē.

It is better to die than live in ignominy. There is only a second of madness before death. But when one is insulted, the sorrow remains for the entire life.

17. Priyavākyapradānēna sarvē tusyanti jantavah.
Tasmāttadēva vaktavyam vacanē kā draridratā.

All creatures enjoy listening to sweet voice. Then why hesitate to speak sweetly?

18. Sansāravisavrksasya dvē phalē amrtōpamē.
Subhāsitanca susvādam sangatih sujanē janē.

The universe is a poison tree, which has two ambrosic fruits. One is good speech which is used for other's welfare and the second is the company of good men.

19. Bahujanmasu cā abhyastam dānam adhyayanam tapah.
Tēnaivābhyāsayōgēna dahīcābhyasyatē punah.

The man keeps doing repeatedly the donations he has given, the learning he has had, the penances he has practised in many lives.

20. Pustakēsu ca yā vidyā parahastēsu tat dhanam.
Utpannēsu ca kāryēsu na sā vidyā na tat dhanam.

The knowledge in books, the wealth in others hands, will not be useful to anyone during the need.

Chapter-17

1. Pustakapratyayādhītam nādhītam gurusannidhau.
Sabhāmadhyē na śōbhantē jāragarbhā iva striyah.

Those who haven't been educated by a guru, never look lessons from the learned men are just like a woman who becomes pregnant immorally lose respect in the society.

2. Krtē pratikrti kuryād hinsanē pratihinsanam.
Tatra dōsī na patati dustē daustyam samācarēt.

Do unto others as they do unto you, gratitude to those who show gratitude, violence towards violent, evilness towards evil. We will never suffer any sin if we follow these.

3. Yaddūram yaddūra ārādhyam yacca dūrē vyavasthim.
Tatsarvam tapasā sādhyam tapō hi durati kramam.

It is difficult to admire something which is very fat or very high or difficult to reach. It can be got only by doing penance.

4. Lōbhaścēdagunēna kim piśunatā yadyasti kim pātakaih
Satyam cēt-tapasā ca kim śucimanah yadyasti tīrthēna kim.
Saujanyam yadi kim gunaih sumahimā yadyasti kim mandanaih
Sad - vidyā yadi kim dhanaih apayaśō yadyasti kim mrtyunā.

There is no need for any other bad qualities if a man has greed,

There is no need for any other sin if a man is a cheat,

There is no need for any other penance if a man is truthful

There is no need of going to any places of pilgrimage if a man's heart is pure.

5. Pitā ratnākarō yasya laksmī yasya sahōdarī.
Śankhō bhiksātanam kuryānna ādattam upatisthatē.

The mighty ocean is the father of a conch, Lakshmi is the sister of conch, the conch glitters like the moon. When somebody blows the conch and asks for alms, it has to be understood that one cannot gain respect without donating something.

6. Aśaktastu bhavēt sādhuh brahmacārī ca nirdhanah.
Vyādhisthō dēvabhaktah ca vrddhā nārī pativratā.

A weak person becomes a sage or a good man, a penniless person a celibate, an unwell person a devotee and an old woman becomes very pure.

7. Na annōdakam samam dānam na tithih dvādaśī samā.
Na gāyatryāh parō mantrō na mātuh param daivatam.

There is no purer donation that rice or water, no auspicious day than dwadashi, no chant as powerful as Gayatri and no God equivalent to a mother.

8. Taksakasya visam dantē maksikāyāh śirō visam.
Vrścakasya visam pucchē sarvāngē durjanam visam.

The venom of a snake is in its teeth, the venom of a bee is in its forehead, the venom of a scorpion is in its tail, but the venom in an evil man if found in all parts of his body.

9. Patyurājñām vinā nārī upōsya vratacārinī.
Āyusyam haratē bhartuh sā nārī narakam vrajēt.

The lady who keeps a vow or fasts without taking her husband's permission, not only reduces her husband's life span but goes to the hell herself.

10. Na dānaih śudhyatē nārī na upavāsa śataih api.
Na tīrthasēvayā tadvad bhartuh pādōdakaih yathā.

A woman does not become pure by donating or fasting or going on pilgrimage. She becomes pure when she serves her husband.

11. Dānēna pāninah tu kankanēna snānēna śuddhih na tu candanēna.
Manēna trptih na tu bhōjanēna jñānēna muktih na tu mandanēna.

The beauty of hand gets enhanced with donation and not with a bracelet. The body gets cleaner by bath and not by the application of sandal paste, man is satisfied with respect and not food and attains salvation by knowledge and not by prostrating.

12. Nāpitasya grhē ksauram pāsānē gandhalēpanam.
Ātmarūpam jalē paśyēna śakrasyayāpi śriyam harēt.

The glory of a man is equivalent of Lord Indra, will diminish if he goes to a barber's house for a hair cut, applies sandal paste on stones and looks at his reflection in the water.

13. Sadyah prajñāharā tundī sadyah prajñākarī vacā.
Sadyah śaktiharā nārī sadyah śaktikaram payah.

The brain gets temporarily addled when kunduru is eaten, the brain's power increases when vakk is eaten. The woman loses her strength in an instant and milk gives strength in an instant.

14. Parōpakaranam yēsām jāgarti hrdayē satām.
Naśyanti vipadah tēsām sampadah syuh padē padē.

A man's difficulties reduce and he gets wealth in every step of his life if he has the feeling of helping others.

15. *Āhāranidrābhayamaithunam ca sāmānyam ētat paśubhih narānām.*
Dharmō hitēsām adhikō viśēsō dharmēna hīnāh paśubhih samānā.

Eating, sleeping, getting scared are emotions commonly felt both by man and beast. But it is the feeling of righteousness which separates man from beast. One who is not righteous is equivalent to beast.

16. *Dāna arthinō manukarā yadi karna tālaih*
dūrīkrtāh karivarēna madāndhabuddhayā.
Tasyaiva gandayugamandanahānih ēsā bhrngā
punah vikacapadmavanē vasanti.

When an elephant swats away the black bees perching on its forehead with its long ears with frenzy, no harm occurs to the bees. They just go and perch on the lotus flowers. But the beauty of the elephant's forehead is lost.

17. *Rājā vēśyā yamō hyagnih taskarō bālayācakau.*
Paraduhkham na jānanti astamō grāmakantakah.

A king, a prostitute, Lord Yama, fire, thief, child, beggar and one who troubles the villagers, do not understand other's sorrow.

18. *Adhah paśyasi kim vrddhē patim tava kim bhuvi.*
Rē rē mūrkha na jānāsi gatam tārunya - mauktikam.

A youth asked a woman bent with age if she had lost something. The old woman replied, "O' foolish fellow! You don't realise that I have lost the pearl of my youth."

19. *Vyāla āśrayā api viphalāpi sakantakā api*
vakrā api pankila bhavā api durāsadā api.
Gandhēna bandhurasi kētaki sarvajantōh ēkō
gunah khalu nihanti samasta dōsān.

Snakes are entwined in ketaki flowers, these plants don't produce fruits, there are thorns in it, it goes in a bog, it cannot be got that easily, yet its fragrance intoxicates everyone.

SECTION-3

SELF, TIME, THINGS-METHODICAL

CHANAKYA'S COMPLETE FORMULA/ RULE

Chanakya's Rule

1. *Sukhasya mūlam dharmah*

   Righteousness is the base for comfort.

2. *Dharmasya mūlam arthah.*

   Wealth is the base for righteousness.

3. *Arthasya mūlam rājyam.*

   The administration is the base for wealth.

4. *Rājyamūlam indriya-jayah.*

   The base for a good administration is the control of senses.

5. *Praketi sampadā hyanāyakam-api.*

   If there is natural wealth, even a king who does know how to administer, continues to do so.

6. *Vinayasya mūlam vrddhōpasēvā.*

   Service to the aged is a sign of humility.

7. *Vrddhasēvāyā vijñānam.*

   One achieves knowledge by serving the aged.

8. *Vijñānēna ātmanam sampādayēt.*

   Knowledge purifies the soul.

9. *Sampāditaātmā jitātmā bhavati.*

   The righteous soul is able to achieve control over the soul.

10. *Jitātmā sarvārthaih sanyujyēt.*

    One who has control over his soul becomes successful in achieving all kinds of wealth.

11. *Arthasampat prakrtisampadam karōti.*

    The natural wealth is more easily collected than any other wealth.

12. *Indriyajayasya mūlam vinayah.*

    Humility is the best weapon to control the senses.

13. *Prakrti kōpah sarvakōpēbhyō garīyān.*

The fury of nature is more terrifying than any other fury.

14. *Avinītasvāmi lābhāda asvāmi lābhah śrēyān.*

It is better to lead a life without a master rather than being under an unethical or a cruel master.

15. *Sampādyasata ātmānam anvicchēt sahāyavāna.*

One should work with competent people after becoming refined and competent oneself.

16. *Nā sahāyasya mantraniścayah.*

It is difficult to take a proper decision without competent people. The decisions taken by incompetent people cannot be followed.

17. *Na ēkam cakram paribhramayati.*

A solo wheel cannot run by itself.

18. *Sahāyah sama-duhkha sukhah.*

One should help, be helpful and share one's joys an sorrows.

19. *Mānī pratimānina ātmāni dvitīyam mantram utpādayēt.*

An arrogant person always feels that a useless topic has to be brought forth and discussed again and again.

20. *Avinītam snēhamātrēna na mantrē kurvīta.*

One must not invite an unethical person even if he is a friend.

21. *Śrutavantam upadhā śuddham mantrinam kurvīt.*

One has to seek advice only from a knowledgeable person who does not have cunningness or deception.

22. *Mantramūlāh sarvārambhāh.*

Work has to be commenced only after deliberations.

23. *Mantraraksanē kārya siddhih bhavati.*

The work will succeed only if the thoughts and decisions are kept a secret.

24. *Mantravisrāvī kāryam nāśayati.*

Difficulties arise when the thoughts and decisions are revealed.

25. *Pramādād dvisatām vaśam upāsyati.*

The delay or carelessness will reveal the secret and increase the difficulties.

26. *Sarvadvārēbhyō mantrō raksitavyah.*

When a secret gets revealed it is necessary to safeguard from all sides.

27. *Mantrasampadā hī rājyam vardhatē.*

There will be four fold development with proper thought and resolution.

28. *Śrēsthatamām mantraguptimāhuh.*

The concealment of advice is supposed to be very eminent.

29. *Kārya-andhasya pradīpō mantrah.*

The sage advice is like a light when given to work shrouded in darkness.

30. *Mantrakālē na matsarah kartavyah.*

One should not be jealous while getting the advice.

31. *Mantracaksusā paricchidrānyavalōkayanti.*

The weaknesses of the enemy can be scrutinised through the eyes of advice.

32. *Trayānāmmēkavākyē sampratyayah.*

It is of paramount importance to become one with a man who advices thrice.

33. *Kārya akārya tattvārthadarśinōmantrināh.*

One who can differentiate between doable and non doable things can only become a minister.

34. *Sat-karnād bhidyatē mantrah.*

If the secret advice falls in six ears, its secret gets revealed.

35. *Mitra-sangrahanē balam sampadyatē.*

Strength is gained through the increased number of friends.

36. *Alabdha-lābha-ādi catustayam rājatantram.*

The gains etc are the four pillars of politics.

37. *Alabdhalābhō na ālasya.*

One cannot receive the gains in a delayed manner.

38. *Ālasya labdhaapi raksitum na śakyatē.*

Ones that are received slowly cannot be safe guarded.

39. *Na ca ālasasya raksitum vivardhatē.*

Anything saved cannot be safeguarded by a lazy person.

40. *Na bhrtyān prēsayati.*

The servants of a lazy person also do not praise him.

41. *Balavāna labdhalābhē prayatatē.*

The mighty tries to acquire profits.

42. *Rājya-tantrāyattam nītiśāstram.*

The basis of administration is political science.

43. *Rājatantra ēsvāyatau tantrāvāpau.*

The internal as well as external duties are a part of administration.

44. *Tantram svavisaya krtya ēsvāyattam.*

The development of one's own kingdom is the work of an administration.

45. *Hīyamāna sandhim kurvīta.*

A weak king should compromise. And seek treaty.

46. *Sandhivigraha yōnih mandalah.*

The cabinet ministers decide about the relation ship with neighbouring kingdome etc.

47. *Nītiśāstrānugō rājā.*

A king should abide by political Science.

48. *Anantara prakrtih śatruh.*

The neighbouring kindoms automatically become the enemies.

49. *Ēkāntaritam mitram isyatē.*

The common enemies of a kingdom become develop friendship between themselves.

50. *Hētutah śatru mitrē bhavisyatah.*

An enemy becomes a friend only with an ulterior motive.

51. *Āvāpō mandala nivistah.*

It is the responsibility of the council of ministers to have a relationship, legal dealings etc with the neighbouring kingdoms.

52. *Hīyānē na sandhi kurvīta.*

Never form a treaty with weak.

53. *Nātapta-lōhō lōhēna sandhīyatē.*

The cold metal cannot mix with metals.

54. *Tējō hi sandhāna-hētuh-tadarthānām.*

The treaty occurs only due to the glory of kings.

55. *Ariprayatnam abhi samīksayēt.*

One should have a review of the attempts of the enemy.

56. *Na jyāyasā samēna vā.*

One should not have enmity with people who are stronger or equally strong.

57. *Gajapādayuddham iva balabadvigrahah.*

Fighting with a strong person is like the foot soldiers fighting with a troop of elephants.

58. *Āmapātram āmēna saha vinaśyati.*

Even if an imperfect vessel hits another imperfect vessel, it still breaks.

59. *Balavāna hīnēna vigrahanīyāt.*

The strong one should annex the enemies thinking that they are weak.

60. *Sandhi aikatō vā.*

One should be cautious even after treaty and unity.

61. *Amitra virōdha ātmaraksām avasēt.*

One should safeguard oneself from one's enemies.

62. *Śaktihīnō balavantē āśrayēt.*

The meek should seek the shelter of a strong man.

63. *Durbala āśrayō duhkham-āvahati.*

The shelter with a weak person is like an invitation to difficulties.

64. *Agnivadrā jñānam āśrayēt.*

One should take shelter with another only after understanding that he is as potent as fire.

65. *Rājñah pratikūlam na ācarēt.*

A king should not behave unethically.

66. *Uddhatavēsadharō na bhavēt.*

The king should not behave in an excited or frenzied manner.

67. *Na dēvacaritam carēt.*

One should not try to follow the characteristics of Gods.

68. *Dvayōh api īsryatōh dvaidhībhāvam kurvīta.*

If there are two people who are jealous, one should create enmity between them.

69. *Na vyasanaparasya kārya avāptih.*

One who is addicted to vices cannot do any work.

70. *Indriyavaśavartī caturanga avānapi vinaśyati.*

One who is addicted to vices, lust, gambling and drinking etc even if he has elephants, horses, chariots and foot soldiers, he will get destroyed by these vices.

71. *Nāsti kāryam dyūta-pravrttasya.*

The work of gamblers never gets completed. This results in his destruction.

72. *Mrgayāparasya dharmāthō vinaśyatah.*

The virtue and wealth of a person is lost if he is addicted to some vice.

73. *Arthēsu pāta vyasanī na gamyatē.*

The work mof a drunkard never gets completed.

74. *Na kāmāsaktasya kārya anusthānam.*

The lustful man can never do any work.

75. *Agni dāhāda api viśistam vākpārusyam.*

The cruel words sear us worse than a flame.

76. *Dandapārusyāt sarvajanadvēsyō bhavati.*

The public ridicule is worse than getting scolded in anger.

77. *Arthatōsinam śrīh parityajati.*

Lakshmi gives up the house oif greedy.

78. *Amitrō dandanītyām āyattuh.*

The enemy will be well versed in the art of warfare.

79. *Dandanītim adhisthan prajāh sanraksati.*

The legitimate usage of the warfare results in the safety and security of the common people.

80. *Dandah sampadā yōjayati.*

Wealth increases when punishment is given.

81. *Danda abhāvē mantrivarga abhāvah.*

The power of ministers diminishes with the scarcity of punishment.

82. *Na dandāda akāryāni kurvanti.*

In the absence of punishment, people start doing unethical things.

83. *Dandanītya āmāyattam ātmaraksanam.*

Self defence occurs due to the art of warfare.

84. *Ātmani raksitē sarvam raksitam bhavati.*

Self defence leads to the security of every body.

85. *Ātma āyattau vrddhivināśau.*

The development stops when there is no self respect.

86. *Dandō hi vijñānē pranīyatē.*

The punishment should be justified.

87. *Durbalō api rājā na avamantavyah.*

One should not mock even a weak king.

88. *Nāstya agnē daurbalya.*

There is no weakness in the fire.

89. *Dandē pratīyatē vrtih.*

One can get to know the character of a person only through the art of punishment.

90. **Vrtti mūlam arthalābhah.**

The root of every profession is the benefit of wealth.

91. **Arthamūlau dharmakāmau.**

The virtue and work depend on wealth.

92. **Arthamūlam kāryam.**

The root of wealth is duty.

93. **Yad alpa prayatnāt kārya siddhi bhavati.**

The work is easily finished with the help of wealth.

94. **Upāya pūrvam na duskaram syāt.**

All work get done through ideas, nothing remains difficult.

95. **Anupāya pūrvam kārya krtam api vinaśyati.**

The work done without a proper idea gets spoilt.

96. **Kārya arthinām upāya ēva sahāyah.**

The idea is the friend of a worker.

97. **Kāryam purusakārēna laksyam sampadyatē.**

If one decides on the method of work, then that becomes one's aim.

98. **Purusa kāram anuvartatē daivam.**

Luck weds the industrious.

99. **Asamāhitasya vrttih na vidyatē.**

The thoughts of people with unsteady mind will not be steady.

100. **Pūrvam niścitya paścāt kāryam ārambhayēt.**

One should begin work only after deciding it first.

101. **Kāryāntarē dīrghasūtritā na kartavyā.**

One should not delay or defer once the work commences.

102. **Na cala cittasya kāryāvāptih.**

The work of fickle minded people never gets over.

103. **Hastagata avamānanāt kāryavyatikramō bhavati.**

The delay in work occurs when there is no efficiency in work.

104. **Daivahīnam kāryam susādhyam api duhsādhyam bhavati.**

When ill luck occurs, even the easiest job becomes very difficult.

105. **Duh-anubandham kāryam na ārambhēt.**

One should not commence an inauspicious or bad jobs.

106. **Kālavit kāryam sādhayēt.**

One should complete work within the specified time.

107. *Kāla atikramāt kāla ēva phalam pibati.*

The fruits of work get sucked by time if a man does not work according to time.

108. *Ksanam prati kālaviksēpam na kuryāta.*

Do not neglect even for a minute your work.

109. *Dēśa phala vibhāgau jñātvā kāryam ārambhayēt.*

One should commence work after knowing the country and the results.

110. *Dōsa varjitāni kāryāni durlabhāni.*

It is impossible for the work to be faultless.

111. *Nītijñō dēśakālau parīksēt.*

The intelligent and the virtuous examine the country and time much before hand.

112. *Parīksyakārinī śrīh ciram tisthati.*

If work is done after a lot of thought, then wealth remains for a long time.

113. *Sarvāh ca sampadah sarva upāyēna parigrahēt.*

All kinds of wealth should be accumulated using all ideas and means.

114. *Bhāgyavantam aparīksyakārinam śrīh parityajati.*

Lakshmi leaves the person who works without any thought or plan.

115. *Jñānēna anumānaih ca parīksā kartavyā.*

We have to stabilize our thoughts through knowledge, questioning and doubt.

116. *Ajñāninā krtamaapi na bahu mantavyam.*

One hould not give much importance to the work of ignorant people.

117. *Ādrcchikatvāta krmih-api rūpāntarāni karōti.*

Even an insect can change the situation through a given opportunity.

118. *Yō yasmin karmani kuśalastam tasminnēva yōjayēt.*

One should only be doing the work in which one is a specialist.

119. *Siddhasyaiva kāryasya prakāśanam kartavyam.*

One should publicize the work only after its completion.

120. *Jñānavatām api daivam mānusa dōsat kāryāni dusyanti.*

Even the work of knowledgeable sometimes get bad mouthed due to luck or faults of people and remain half done.

121. *Daivam śānti karmanah pratisēddhavyam.*

The luck has to be appreciated very calmly.

122. *Mānusīm kārya vipattim kauśalēna vinivārayēt.*

The difficulties brought by people should be sorted out very intelligently.

123. *Kāryavipattau dōsān varnayanti bāliśāh.*

Fools find fault when they face difficulty while doing a work.

124. *Kāryārthinā dāksinyam na kartavyam.*

One should not be unduly generous for getting the work done.

125. *Dugghārthī vatsō mātuh udhah pratihanti.*

The calf or an infant always kicks the chest of its mother.

126. *Aprayatnāt kārya vipattih bhavati.*

There will be obstacles to work if one doesn't put effort.

127. *Na daivapramānānām kāryasiddhih.*

The work of those doesn't get completed who do not believe in luck.

128. *Kāryabāhyō na pōsayatya āśritān.*

Those who escape their duty will not be able to take care of their kith and kin.

129. *Ya kāryam na paśyati sa andhah.*

One who cannot see his duty is blind.

130. *Pratyaksa-parōksa anumānaih kāryāni parīksēt.*

The work has to be examined keeping in mind the visible and invisible things.

131. *Aparīksyakārinam śrīh parityajati.*

Lakshmi leaves the person who works without examining it first.

132. *Na parīksya kārinām kārya vipattih.*

If work is performed without examining it, it might fall into trouble.

133. *Parīksya tāryā vipatti.*

The danger has to be removed through examining, testing.

134. *Sva-śaktim jñātvā kāryam ārambhēt.*

One should begin work only after knowing one's strength.

135. *Svajanam tarpayitvā yah śēsabhōjī sa amrtabhōjī.*

One who eats the remaining food after feeding others, drinks the ambrosia.

136. *Sarva-anusthānada āya mukhāni vardhantē.*

The span of life increases by following all religious practices.

137. *Nāsti bhīrōh kāryacintā.*

A coward is never worried of work.

138. **Svāmīnah śīlam jñātvā kāryārthī kārya sādhayati.**

A worker works knowing the behaviour of his boss.

139. **Dhēnō śīlajñah ksīram bhunktē.**

One who knows the characteristic of a cow will be able to relish its milk.

140. **Ksudrē guhya prakāśanam ātmavānna kuryāt.**

One should not speak a secret or one's inner thoughts in the presence of an evil man.

141. **Āśritaih apya avamanyatē mrdusvabhāvah.**

A meek person gets insulted by even his well wishers.

142. **Tīksna dandah sarvai ruddhē-janīyō bhavati.**

All people hate severe punishment.

143. **Dandakārī syāt.**

The one who gives proper punishment is great.

144. **Alpasāram śrutavantam api na bahu manyatē lōkah.**

A lowly pundit doesn't get any respect by being very sober.

145. **Sāram mahājana-sangraha pīdayati.**

A detailed explanation by a learned person only brings pain to people.

146. **Atibhārah purusam avasādayati.**

An obese person tires quickly.

147. **Yah sansadi paradōsam śansati sa svadōsa bahutvam prakhyāpayati.**

One who finds faults with others in an open forum, actually reveals his own faults.

148. **Ātmānam ēva nāśayati anātmavatām kōpah.**

The anger of fools destroys them.

149. **Nāstya aprāpyam satyavatām.**

There is nothing unobtainable for people who tell the truth.

150. **Sāhasēna na kāryasiddhih bhavati.**

One cannot attain success in work with just fearlessness.

151. **Vyasanārtō vismaratya apravēśēna.**

One who is addicted to bad habits stops even before he reaches his goal.

152. **Nāstya antarāyah kālaviksēpē.**

One who doesn't keep track of time, always faces difficulties in his life.

153. **Asanśaya vināśāt sanśaya vināśah śrēyān.**

The destruction after doubting is better than the destruction without any doubting.

154. *Paradhanāni niksēptuh kēvalam svārtham.*

Differenciating others wealth is bad.

155. *Dānam dharmah.*

Donating is a virtue.

156. *Nāryāgatō arthavad viparītō anartha bhāvah.*

If people follow the path shown by ignorant, it will result in destruction.

157. *Nyāya āgatō artha.*

True wealth is one which is acquired through fair means.

158. *Tada viparītā artha ābhāsah.*

If wealth is acquired through foul means then it is vulgar.

159. *Yō dharma arthau na vivardhayati sa kāmah.*

One who doesn't work for the increase of wealth and money is a lustful person.

160. *Tad-viparī tō anartha sēvī.*

One who goes in the wrong way of accumulating wealth and money does a very wrong thing.

161. *Rjusvabhāvō janēsu durlabhah.*

It is difficult to get a person who is calm and having common sense.

162. *Avamānēna āgata-aiśvaryam avamanyatē sādhuh.*

Saints and good people do not respect the wealth gotten through foul means.

163. *Bahūnapi gunāna ēkō dōsō grasati.*

One fault can remove many good qualities.

164. *Mahātmanā parēna sāhasam na kartavyam.*

One should not dare to do something on someone else's strength.

165. *Kadācit api caritram na langhayēt.*

One should not sacrifice the characteristic good qualities.

166. *Ksudhārtō na trnam carati sinha.*

The lion does not eat grass even if it is very hungry.

167. *Prānāt api pratyayō raksitavyah.*

One should safeguard trust better than even life.

168. *Piśunah śrōtā putra dārā api tyajyatē.*

The wife and son of a man listening to rumours will leave him.

169. *Bālāt apyartha jātē śrrnuyāt.*

One should understand the useful talk of children.

170. *Satyam apya aśraddhēyam na vadēt.*

Even if the truth is not right, then one should not do it.

171. *Na alpa dōsād bahugunāh tyajyantē.*

One should not sacrifice all the good qualities because of a few normal or bad qualities.

172. *Vipaścitah api sulabhā dōsāh.*

Even the saints can have faults.

173. *Nāsti ratnam khanditam.*

The diamond remains a diamond even after it is cut. Therefore the cut diamond is not a diamond.

174. *Maryādātītam na kadācita api viśvasēt.*

One should never believe those who neglect to respect and honour others.

175. *Apriyē krtam priyamapi dvēsyam bhavati.*

The loving work done by the enemy should only be thought of as faulty.

176. *Na mantsa api tulākōtih kūpōdakaksayam karōti.*

The appliance also bows its head when it takes water from the well. People cheat others only with sweet words.

177. *Satām matam na atikramēt.*

Never go against the advice of a good man or thousands of people.

178. *Gunavada āśrayā nirgunō api gunī bhavati.*

Living under the care of good charactered people, even the evil natured become good.

179. *Ksīra āśritam jalam ksīram ēva bhavati.*

The water mixed in the milk also becomes milk.

180. *Mrt pinda api pātali-gandham utpādayati.*

The mud also spreads the fragrance of flowers.

181. *Rajatam kanakasangāt kanakam bhavati.*

The silver when mixed with gold, becomes gold.

182. *Upakartah apakartum icchatya abadhuh.*

A fool harms the person who does good to him.

183. *Tad-viparītō budhah.*

The knowledgeable do good to those who harm them.

184. *Matsya arthivaj jalam upautyārtham grhanīyāt.*

The fisherman can get something only by venturing into the water.

185. *Utsāhavatām śatravaapi vaśībhavanti.*

The enemy also falls into the net of an excited person.

186. *Vikramadhanā rājānah.*

A king can amass wealth only through his power and might.

187. *Na astya alasasya aihikāma usmikam.*

The lazy do not have either the present or the future.

188. *Nirutsāhāda ēva patati.*

The destruction of a listless person is certain.

189. *Na pāpakarmanām ākrōśa bhayam.*

People who do evil things are never afraid of anger or fear.

190. *Aviśvastēsu viśvāsō na kartavyah.*

One should never believe a stranger.

191. *Visam visam ēva sarvakālam.*

The poison remains the poison in every situation.

192. *Artha samādānē vairinām sanga ēva na kartavyah.*

One should not work in concert with the enemy.

193. *Ārya artham ēva nīcasya sansargah.*

One should keep the company of poor for the welfare of good people.

194. *Arthasiddhau vairinam na viśvasēt.*

Never believe the enemy just for the sake of completion of some work.

195. *Arthādhīna ēva niyata sambandhah.*

The proof of relation is dute to some reason.

196. *Śatrōh api sutah sakhā raksitavyah.*

One must safeguard the children of the enemy and friends.

197. *Yāvacchatrōh chidram paśyati tāvata astēna vā skandhēna vā vāhyah.*

Keep the enemy as friend until you find his weakness.

198. *Śatrum chidrē praharēt.*

One should attack only the weakness of the enemy.

199. *Ātma chidram na prakāśayēt.*

Never show your weakness.

200. *Chidra prahārinah śatravah.*

One who attacks someone who is helpless, is an enemy too.

201. *Hastagatam api śatrum na viśvasēt.*

Never believe the enemy who is arrested by you.

202. *Svajanasya duvrttam nivārayēt.*

One should make the relatives give up dirty habits.

203. *Svajana āvamānō api manasvinām duhkham āvahati.*

People get upset when their kith and kin are treated badly.

204. *Ēkānga dōsah purusam avasādayati.*

The diability of even one part of the body saddens the man.

205. *Śatrum jayati suvrttatā.*

The victory can be gained over the enemy through good behaviour,

206. *Vikrti priyā nīcāh.*

One who likes horrible things is evil.

207. *Nīcasya matih na dātavyā.*

Never advise an evil person.

208. *Tēsu viśvāsō na kartavyah.*

Never believe the evil people.

209. *Supūjitō api durjanah pīdayatya ēva.*

A bad person brings pain to one even though he is venerated.

210. *Candanādīna api dāvāgnih dahatyēva.*

The forest fire will burn even the sandal wood.

211. *Śirasi prasthāpyam ānō-api vahnih dahatyēva.*

The fire will still burn even if held on the head.

212. *Kada api purusam na avamānsatē.*

One should never mock an industrious person.

213. *Ksantavyam iti purusam na bādhēt.*

Never hurt a forgiving person.

214. *Ksamanta iti purusam na bādhēt.*

Never hurt a person worth forgiving too.

215. *Bhatrādhikam rahasya uktam vaktum icchantya abuddhayah.*

The fools reveal the secret told to them by their masters in secrecy.

216. *Anurāgah tu phalēna sūcyatē.*

The result of love is knowledge.

217. *Jñāna phalam aiśvaryam.*

Wealth is the result of knowledge.

218. *Dātavyam api bāliśah klēśēna paridāsyati.*

A fool feels sad to donate.

219. *Mahad aiśvaryam prāpya āpya adhrtimān vinaśyati.*

A fool gets destroyed inspite of his acquiring vast wealth.

220. *Dhrtayā jayati rōgān.*

Diseases can also be conquered through patience/bravery.

221. *Na astya dhrtē aihikam usmikam.*

One who doesn't have patience has neither present nor future.

222. *Gunavāna api ksudrapaksah tyajyatē.*

A good charactered person gives up the company of mean minded people or mean mindedness itself.

223. *Jīrna śarīrē vardhamānam vyādhi na upēksayēt.*

Never neglect the diseases that grow in a weak body.

224. *Śaunda hastagata payō api avamanyēt.*

Even if a drunkard has milk in his hand, he will still think that it is alcohol.

225. *Kāryasankatēsvartha vyavasāyinī buddhih.*

Commonsense reduces during the time of difficulties.

226. *Mitabhōjanam svāsthyam.*

Limited intake of food will help in remaining healthy.

227. *Pathya apathya ajīrnē nāśnīyāt.*

One should never eat such food which is not worth eating and develop indigestion.

228. *Bhaksyam apya pathyam nāśnīyāt.*

One should never eat such food which though is edible but causes indigestion.

229. *Na durjanaih saha sansargah kartavyah.*

Never stay with an evil person.

230. *Ajīrnē bhōjanam duhkham.*

Eating during indigestion is painful.

231. *Śatrōh api viśisyatē vyādhih.*

Disease is worse than an enemy.

232. *Chānannidhānam anugāmī.*

One must donate only according to one's capacity.

233. *Patutarē trsnāparē sulabham ati sandhānam.*

The clever and the greedy increase their status just like that.

234. *Trsnayā matih chādyatē.*

Greed corrupts the mind.

235. *Kārya bahutvē bahuphalam āyatikam kuryāt.*

While having a lot of work for completion, finish that work which gives maximum profit first.

236. *Svayam ēva āvaśkannam kāryam nirīksēt.*

One has to observe carefully the work which has been done wrongly either by self or by others.

237. *Mūrkhēsu sāhasam niyatam.*

Fools are daring.

238. *Mūrkhēsu vivādam na kartavyam.*

Never argue with fools. 239. Āyasaih āyasam chēdyam.

Iron has to be cut with iron only.

240. *Nāsya adhamitah sakhā.*

Fools do not have friends.

241. *Nāsti dharmasamah sakhā.*

There can be never a better friend than righteousness.

242. *Dharmēna dhāryatē lōkah.*

Righteousness holds the world. The world has to be held only by righteousness.

243. *Prētam api dharma-adharma avanugacchatah.*

Even the spirits follow morality and immorality.

244. *Dharmēna jayati lōkāh.*

Victory in the world is achieved only through righteousness.

245. *Mrtyuh api dharmistham raksati.*

Even death safeguards the one who follows righteousness.

246. *Dharmāda viparītam pāpam yatra prasajyatē tatra dharma avamatih bhavati.*

Righteousness gets disgraced in the presence of sin.

247. *Lōkē praśastah sa matimān.*

One who is well versed in worldly affairs is a smart person.

248. *Sajjana garhitam na prasajyēt.*

A good man should not follow wrong beliefs.

249. *Upasthi vināśānām prakrtya akārēna laksyatē.*

The fact that destruction is inevitable can be learnt from the nature itself.

250. *Ātma vināśam sūcayatya adharma buddhih.*

One can get the message of self destruction through the following of immoral ways.

251. *Piśunavādinō na rahasyam.*

Never reveal any secrets before nit pickers.

252. *Vallabhasya kārakatvam adharmayuktam.*

It is not right to be cruel to one's workers.

253. *Para-rahasyam na śrōtavyam.*

Never listen to others' secrets.

254. *Svajanēh avatikramō na kartavyah.*

Never cross your limits with the relatives.

255. *Mātā-api dustā tyājyā.*

If a mother is evil, then we have to discard her.

256. *Sva hastō api visa digdhah chēdyah.*

If poison is spreading in our arms, it is better to cut the arms.

257. *Parō api ca hitō bandhuh.*

If a stranger is a well wisher, he becomes the brother.

258. *Pratikārēsva anādarō na kartavyah.*

Never ignore the enemies by becoming carteless.

259. *Vyasanam manāga api bādhatē.*

Even a little addiction will give one sorrow.

260. *Amara avadartha jātam arjayēt.*

Collect wealth with the thought that we are immortal.

261. *Arthavāna sarvalōkasya bahumatah.*

The words of a wealthy person is paid heed to everywhere.

262. *Mahēndram api hīnam na bahu manyatē lōkah.*

The words of a poor king is never heede.

263. *Dāridrayam khalu purusasya jīvitam maranam.*

The wretched is considered dead even while alive.

264. *Virūpō arthavāna surūpō.*

If an ugly person is wealthy, he will be considered handsome.

265. *Adātāram api arthavantam athirnō na tyajyati.*

The misers and those who keep asking never miss asking from others.

266. *Upārjitānām vitānām tyāga ēva hi raksanam.*

The sacrifice of amassed wealth is one's armour.

267. *Akulīnō api kulīna adviśistah.*

The rich person of a degraded caste is better than a poor person of high caste.

268. *Nāstya amāna bhayam anāryasya.*

The evil person has no fear of shame.

269. *Na cētana vatām vrttibhayam.*

A skilled workman never fears employment.

270. *Na jitēndriyānām visayabhayam.*

One who has self control will never fall prey to lust.

271. *Na krtaarthānām marana bhayam.*

One who has acquired wealth has no fear of death.

272. *Kasyacid artham svamiva manyatē sādhuh.*

The saints consider all the wealth as theirs.

273. *Paravibhava ēsvādarō na kartavyah.*

Never be greedy for other's wealth.

274. *Na mrtasya ausadham prayōjanam.*

A dead man needs no medicine.

275. *Paravibhava ēsvādarō api nāśamūlam.*

Craving other's wealth will result in destruction.

276. *Alpam api paradravyam na hartavyam.*

One should never grab even a little bit of wealth from someone.

277. *Paradravya apaharanam ātmadravya nāśa hētuh.*

Grabbing others wealth will result in the loss of our wealth.

278. *Na cairyāt param mrtyupāśah.*

There is no worse death sentence than thieving.

279. *Āvāgūh api prānadhāranam karōti lōkē.*

Even a parched grain can save a life in the world.

280. *Samakālē svayam api prabhutvasya prayōjanam bhavati.*

It is the duty to retain the ownership during normal times.

281. *Nīcasya vidyā pāpakarmani yōjayanti.*

The immoral education trains in performing sinful deeds.

282. *Payahpāna api visavardhanam bhujangasya na amrtam syāt.*

The venom of a snake increases when it is given milk. It doesn't turn into nectar.

283. *Nahi dhānyasamō artham.*

There is no wealth other than food.

284. *Na ksudhāsamah śatruh.*

There can be no enemy like hunger.

285. *Akrtēh niyatā ksut.*

A lazy person has to bear the pangs of hunger.

286. *Nāstya aksyam ksudhitasya.*

A hungry person will eat even the inedible things.

287. *Indriyāni jarāvaśam kurvanti.*

Increased usage of the senses will hasten old age.

288. *Sānukrōśam bhartāh mājīvēt.*

One should serve only a rich and kind master.

289. *Lubdhasēvī pāvakēcchāyā khadyōtam dhamati.*

Trying to get something froma miserly and greedy master is like getting fire out ofa fire fly.

290. *Viśēsajñam svāminam āśrayēt.*

A knowledgeable [erson should seek the shelter of a master.

291. *Purusasya maithunam jarā.*

A man become old if he indulges in sexual act too much.

292. *Strīnāmaithunam jarā.*

The woman ages farter if she has no sexual relationship.

293. *Na nīca uttamayōh vivāha.*

There should not be a marriage between the evil and the knowledgeable.

294. *Agamya āgamanāda āyuh yaśah punyānī ksīyantē.*

If one lives with prostitutes and other immoral women, one loses one's life span, fame and piousness.

295. *Na astya ahankāra samah.*

There is no greater enemy than arrogance.

296. *Sansadi śatrum na parikrōśēt.*

Never anger the enemy in an open court.

297. *Śatru vyasanam śravana sukham.*

Listening to the dirty habits of enemy gives one pleasure.

298. *Adhanasya buddhih na vidyatē.*

Poor person does not have intelligence.

299. *Hitam apya dhanasya vākyam na śrrnōti.*

No one listens to the useful words of a poor person.

300. *Adhanah svabhāryāyā apya avamanyatē.*

The wife of a poor amn also doesn not listen to him.

301. *Puspahīnam sahakāram api na upāsatē bhramarāh.*

The honey bee vacates the plant when it stops flowering.

302. *Vidyā dhanam adhanānām.*

Education is the wealth of apoor man.

303. *Vidyā cairaih api na grāhyā.*

No thief can steal the wealth of education.

304. *Vidyayā khyāpitā khyātih.*

Education brings fame to a scholar.

305. *Yaśah śarīram na vinaśyati.*

The body of fame never perishes.

306. *Yah parārtham upasarpati sa satpurusah.*

One who spends his time for the welfare of others is a teue human being.

307. *Indriyānām praśamam śāstram.*

The knowledge of scriptures help in controlling the senses.

308. *Aśāstra kāryavrttau śāstra ankuśam nivārayati.*

Only the knowledgeable scripture can stop a man going in unethical way.

309. *Nīcasya vidyā na upētavyā.*

One should not follow the knowledge given by evil persons.

310. *Mlēccha abhāsanam na śiksēt.*

One should not learn the foul language of evil people.

311. *Mlēchānāma api suvrttam grāhyam.*

One should assimilate the good thoughts of even an evil man.

312. *Gunaih na matsarah kartavyah.*

One should not feel jealous of others characters.

313. *Śatrōh api sugunō grāhya.*

One should learn the good qualities of even the enemies.

314. *Visād apya amrtam grāhyah.*

If there is nectar in the poison, then one should drink it.

315. *Avasthayā purusah sammānyatē.*

A man gets respect only in a special way.

316. *Sthāna ēva narāh pūjyantē.*

A man will be respected only if he stays within his limits.

317. *Āryavrttam anutisthēt.*

One should behave only like the kings.

318. *Kadāpi maryādā na atikramēt.*

Never destroy the self respect.

319. *Na astyarghah purusa ratnasya.*

Scholars and knowledgeable persons are the precious stones of the society.

320. *Na strīsamam ratnam.*

There is no greater gem than a woman.

321. *Sudurlabham ratnam.*

It is very difficult to get the gems.

322. *Ayaśō bhayam bhayēsu.*

The fear of disgrace is far worse than all other fears.

323. *Na asti alasasya śāstra adhigamah.*

The lazy man does not get the knowledge of scriptures.

324. *Na strainasya svargāptih dharma krtyam ca.*

The one who is preoccupied with thoughts on woman does not attain heaven not good deeds.

325. *Striyō api strainam avamanyatē.*

A woman also belittles a eunuch.

326. *Na puspārthī sinhcati śuskatarum.*

One who desires flowers won't water the dry tree.

327. *Adravya aprayatnō bālukā kvāthana ādananyah.*

Trying to acquire wealth without any toil is like taking out oil from gravel.

328. *Na mahājanahāsah kartavyah.*

Never mock the great people or greatness.

329. *Kāryasampadam nimittāni sūcayanti.*

The method of working itself will give us an idea of the work's success or failure.

330. *Naksatrādapi nimittāni viśēsayanti.*

One can know about the success of a work through the stars.

331. *Na tvaritasya naksatra parīksā.*

One who wants to complete his work quickly does not depend on stars.

332. *Paricayē dōsā na chādyantē.*

Shortcomings cannot be hidden after getting to know one well.

333. *Svayam aśuddhah parāna āśankatē.*

One who is impure, always thinks of impurity in others.

334. *Svabhāvō durati kramah.*

Changing one's behaviour is difficult.

335. *Aparādha anurūpō dandah.*

Punishment should depend on the crime.

336. *Kathā anurūpam prativacanam.*

Answer only to the question.

337. *Vibhava anurūpam ābharanam.*

One should dress according to one's status.

338. *Kula anurūpam vrttam.*

Work according to one's family.

339. *Kāryānurūpah prayatnah.*

Satisfy according to the work.

340. *Pātra anurūpam dānam.*

Give alms according to the role.

341. *Vayō anurūpō vēśah.*

Dress according to the age.

342. *Svāmya anukūlō bhrtyah.*

The servant should be similar to his master.

343. *Bhartrvaśavartinī bhāryā.*

A wife should follow her husband's foot steps.

344. *Guruvaśānuvartī śisyah.*

A disciple should follow his teacher.

345. *Pitrvaśānurtī putrah.*

The son should be under the control of his father.

346. *Ati upacārah śankitavyah.*

Never doubt the extended hospitality.

347. *Svāmina kupitē svāminā ēva anuvartatē.*

Always follow the master when the master is angry.

348. *Mātrtāditō vatsō mātah ēva ānurōdati.*

The child who is punished by his mother still goes and cries before her.

349. *Snēhavatah svalpō hi rōsah.*

The anger of peace loving people lives for a very little time.

350. *Ātmachidram na paśyati parachidram ēva paśyati bāliśah.*

A foolish man never knows his faults, he only sees the faults of others.

351. *Sa upacārah kētavah.*

An evil person works under others for his selfish ends.

352. *Kāmyaih viśēsah upacāranam upacārah.*

An evil person gives presents for fulfilment of his desires.

353. *Ciraparicitā nāma ati upacārah śankitavyah.*

If a person known from a long time suddenly starts serving a lot, then he has to be doubted.

354. *Gauh duskarāśvasahasrāda ēkākinī śrēyasī.*

One obstinate cow is better than a hundred dogs.

355. *Śvō mayūrādadya kapōtō śrēyasō.*

Today's pigeon is better than yesterday's peacock.

356. *Śvah sahasrādadya ēkākinī śrēyasī.*

One single shell of today is better than a thousand shells of yesterday.

357. *Ati sangō dōsam utpādayati.*

An extra eager person leans bad qualities very easily.

358. *Sarvam jayatyaakrōdhah.*

Calm and even tempered man wins over all.

359. *Yadyaapakārinī kōpah kōpē kōpa ēva kartavyah.*

Before getting angry on an evil person, one has to get angry on oneself.

360. *Matimatsu mūrkhamitraguru vallabhēsu vivādō na kartavyah.*

An intelligent man should not argue with fools, friends, teacher and kin.

361. *Na asti piśācam aiśvaryam.*

Evil spirits do not have wealth but wealth can make one evil spirited.

362. *Nāsti dhanavatām sukarmasu śramah.*

A rich man doesn't have to strain too much while doing good deeds.

363. *Nāsti gatiśramō yānavatām.*

One who travels by vehicle cannot walk.

364. *Na samādhih strīsu lōkajñatā ca.*

A woman does not have dignity but has fickleness.

365. *Yō yasmin kuśalah sa tasmin yōktavyah.*

One should do or made to do only that work in which one is excellent.

366. *Duskalatram manasvinām śarīrakarśanam.*

An evil lady weakens the body of even a scholar.

367. *Apramattō dārān nirīksēt.*

Never neglect to keep an eye on woman, or wife.

368. *Strīsu kinchidapi na viśvasēt.*

Never believe a woman.

369. *Alaumayam nigadam kalatram.*

A woman is a shackle sans iron.

370. *Vaidusyam-alankārēna-ācchādyatē.*

Beauty and knowledge gets hidden due to make up.

371. *Gurunām mātā garīyasī.*

The place given to the mother of teachers is very great.

372. *Sarva avasthāsu mātā bhartavyā.*

A mother has to be taken care of in every phase of life.

373. *Strīnām bhūsanam lajjā.*

Modesty is the ornament of a woman.

374. *Viprānām bhūsanam vēdah.*

Knowledge is the ornament of a priest.

375. *Sarvēsām bhūsanam dharmah.*

Righteousness is the ornament of all.

376. *Bhūsanānām bhūsanam savinayā vidyā.*

The greatest ornament is that education or knowledge which has humility in it.

377. *Ana upadravam dēsam-āvasēt.*

Live in a peaceful country.

378. *Sādhujana bahulō dēsah.*

Live where there is a large number of good men residing.

379. *Rājñō bhētavya sarvakālam.*

Always fear the king.

380. *Na rājñah param daivatam.*

There is no greater God than a king.

381. *Sudūram api dahati rājavahni.*

The fire of king burns very far,.

382. *Riktahastō na rājānam abhigacchēt.*

Never go empty handed to a king.

383. *Gurum ca daivam ca.*

Never go empty handed to a guru or a God.

384. *Kutumbinō bhētavyam.*

Never keep differences, hatred or curtness with relatives.

385. *Gantavyam ca sadā rājakulam.*

People have to keep coming and going in royal households.

386. *Rājapurusaih sambandham kuryāt.*

Maintain relationship with the royalty.

387. *Rājadāsī na sēvitavyā.*

Never become intimate with the king's servant.

388. *Na caksusa api rājadhanam nirīksēt.*

Never even look at the wealth of a king.

389. *Putrē gunavati kutumbinah svargah.*

If the son and the family are of good character, then the house becomes a heaven.

390. *Putrā vidyānām pāram gamayitavyā.*

Make your son adept in every kind of education.

391. *Janapadārtham grāmam tyajēta.*

One has to sacrifice the town for the sake of population. The population should be safeguarded even after sacrificing the town.

392. *Grāmārtham kutumbah tyajēt.*

One has to sacrifice the family for the sale of the town. The town has to be safeguarded inspite of sacrificing the family.

393. *Atilābhah putralābhah.*

The greatest profit in life is the begetting of a son.

394. *Prāyēna hi putrāh pitaram anuvartantē.*

The son follows the foot steps of his father after the passing away of the father.

395. *Durgatēh pitarau raksati sa putrah.*

One who safeguards his father and the rest during trouble is a real son.

396. *Kulam prakhyāpayati putrah.*

A son brings glory to his family.

397. *Yēna tatkulam prakhyātam sah purusah.*

A true man is one who brings glory to his lineage.

398. *Na anapatyasya svargah.*

One cannot reach heaven if one doesn't have a son.

399. *Yā prasūtē sā bhāryā.*

A woman is considered a true wife if she begets a son.

400. *Satīrthā abhigamanād brahmacaryam naśyati.*

The purity of brahmacharya is lost if the students maintain a close relationship with their class mates in the school.

401. *Putrārthā hi striyah.*

A woman is acquired to beget a son.

402. *Na paraksētrē bījam viniksēpēta.*

Never sow a seed in a strange place and never impregnate a strange woman.

403. *Upasthita vināśah pathya vākyam na śrrnōti.*

No one heeds to the words of advice during the time of destruction.

404. *Nāsti dēhinām sukha duhkha abhāvah.*

An incarnate will never have any scarcity of comfort or sorrow.

405. *Mātaram iva vatsāh sukha duhkhāni kartāram ēvā anugacchati.*

Joy and sorrow follow a man all through his life just like a calf follows its mother.

406. *Tilamātram upakāram śailamātram manyatē sādhuh.*

A man considers a small favour to be a mountain size.

407. *Upakārō anāryēh na kartavyah.*

Never help the evil people.

408. *Pratyupakāra bhayāda anāryah śatruh bhavati.*

The evil person becomes an enemy while paying the price of the favour received.

409. *Svalpam upakāra krtē pratyupakāram kartum āryō na svapiti.*

A good man cannot sleep peacefully if he doesn't reciprocate a small favour with a really large one.

410. *Na kadāpi dēvatā avamantakā.*

Never insult Gods.

411. *Na caksusah samam jyōtih asti.*

There is no better light than the eyes.

412. *Caksuh hi śarīrinām nētā.*

The eyes are the leaders.

413. *Apacaksusah kim śarīrēna.*

What is a body without eyes?

414. *Na apsu mūtram kuryāt.*

Never urinate on water.

415. *Na nagnō jalam praviśēt.*

Never enter naked in water.

416. *Yathā śarīram tathā jñānam.*

The knowledge is the same as the body.

417. *Yathā buddhih tathā vibhavah.*

A man's glory will depend on his intellect.

418. *Durlabhah strī bandhanāna mōksah.*

To get detached from a relationship with a woman is very difficult.

419. *Strī nāma sarva aśubhānāma ksētram.*

Women are the cause of all evil and difficulties.

420. *Strīnām manah ksanikah.*

A woman's mind remains steady just for a second.

421. *Agnāva agnim na niksēpēt.*

Never pour fire into fire.

422. *Tapasvinah sadā pūjyanīyāh.*

Sages are always worshipped.

423. *Paradārān na gacchēt.*

Never go to the strange women or other's women.

424. *Annadānam bhrūnahatyām-api māsrti.*

By donating food, one can be atoned even for the killing of foetus.

425. *Na vēdabāhyō dharmah.*

There is no righteousness other than vedas.

426. *Na kadācit api dharma nisēdhayēt.*

Never oppose the righteousness.

427. *Svargam nayati sūnrtam.*

Even the heaven bows down before the truthful speech.

428. *Nāsti satyāt param tapah.*

There is no greater penance than uttering of truth.

429. *Satyam svargasya sādhanam.*

Truth is the means of attaining the heaven.

430. *Satyēna dhāryatē lōkah.*

Truth has taken the shape of the world.

431. *Satyād dēvō varsati.*

God's blessings showers on the truth.

432. *Na mīmānsyā guravah.*

Guru can never be questioned or discussed.

433. *Khalatvam na upēyāt.*

Never accept evilness.

434. *Nanrtāt pātakam param.*

There is no greater sin than false hood.

435. *Nāsti khalasya mitram.*

There can never be any friend to an evil man.

436. *Lōkayātrā daridram bādhatē.*

The journey of a penniless man in the life is sorrowful.

437. *Ati śūrō dānaśūrō.*

The bravest is the one who is a great donor.

438. *Gurudēvabrāhmanēsu bhakti bhūsanah.*

Devotion is the jewel to a guru, God and Brahmin.

439. *Sarvasya bhūsanah vinayah.*

Humility is the ornament of everyone.

440. *Akulīnō api vinītah kulīnādvi aśistah.*

If the one who is born in a lowly caste is very humble, he is better than an evil man of a superior caste.

441. *Na arthisva avajñā kāryā.*

Never humiliate or ignore the seekers.

442. *Priyam apya ahitam na vaktavyam.*

Never speak words which are destructive even if couched in sweet tones.

443. *Bahujana virōdham ēkam na anuvartēt.*

One who opposes the majority cannot agree to one person.

444. *Na durjanēsu bhāgadhēyah kartavyah*

Never connect your fortune with a wicked person.

445. *Ācārāda āyuh vardhatē kīrtiśca.*

A man's life and renown grows if he follows righteous path.

446. *Na krtārthēsu nīcēsu sambandhah.*

Never form a relationship with an evil person even if he is rich.

447. *Rnaśatruvyādhisva aśēsah kartavyah.*

Always close the debt, enemy and disease.

448. *Bhūtya anurvanam purusasya rasāyanam.*

Following the path of goodness gives the strength of life to people.

449. *Duskaram karmam kārayitvā kartāram avamanyatē nīcah.*

After getting the work done from a person, man generally insults that person.

450. *Na akrtajñasya narakāni vartanam.*

Hell is certain to an ungrateful person or one who doesn't accept help.

451. *Jivāyattau vrddhi vināśau.*

Too much of talk only results in destruction.

452. *Visa amrtayōh ākarō ji"vā.*

Tongue is both a poison and ambrosia.

453. *Svadharma hētuh satpurusa.*

A man is called a gentleman only if he follows righteousness.

454. *Stutā api dēvatā stusyanti.*

Even Gods get pleased when prayed to.

455. *Anrtam api durvacanam ciram tisthati.*

People remember bad words for a longer time.

456. *Rājadvistam na ca vaktavyam.*

Never speak words which show animosity towards the king.

457. *Śrutisukhāt kōkila ālāpā tusyanti.*

People enjoy listening to the melodious music of the cuckoo.

458. *Priya vādinō na śatruh.*

There is no enemy to a person who speaks loving words.

459. *Na astya arthinō gauravam.*

A seeker loses his self respect.

460. *Strīnām bhūsanam saubhāgyam.*

A woman's ornament is her life when her husband is alive.

461. *Śatrōh api na patanīyā vrttih.*

Never kill even the enemies.

462. *Sujīrnō api picumandō na śankulāyatē.*

An old neem tree cannot still give a nut cracker. One can only do that work which one is capable of.

463. *Ērandam avalambya kujaram na kōpayēt.*

An elephant cannot be made angry with a castor seed tree.

464. *Ati pravrddhā śālmalī vārana stambhō na bhavati.*

An elephant cannot be tied even to an old shaal tree.

465. *Ati dīrghō api karnikārō na musalī.*

However big a piece of wood may be it still cannot become a pestle.

466. *Atidīptō api khadyōtō na pāvakah.*

However bright the embers maybe, it can still never become fire.

467. *Na pravrddhatvam gunahētuh.*

One cannot become a virtuous person just by becoming rich.

468. *Aprayatnādēkam ksētram.*

Farming has to be done only where free and plentiful water is available.

469. *Yathā bīnja tathā nispatti.*

You will reap the fruit of the seed that you sow.

470. *Yathāśrutam tathā buddhih.*

Education is according to the intellect.

471. *Yathākulam tathā ācāram.*

Behaviour depends on the lineage.

472. *Sanskrtah picumandō na sahakārō na bhavati.*

An embellished neem cannot become a mango.

473. *Na ca āgatam sukham parityajēt.*

Never give up the comfort that you have acquired.

474. *Svayam ēva duhkham adhigavchati.*

Sorrow will arrive on its own.

475. *Śāstrapradhānā lōkavrttih.*

Public service should always follow the scriptures.

476. *Niśāyā na carēt.*

Never venture out at night.

477. *Na ca arddharātram svapēyāt.*

Never be awake till late at night.

478. *Anadhikārē na praviśati grhē.*

Never enter somebody's house without prior permission.

479. **Paradravyam haranam aparādhah.**

It is illegal to grab others' wealth.

480. **Tad vidvadbhih parīksēta.**

One should always take the advice of knowledgeable people before starting on work.

481. **Paragrham akāranatō na praviśēt.**

Never enter anyone's house without reason.

482. **Jñātvā api dōsam ēva karōti lōkah.**

People commit sins knowingly.

483. **Śāstra abhāvē śistācāram anugacchēt.**

When one is not aware of scriptures, it is better to follow the advice of knowledgeable people.

484. **Na caritāh śāstram garīyah.**

Scriptures are not greater than discipline.

485. **Durastham api cāracaksuh paśyati rājā.**

A King gets the information of even the farthest place through his spies.

486. **Gatānugatikō lōkah.**

Common people follow the popular conventions.

487. **Yama anujīvēttam na apavadēt.**

Never insult that which provides livelihood.

488. **Tapahsāra indriya nigrahah.**

Controlling of senses is the gist of penance.

489. **Aśubha-dvēsinah strīsu na prasaktāh.**

The women who are away from misfortune are never given a second look.

490. **Yajña-phalajñāh trivēdavidah.**

One who knows the three vedas only knows the summary of them.

491. **Svargasthānam na śāśvatam.**

Life in heaven is not permanent.

492. **Yāvat punyaphalam tāvadēva svargaphalam.**

It is heaven as long as there is sacredness.

493. *Na ca svagāt patanāt param duhkham.*

It is not a matter of great sorrow if one gets destroyed from heaven.

494. *Dēhī dēham tyaktvā aindrapadam na vānchati.*

A man does not aspire for Indra's post by sacrificing his life.

495. *Duhkhānām ausadham nirvānam.*

Relief from sorrow is achieved only through salvation.

496. *Anārya sambandhāt uttama ārya śatrutā.*

It is better to be an enemy with a virtuous man rather than be friend of an evil man.

497. *Nihanti durvacanam kulam.*

The race gets destroyed by the evil saying.

498. *Na putra sansparśāt param sukham.*

There is no greater comfort than the comfort one gets from one's son's touch.

499. *Vivādē dharmam anustarēt.*

Always follow the righteous path during argument.

500. *Niśāntē kāryam cintayēt.*

Always plan the day's activity early in the morning.

501. *Upasthita vināśō durnayam manyatē.*

Man treads the unethical path during the time of destruction.

502. *Ksīrāthirnah kim karinyā.*

What is the use of an elephant to a man wanting milk?

503. *Na dāna samam vaśyam.*

There is nothing more attractive than donation.

504. *Parāyattēsu utkanthām na kuryāt.*

Never be greedy for acquiring others wealth.

505. *Asat samrddhih asad ēva bhujyatē.*

Only the evil people enjoy the ill gotten wealth.

506. *Nimbaphalam kākaih bhujyatē.*

Only crows eat the neem fruits.

507. *Na ambhōdhih trsnām upōhati.*

One cannot quench the thirst with the sea water.

508. *Bālukā api svagunam āśrayēt.*

Both the bear and the evil person never change their character.

509. *Santō asatsu na ramantē.*

Virtuous people do not discuss with evil people.

510. *Na hansāh prētavanē ramantē.*

The swans don't reside in the grave yards.

511. *Artha-artham pravartatē lōkah.*

People are always preoccupied in the acquisition of wealth.

512. *Āśayā badhyatē lōkah.*

This world is entwined in desires.

513. *Na ca āśa aparaih śrīh sahatisthati.*

Wealth cannot be acquired by merely desiring it.

514. *Āśā aparē na dhairyam.*

Desire does not have fearlessness.

515. *Dainyān maranam śrēstham.*

It is better to die than lead a wretched life.

516. *Āśā lajjām vyapōhati.*

Greed makes a person shameless.

517. *Ātmā na stōtavyah.*

Never indulge in self praise.

518. *Na divā svapnam kuryāt.*

Never day dream.

519. *Āyuh ksayī divā nidrā.*

Life span reduces if we sleep during the day.

520. *Na ca āsannam api paśyatya aiśvarya andhah na śrrnōtistam.*

A blind man cannot see the people around him nor can he hear good words for the sake of wealth.

521. *Strīnām na bhartuh param daivatam.*

There is no greater God than husband to a woman.

522. *Tada anuvartanam ubhaya saukhyam.*

A woman gets the joy of the earth and the heaven with the arrival of her husband.

523. *Atithim abhyāgatam pūjayēt yathāvidhi.*

Treat the invited guest with respect according to your means.

524. *Nityam sanvibhāgī syāt.*

Make everyone an equal partner everyday.

525. *Nāsti havyasya vyāghāt.*

The donation given never gets destroyed.

526. *Śatruh api prabhāvī lōbhāt.*

The enemy can be destroyed through greed.

527. *Mrgatrsnā jalavad bhāti.*

The mirage looks like water.

528. *Upālambhō na asti-pranayēsu.*

It is useless to scold an obedient person.

529. *Durmēdha sāmahca śāstram mōhayati.*

People without common sense are attracted towards vile literature.

530. *Satsangah svargavāsah.*

Good company is like living in heaven.

531. *Āryah svayam iva param manyatē.*

A good person thinks of others as having his qualities.

532. *Viśvāsaghātinō na niskrti.*

A betrayer never gets salvation.

533. *Putrō na stōtavyah.*

Never praise your son.

534. *Śaktau ksamā ślāghanīya.*

Forgiveness is far superior to physical might.

535. *Śvah kāryam adya kurvīt.*

Better do today, that you wish to do tomorrow.

536. *Tattvajñānōnryam ēva prakāśayati.*

Philosophy can be understood only through deeds.

537. *Ātmā hi vyavahārasya sāksī.*

Our soul is the witness of our deeds.

538. *Prachanna pāpānām sāksinō mahābhūtāni.*

Five great spiritual philosophies are the proof to the evil deeds done secretly.

539. *Ātmanah pāpam ātmā ēva prakāśayati.*

A sinner reveals his sin by himself.

540. *Ahinsā laksanō dharmah.*

Non-violence is a quality of virtue.

541. *Sarvamanityam bhavati.*

Everything is perishable.

SECTION-4

THOUGHTS ON MANAGEMENT, KAUTILYA'S ARTHASHASTRA

First Case	:	Courtesy
Second Case	:	Publicity of Rules
Third Case	:	Virtue
Fourth Case	:	Difficulty in Reformation
Fifth Case	:	Plan of Conduct
Sixth Case	:	Origin of Sphere
Seventh Case	:	Six Qualities
Eighth Case	:	Addiction to Habits
Nineth Case	:	Duty of Practice
Tenth Case	:	Association
Eleventh Case	:	Plan of Society
Twelfth Case	:	Weaknesses
Thirteenth Case	:	Art of Longevity of Fort/Stronghold
Fourteenth Case	:	Treatise
Fifteenth Case	:	Bases on Principles

First Case – Courtesy

Nama Shukra Brihaspatibhyam. Chanakya began writing the book on arthashastra after praying to Brihaspati- the teacher of the Gods and Shukracharya – the teacher of the demons. He wrote in the book, the various ways one can reign control over the Earth and the wealth of the Earth, how to gain profit over it, how to keep it well established and safe so that there is good administration, so that comfort is provided, so that peace reigns, so that there is prosperity, so that for generations together people live happily, so that respect and prestige is prevalent and salvation can be attained in the end.

Knowledge is very essential to gain all the above things. An ignorant person cannot do anything while the mighty person can get destructed through arrogance. It is only the enlightened person who can ponder calmly, stabilize the thoughts and successfully attain that which he wants to attain. Chanakya has written all that is required to attain all the above.

Discussion on Education

Meditative, Trio, Information and Ethics of government – these four are required for the rule, administration and for acquisition of wealth which is useful for the humanity. It keeps the mind steady through joy-sorrow, and makes us adept in thinking-deciding-speaking-doing. The meditative education is the light among all these learning, is a means to achieve all goals and is a solace to all faiths.

Statistics, Yoga and atheist views come in this part.

Trio contains virtue-vice, news-fortune-misfortune and the ethics of the government contains able administration and bad administration.

Virtue and Deed

One has to gain complete knowledge of Rig, Yajur, Sama and Atharva vedas, history, education, medical treatment, grammar, etymology, metre, astrology, Ayurveda, archery, economics, law, code of hindu law, puranas, Upanishads, Forestry. This is useful for all in the world because it contains in itself the complete knowledge.

1. A Brahmin is one who is a learner-teacher, who performs yagas, sacrifices, who donates and counsels.

2. A Kshatriya is one who practices, performs yagas, donates, finds his means of livelihood through his physical strength and valour.

3. A Vysya is one who practices, performs yagas, donates, who does agriculture, animal husbandry and business.

4. A shudra is one who doesn't specialize in any work, but works as a servant, tends to animals, does business, carves statues, works in factories, sings, plays music, is a bard and a minstrel.

Everyone should perform one's tasks correctly, earn for one's livelihood, marry within and outside one's lineage, mature and lead their lives with the wealth remaining after donating to Gods, forefathers, guests and workers.

The duty of a brahmachari is to perform regulated rituals, keep the environment pure by performing penances, acquire and spread the knowledge.

The duty of a vanaprashthi is to live on fruits and herbs, not to amass wealth, to acquire knowledge and serve the society.

A sanyasi should subdue his senses, not perform any worldly task, be away from greed and desire and be pure in thought, word and action.

The rule of every varna and every ashrama is such that one should not indulge in violence, utter only the truth, be pure, be compassionate and forgive others. One should lead the life with only what is acquired and only then will everyone be healthy and happy.

Victory over Senses

Self control or self discipline is required for success. Only when a man has self discipline, can he discipline his people and the others. This self-control or the self-discipline is nothing but control over one's senses. One must not become immersed in the auditory, tactile, visual, sensual and olfactory senses. One should live with self control and keep away from the enemies like lust, anger, greed, desire and jealousy so that these emotions do not rule over the man but the man rules over them.

Information or Work and Punishment or Administration

Agriculture, animal husbandry and business fall under work. It makes use of the available resources on the earth. These are highly uselful because the livelihood of all is dependent on these.

In order that work is completed usefully and correctly, administration and punishment is required. If there is no administration or punishment, then people will veer away from virtue.

People who commit mistakes have to face punishment accordingly. Sever punishment will only result in hatred and discontent where as good good administration is dependent on pity and compassion.

The Work of Rule – Administrator

One has to let go of six enemies like lust, anger etc and gain victory over the senses, maintain equilibrium that one remains a follower and not an enemy, keep working without hindering virtue or wealth.

Gain knowledge by being in the company of learned men.

Know the news about one's country and other's country through the secret agents.

Maintain good health of the country through honest labour.

Keep a control on workers and related people through the laws of governance.

Make everyone educated through the publicity and propaganda of education.

As far as possible, maintain popularity among the people by donating wealth and maintaining good health.

Be eager to help others.

Always give up the relationship with other women, needing the wealth of others, indulging in violence.

Never sleep at the wrong time of the day, never be inconsistent, never utter lies, never do unethical work.

Maintain equilibrium as inequilibrium will drown us.

Decide on the manner the great scholars and personalities have to be treated and respectly and follow the same implicitly.

Neither a small nor a large organization can run on one wheel. It requires co-operation. In order to get the co-operation from others, be co-operative first.

Commissions/Appointments

The rules, administrator, director and president should appoint their close friends in important posts or appoint those whose antecedents have been verified, who are trustworthy and who have the ability of managing their posts. While appointing a person, his lineage, ability, experience, knowledge, courage, character, mistakes, roles and trustworthiness should be taken into consideration over the personal relationship. A stranger or an incapable person should never be appointed thoughtlessly.

While appointing a person, the following characteristics should be given priority :

Citizen of the country	Noble descent	Character
Authority on economics	Knowledge in fine arts	Good memory
Clever	Eloquent in speech	Effective in speech
Capable of remediation	Effective	Tolerant
Steady	Calm demeanour	Hatred-free

More than half of the people appointed should have these above characteristics. Never appoint less than half the number. They should be verified overtly and covertly and any doubts should be clarified. The administrator should not do the verification himself nor appoint his family member for the same.

The following things have to be found out from the employed people.

Address	Economic condition	Capability
Knowledge of scriptures	Intellect	Tradition/memory
Cleverness	Eloquence in speech	Intelligence
Art of speaking	Enthusiasm Tolerance	
Sanctity of work	Firm mindedness	Fidelity
Modest	Strong	Healthy
Respected	Steadfastness	Amicable

Appointment of Secret Agents

It is not just companies who can appoint secret agents. Anyone requiring their services can appoint them. This chapter and the later chapters deal with the detailed description on the methods of appointing the secret agents. Secret agents are of various kinds.

The following are called stationary secret agents because they stay in the same place and glean information.

1. **Kapatik**: One who knows others' secrets, is a good orator, lives in the disguise of a student is called Kapatik.

2. **Udasthith**: Intelligent, virtuous, lives in the disguise of a mendicant and is trustworthy.

3. **Gruhapathik**: Intelligent, pure hearted and lives in the disguise of a farmer.

4. **Vaidehik**: Intelligent, pure hearted and lives in the disguise of a poor businessman.

5. **Tapas**: One who has either tonsured his head or grown long hair.

Thw following are called the mobile secret agents. They travel far and wide in their work. Their work involves taking care of external wealth also.

6. **Satri**: The agent who is not related to the administrator but is required by the administrator for his livelihood, one who is adept in palmistry and astrology, one who is well versed in science of enchantment, omen, ornithology, kamasastra and is adept in song and dance is called Satri.

7. **Teekshan**: The secret agent who does not bother about the safety of his life but gets into the crux of the matter for the sake of his country is called Teekshan.

8. **Rasad**: The agent who has no attachment to his kith and kin, who is cruel and lazy by nature is called Rasad or venomous.

The following are called the travelling secret agents. They keep an eye on the other secret agents too and keep giving information of them.

9. **Parivrajika**: The agent who is interested in earning her livelihood, poor,old or widowed Brahmin, one who enters the houses dressed as a reputed sanyasini is called Parivrajika.

10. **Munda** : One who tonsures her hair and disguises as a beggar.

11. **Vrushali**: The agent who is a shudra.

12. **Sood** : A cook

13. **Aralik**: A person who cooks meat.

14. **Snaapak**: One who helps in bathing.

15. **Savahak**: One who massages arms and legs.

16. **Aastarak**: One who spreads the matters.

17. **Kalpak**: A barber

18. **Prasaadhak**: A beautician

19. **Udak-Paricharak**: One who fills water

20: **Siddha vesha dhaari guptchar**: The people who are safe guarded by these people.

Advice on the Conduct of Virtue

There are ministers and officials today to run the government. There are certain laws and regulations to be followed while conducting the business. They are called the managers and they too have an advisory committee. One has to learn a lot from Chanakya in this matter. There is a need for reference on the important and significant matter of the present conditions and boundaries.

There is a great necessity of following Chanakya's advice in the modern context because the kind of hostilities which are found among the countries, between the continents, between the business organizations, between small scale businessmen, even between criminals today was not heard of or read of in any age before. One reason could be division of a large unit to many smaller units and each independent unit wanting fame and fortune.

Wherever there is a meeting a lot of discussion and critique has to take place. There has to be a meeting on delivery too. Now a days though the production of goods has become very easy, distributing it has become very difficult. The figures shown are not the actual numbers because the goods manufactured in the factories are lying in the godowns of the wholesalers. They don't reach the consumers. All the shops and factories are glutted with goods. Those who were never bothered with villages are bent on selling their goods there. The consumers in the cities have already purchased goods more than they ever need. They are finding it difficult to safe guard them. They do not have any space left to keep their goods, car and appliances.

As a result the sellers are in search of buyers with the inducement of buy one and take one free or 75% discount or 50% discount. What is happening? What should happen? There has to be proper advice on this matter too.

While such a meeting is organised no outsiders can enter the meeting hall without first obtaining the permission to enter from the president. The meeting hall should be such that no voices from inside should be heard outside. Even a minute information of the meeting should not be leaked out.

The meeting room should be such that there should not be place for birds to even flap their wings, no one can peep inside and no sound from inside can be heard outside. No one can enter the hall without the invitation of the president. Chanakya is called Kutil and his Arthashastra Kautilya's Arthashastra because he has written that one who reveals the contents of the secret meetings has to be ruined and the most severe kind of punishment has to be announced for such acts.

Five Parts of the Meeting

1. The method of commencing the work
2. The wealth, the labour, the property
3. The division of the country – time
4. Impediments – Retaliation
5. Success of work

Only after finalising in the secret meeting can one be employed for work.

The Work of an Administrator

The workers and others stand to gain if the administrator is efficient or successful. Hence the administrator or the head of the planning committee cannot relax for even a moment. The person holding that senior post should divide his day into four parts. Now-a-days there are personnel secretaries to do the work- like the earlier kings had, various time saving gadgets, ability to work till late in the evening due to the availability of electric lights etc. The timing of the meeting and the time of the people who have to attend should be pre decided.

According to Chanakya, an administrator should work for 16 hours. He has to divide his day into 8 parts of two hours each and use those 8 parts in the following manner.

1. In the first part, supervise the work happening and review the previous day's work

2. In the second part, supervise the work of the labourers inside and outside the organization.

3. In the third part have the ablutions and eat food.

4. In the fourth part, manage the income, decide on the expenditure and employ and counter employ etc.

5. In the fifth part send mails and correspondene, meet the secret agents.

6. In the sixth part have contemplative individual thought.

7. In the seventh part check the factories and production.

8. In the eighth part have meetings with important people and give directions.

One most important instruction should be that all the items and the papers which enter the organisation should be stamped. This usually happens in huge organizations and government offices.

There is also a detailed description on self protection and on safety measures for keeping the residences safe.

2

Second Case— Publicity of Rules

Offices and Institutions

Chanakya had suggested opening of offices and branches in every possible place and invest on good roads for the public to modernize, expand and to facilitate good administration. The different offices and branches should have clearly designated jurisdiction. For area administration and for administration of different places, Regional Offices and for central administration selection of proper centres and deployment of proper personnel should be done with great care. Chanakya had classified these as *Sangrahan*—Head Office, *Karvatik*—Administrative Office, *Dronmukh*—Area Office and *Sthaniya*—Branch Office.

If you consider the construction of modern buildings, it has to be admitted that they are not safe and strong. The buildings of financial institutions are not secure and strong. Take the case of ATMs which are being opened in every towns and cities and in every street. The looting of these ATMs clearly shows that in spite of having security guards, they are not safe. The shopping centres, places of worship and other crowded places are declared as sensitive areas. All places have become insecure. The insecure journey of life begins from mother's womb. When the child grows up, he is drawn into child labour engaging him in most dangerous jobs. The School and College buses kill the students in accidents. The fake drugs are killing; food items sold after the expiry date also are killing. Neither the present nor the future is secure. When the entire nation is mired in corruption, who has got the time to think about the security of its people?

The lopsided development of the country has taken a quick toll of our mainstay, agriculture, which is the backbone of our economy and which was catering to the prime requirement of life. No one is interested to stop and think for a while that with the construction of all the skyscrapers and towers and broad roads across the country, the agricultural land available for cultivation is steadily shrinking. The villages should not have this kind of development at all. Otherwise the farmer will begin to lose interest in agricultural activities. Fake sympathies are being expressed, but the matter of fact is that, bullocks, plough and indigenous implements are disappearing from the scene and migration of farm labourers is rampant. The dependence of the farmers on petrol, diesel, chemical fertizers and imported seeds have resulted in incurring loss on every harvest. The maintenance cost of roads and buildings are also expensive and the courts and primary schools started in villages soon after the independence of the country have disappeared from these villages, making one wonder whether hunger can be quenched by currency notes and cheques, bricks and cement! Unplanned development is not progress; it is sure way to destruction.

Chanakya has pronounced that the farmer and his dependents should be saved from punishment, forced labour, taxes, theft, attacks by wild animals, use of poison, diseases and other harassments.

Dhand-Vishisht kar aavadhai: rakshed uphataam krushim
Sten vyalvishgrahai: vyadhibi: cha pashuvranjan

Chanakya has further stated that the top administrators of the government, employees of organizations and the security personnel should provide necessary protection and services to farmers and merchant class.

Vallabhai:karmikai: stenai: antpalai: va peeeditham
Shodhyeth pashu sanghai: ksheeyamanam vanikyadham

But no one is getting protection from anyone. All security measures have been proved to be of no avail; the scams and criminality that comes out like a can of worms clearly establishes that government servants, top administrative officials, the security wings and taxation authorities are exploiting the people, whom they are expected to protect, in the hours of their needs. They have not even spared the government and the governmental work with their devious deeds.

Chanakya has again opined that the government should protect forest wealth, forest animals, bridges, mineral wealth and the mines. However, what is happening today is just the contradictory. It is under government direction that the plunder is taking place, and when they have bled them dry, they give direction to close the mines. New roads and bridges have to be constructed, and, indeed, they are being constructed — but are being used to facilitate the plundered goods to be transported to the other end to be sold at exorbitant price. The railways are busy in this transport; lakhs of tractors and trucks also are engaged in transporting the loot. Everyone turns a blind eye to the goings on and the act of exploitation and destruction goes on unabated. According to government's own admission, between 2006 and 2011, 350 kilometers of forest land has been lost. As far as animal wealth is concerned in majority of states, there are no wild animals, or agriculture related animals, or fauna, even though there are separate departments in the government to look after the individual interests. When the saviours themselves become destroyers, it leads to anarchy in governance. The entire nation is bogged by this misrule. Everyone lives in fear and nobody feels safe. However, safety and security have to be their prime concern and responsibility.

Evam Dravya Dweep Vanam Sethubandham Yadhakaran
Rakshetu Purv Krutan Raja Nava: Cha Abhipravartayet I

Treasury Management

This should be entrusted to the senior most official of the government. He is responsible for reasonable, established, revenues, expenditure and audit the surplus generation and manage efficiently. His work is sub-classified as under:

1. **Reasonable**: These are of 6 types: Institutional, propaganda, travel, Exchange, community welfare and derivatives.

2. **Established**: This again is of six types: fund paid as tribute, royal expenses, outstanding expenses, next year's fixed expenses, governance related and entrance.

3. **Sesh—Others**: This is classified into 6: Fixed main collection, penalty levied, compulsory (prati stabdh, avasrusht), minor levies and very minor levies.

4. **Revenue**: This is of three classes: Fixed regular tax, surtax and supertax.

5. **Expenditure**: are categorized into four: Regular, regular productive, returns and returns-productive

6. **Surplus**: After accounting for all the revenues received and expenses incurred, the balance is known as surplus. The surplus are classified into positive and negative.

The Recovery of the Sums Defrauded by the Employees

Man never lives within his means. Sometimes, he is led astray by his greed. On some other occasion his arrogance drowns him. Other times his desire for sensual pleasure leads to his falling from grace. He is also entangled by his aspirations. Hence crooked persons and thieves were active then and are active even now. Scams were happening then, and are happening now. The difference is that while in the ancient times, the defrauded amount was recovered, whereas it is not being retrieved now. Fraudsters prefer to go to jail and there ends the matter.

To keep a check on this, every one had to submit the statement of accounts at the beginning of rainy season, i.e. month of July. This date was fixed after taking into account the work pressure, which will be the least at the beginning of rainy season. Now this is being done in March, which is a wrong choice because the work pressure will be there in the month of March. After winter, everybody will be fit for work, whereas a major part of the work will be closed during rainy season. Transport including the railways will be badly affected.

There was a rule prevalent that unless a person submits his accounts, he will not even be allowed to meet anyone. Punishment was given for late submission. Of course fraudsters were being punished.

Types of Scams and Frauds

Chanakya has enumerated eight reasons for the depletion of treasury money: prevention, usage, business, harassment, mismanagement, enjoyment, substitute and negligence.

1. **Prevention**: Not collecting; after collecting not keeping the amount in custody; after taking custody of the amount not remitting to the treasury – these are the three types of non performance or duty. The punishment meted out to such persons should be ten times the amount lost.

2. **Usage**: Using the money of the treasury for lending and thereby benefiting is known as usage. Such persons should be levied a penalty of twice the quantum of money so misused.

3. **Business**: Doing personal business with the public fund goes by this name. Such officials are levied a penalty of twice the quantum they diverted for their business.

4. **Harassment**: Not collecting the dues in time and with an ulterior motive to pocket some money, harassing the payer and threatening him with dire consequences and collecting more than what is due and pocketing the excess goes by this name. Such errant official should be levied five times the quantum of amount.

5. **Mismanagement**: Is fall in income and rise in expenditure. The president should be levied a penalty of four times the shortfall.

6. **Enjoyment**: Using the collected amount for self-enjoyment or spending it for others' enjoyment is called depletion on account of enjoyment. Those misappropriating precious stones and gems are to be given life imprisonment; misusing valuable liquids should be given a medium term punishment and others misusing some ordinary items should be asked to return the materials.

7. **Substitution**: Substituting items of king's treasury with some other items is called substitution. The punishment to be meted out to these persons is similar to those of enjoyment.

8. **Negligence**: Not recording the collections immediately, recording expenses and not spending the money, denying remaining amount or the balance – these three are acts of negligence. The penalty levied should be twelve times the amount.

Forty Types of Frauds

1. Not recording the first collection at the time of collection and merging it with the next collection and making entry in the records at the time of second collection.

2. Merging a part of the second collection with the first one.

3. Waiving the dues after taking bribe.

4. Collecting taxes in tax free zones.

5. Not recording the collection in records.

6. Recording as collected the revenues not collected.

7. After collecting only part of the amount, recording the full amount.

8. After collecting full amount recording only part of the amount.

9. After collecting a particular item, recording it as something else.

10. Giving credit to a different person while the revenue is collected from some other person.

11. Not giving the rightful dues,

12. Giving dues which are not rightful.

13. Not giving the dues on time.

14. Giving dues before time after taking bribe.

15. Giving more items and recording less.

16. Giving less and recording more.

17. Giving a different item than the one specified.

18. Delivering the item to a different person.

19. Not depositing the levy collected into the treasury.

20. Without collecting the levy, recording in the books.

21. Not paying the full amount after making purchases.

22. Inflating the purchase price.

23. Recording lesser purchase price.

24. Collecting community tax from all individuals instead of collecting from the community.

25. Collecting from the community what is to be paid individually.

26. Substituting high value items with low value items.

27. Substituting low value items with high value items.

28. On getting a bribe, inflating the prices in the market.

29. On getting a price, deflating the prices in the market.

30. Showing the wages paid for a few days as more days.

31. Sowing the wages paid for more days, as wages paid for few days.

32. Showing normal rainfall as untimely rainfall.

33. Recording the number of days as more or less.

34. Inflating the numbers of employees.

35. Crediting to a wrong head the income received.

36. Keeping part of the amount of charity for oneself.

37. Deviously misappropriating the amount.

38. Collecting more for the community levy.

39. Misappropriating the amount through jugglery in accounts.

40. Showing the size of the bags as small when big bag of goods are received.

Punishment and Reward

1. Once a person brings to the notice and is proved, he will be rewarded one-sixth of the collection.

2. If proved wrong, then the person who had made wrong allegation will be punished.

3. If the person, after bringing to the notice a fraud, takes the side of the accused, will be given life imprisonment.

4. The person who has misappropriated funds and his aide should be given rigourous imprisonment.

5. The person circulating counterfeit coins should be given rigorous imprisonment.

6. The person giving inferior and spoilt food grains should be levied a penalty of twice the amount.

7. For the first mistake committed a penalty of one pana (a quantum of money). Two pana, three pana or four pana will be levied by way of punishment. If the mistake is committed second time, he should be given simple or medium or rigorous punishment. If the person is not reformed by this and commits mistake again, he should be given life imprisonment.

8. The person who steals from the treasury should be given life imprisonment and his abettor should be given half life imprisonment.

9. The person who steals from the treasury should be given life imprisonment and his abettor should be given half life imprisonment.

10. If an employee is deficient in his work, he should be levied a penalty of twice his salary.

11. If an employee does the work as directed and in addition does some useful work on his own volition, he should be rewarded.

12. If an employee harasses the public and collects revenue and promptly deposits the amount in the treasury, he should be sufficiently punished so that he does not harass in future. If he fails to deposit the collected money, he should be levied a penalty of thrice the amount.

13. The officer who saves amount from permitted expenses, thereby denying somebody rightful money, should be given a suitable punishment.

14. If an officer steals from the income of royal house or the general public, then all his assets should be forfeited.

15. The manager with good character should be rewarded on and off.

16. Those stealing minerals should be given punishment of recovery equivalent to eight times the value of stolen goods. Those stealing previous stones and gems should be given life imprisonment.

17. If a person is apprehended while he is attempting to do some wrong act in the night, he should be awarded medium term punishment.

18. If a person is apprehended with arms, he should be punished duly considering the type of the weapon in his possession and his antecedents.

19. If the security guard does not stop a person, who has to be stopped, then he should be punished by levying a penalty of two and a half pana.

20. If a person rapes a concubine or somebody's woman, he should be punished with simple imprisonment.

21. If a person rapes a prostitute, he should be given medium term punishment.

22. If a concubine or prostitute has become somebody's wife and is then raped, rigorous imprisonment should be awarded.

23. If a high born or noble lady is raped, he should be awarded life imprisonment.

24. The old persons, children, sick and destitute prisoners should be released from jail.

25. If an innocent person is jailed by deceit, he should be freed after giving him monetary compensation.

26. All punishment, whether monetary, physical or task, should be bearable to the punished.

27. On special occasions, the prisoners can be freed.

All these are being done even today, however, as punishment is delayed and there is surfeit of cases in the court, there is hardly any effect on the crime or criminals. Most important of all, the court requires proof of crime even if a person is caught in the act of crime. There is no longer trust on the security personnel or even the society.

Systemmatic Writing

It was only during Chanaky's time that organized writings made its first appearance in detail and on scientific lines. He called it 'Governance' and presented in clear writing all classes of treaties and political directives. The maxim that the king and other executives must give importance to the written rather than the word of mouth, was propounded by none other than Chanakya.

Today's demand for 'individual explanation' emanating from all corners had its seed in Chanakya's thoughts. There is however, one difference. Till a few years back, the department used to give explanation as was laid out by Chanakya; now individual himself has to give the explanation. What the explanation should contain is also very clearly specified by Chanakya.

Jathi kulam sthan vay: shrunathi karmardhi sheelanthaya desh kalou
Yon anubandham cha samikshay kaaryadehyatho lekham vidh adhyath
purush anurupam

In letters and articles and treaties or in mutual contracts, apart from the names of individual or individuals they have to clearly specify with due diligence, caste, clan, place, age, qualification, employment, details of assets, eminence, nation time matrimonial details strength or virtues, weaknesses or deficiencies etc.

The letters emanating from controlling offices should have the following 6 attributes"

Ardhakam: sambandg: paripoornath
Madhurya audaye spashtvam iti lekhsampath

1. **Sequence of Meaning**: The main purport of the letter and the less significant issues should be sequenced.

2. **Connection**: There should not be anything contradicting what is said in the first part of the letter.

3. **Completeness**: Subject covered and the word used should be brief; there should not be verbosity; examples to prove the objective and proving with facts clearly perceived and not using unimpressive words constitute this attribute.

4. **Amiability**: Using simple, easily comprehensible words is amiability of the letter.

5. **Liberal**: Using cordial and elegant words constitute this attribute.

6. **Clarity**: Using the apt words in the letter is clarity.

In addition to spelling out these attributes, Chanakya has thrown light on other finer aspects of niceties and complexities of letter-writing. This is one of the reasons for innate skills of writing and clarity in presentation displayed in his books. Probably, he had honed these skills from Takshasila, as a student and later as a teacher. He has further enumerated the negative qualities of writing letters or tendering explanations:

1. **Uncouth:** Writing on paper strewn with ink; writing on dirty paper; writing in incorrigible handwriting; without uniformity of writing, and writing with light ink – all these are uncouth way of writing.

2. **Contradiction:** Where there is contradiction in the substance of second letter to the earlier one or hampers the action to be taken on the basis of earlier letter is contradiction.

3. **Repetition:** To repeat what is already stated.

4. **Bad Grammar:** The wrong usage of gender, words, tense, factors.

5. **Sampalv (Non Completion?):** Not dotting the I's and crossing the Ts and not using the punctuation marks correctly.

It will be befitting if Kautilya's teachings are accepted without demur, because it is only after studying various science that Kautilya or Chanakya has come to these effective conclusions for the benefit of the mankind.

Sarva shastrani anukamy prayogam upalabdh cha.
Autilyen narendrathe shasanasya vidhi: krita:.

The next part of this chapter may not be applicable to business organizations. However it has to be admitted that the elucidation given in depth in these chapters in a scientific manner are replete with rare jewels of wisdom and every single quality of life has been examined and explained from different angles. This is rarely seen in modern writings and it can be said that even books dealing with the examination of jewels does not have this kind of detailed discussion or narration. The details regarding management of mines propounded by him are so complete and comprehensive and it is sad to see that these are being overlooked in contemporary times. The mines are being plundered at will. Chanakya's knowledge in this regard was extensive, deep, practical and commercial. These can be studied and experienced and implemented in full, not in parts.

Sales Management

The first requirement of good sales management is to classify the products and materials of land and water resources and the goods and materials arriving by land and sea:

1. Which goods are popular and in demand?

2. Which are the goods which are not popular and low in demand?

3. What are the enforceable rules and regulations required for decreasing or increasing the supply of goods?

4. The right time to buy the marketable goods and the right time to sell the goods thereby ensuring there is no overstocking in the warehouse.

5. If there is excess stock of marketable goods in high demand, then the selling price should be quietly hiked and when it is felt that sufficient profit is earned, then the price should be reduced.

6. Own goods and our own nation's goods, should be kept and sold at a designated place.

7. Goods from other countries should have many outlets for sale.

8. The sales of indigent and imported materials and products should be managed in such a way that the citizens do not have any inconvenience.

9. If a product on high demand is hurting the consumers, then that product should be taken off temporarily.

10. Hoarding goods which are in high demand with the intention of making a huge profit is highly unjust and punishable.

11. Forcibly cancelling contract of a fast moving item from one and awarding to another is unfair.

12. The goods sold in several places should have the same fixed price.

13. If the sale price comes down in the course of selling, the resultant loss should be borne by the seller.

14. One-sixteenth portion of the value of the goods in safe custody of the warehouse should be given as tax. This is called levy or acceptance levy.

15. 5% (20th portion) of the goods, which are measured and 6% (16th portion)of the goods which are counted have to be given as tax.

16. Every day by close of business accounts have to be submitted and the tax deducted should be deposited.

Export Business

17. In the export business, first and foremost, one has to know which goods area cheap or costly.

18. In addition to the above one has to factor in sales tax, border official's tax, security officials's highway tax, sea route charge, provision for food and expenses, freight charges, etc and assess the profit.

19. If own goods do not yield profit, then one should exchange the goods with the goods available there, which are in popular demand here.

20. Spend one-fourth of the profit and ensure security in the place of business.

21. Establish good relationship with border security force, VIPs of the city and the nation to have a smooth running business.

22. When doing business in overseas, some calamity happens, then the businessman has to protect himself and valuables .If valuables cannot be protected, he should save himself.

23. During the time of staying abroad, pay the local tax prevalent there with due diligence.

24. While trading by sea, businessman should serially take into account 'Transport freight' i.e. the charges of boat and ship, 'Incidentals' i.e. food and other expenses, 'self and others' i.e. clear demarcation of own goods and other's commodities, time of travel and the weather, preventive steps against perceived dangers, safety measures, and tradition, beliefs and habits of the people of the destination country.

25. If trading by sea or land does not generate sufficient profit and there is no safety, it is better to stop that business.

Responsibilies of Heads of Departments

Chanakya has defined the responsibilities of management heads of all the departments and dealt at length their job description, accountability, thefts and prevention thereof and the punishment for lapses. All these are discussed in many of the following chapters. The following are the departmental heads, whose duties are discussed:

1. Manager in charge of markets and produce.
2. Manager in charge of pottery and timber.
3. Manager in charge of publications and science etc.
4. Manager in charge of weights and measures.
5. Manager in charge of ships and harbour.
6. Manger in charge of levies.
7. Manager in charge of yarns and threads.
8. Manager in charge of Agriculture.
9. Manager in charge of excise.
10. Manager in charge of abattoirs.
11. Manager in charge of brothels.
12. Manager in charge of boats.
13. Manager in charge of animal husbandry.
14. Manager in charge of horses.
15. Manager in charge of elephants.
16. Chief of military.
17. Head of finance.
18. Manager in charge of grasslands and meadows.

Third Case—Righteousness

Terms and Conditions

All work, business is dependent on virtue, business, character and principles. Business is greater than virtue, character is greater than the business and the principles are greater than character. There should always be firmness in truth in virtue, proof in business, character in society and the principles in the rulers. One has to believe only in jurisprudence whenever there is a revolt against character, popular conventions and jurisprudence.

The drafting of terms and conditions, business and arguments have to be decided by three judges in the following places.

1. In the boundary of two kingdoms or villages ie. in a populated area.
2. In the collection or centre of the villages.
3. In the centre of 400 villages.
4. In the centre of 800 villages or at a local self government.

The draft of terms and conditions go against rules and regulations they will be considered unconstitutional and punishment will be given

1. If they are conducted in secrecy, inside a house, at night, in the forest, in a cunning manner or while being alone.
2. The one who goes against the regulation has to be given first degree punishment.
3. If someone has heard of theses regulations then they cannot be accepted as anti-regulations.
4. The terms and conditions given by women who are veiled, inheritance of the sick, the property, the trust-money, the prenuptial agreement should be treated as authentic.
5. The work done by the people inhabiting forests in the forests may be considered constitutional.
6. The work of people who lead a secret life may be considered constitutional.
7. If agreements are formed in mutual understanding, then they are considered constitutional.

8. The agreements of angry, sad, intoxicated and insane people cannot be considered constitutional.

There is a detailed description of the legality of marriage and inheritance in this chapter. There is description of the method of construction of house in accordance with vaastu shastra. The sale and purchase of property is also described in this. The rules of collection of deposit, loan and interest are given and the dispute of labour and labourers is also given along with the rules of labour. There is also description of the punishment to be meted out if these are broken.

Punishment for Purchase – Sale, Marriage, Valour etc.

1. If the seller refuses to sell after entering into an agreement, he must be fined 12 panns.

2. The money collected in advance can be returned within a day.

3. The advance for things having a short life span should be paid upon the condition of not reselling it to others. The one who goes against this will be fined 24 panns..

4. If a woman is married off by hiding her faults, then the person will be fined 56 panns.

5. If a groom's flaws are hidden and his marriage is performed, then double the fine ie., 112 panns have to be paid.

6. If any person donates only under the fear of punishment or blame or disease, he has to be given the punishment meant for thieving.

7. Those who create a relationship between a man and a woman, those who try to separate the legally bound couple should be fined 500 or 1000 panns.

8. One who loots a place after informing about it should be fined double the amount.

Verbal Attack Difference and Punishment

Abuse, slander, threat are all verbal attacks. There is no punishment for these in the present day. Hence we have to live bearing with all crimes. Now-a-days foul language is used on public stages too, shoes, slippers and chairs are flung about, but there is no punishment for these. As a result the entire society has become immoral. Touching or hitting people comes under this category and there are five differences.

1. **Body**: If some vulgar word is aiming at some part of the body then three pan has to be paid and if some one slanders falsely then six pan has to be paid as fine. People who comment sarcastically have to pay a fine of 12 panns.

2. **Nature**: If someone attacks verbally on some one's caste and if both belong to the same caste, then the Brahmin has to pay affine of three, six or twelve pan. If he attacks some other caste person verbally then ha has to pay two or four pan.

3. **Hearing**: People have to be punished similarly even if they attack verbally.

4. **Work**: If people attack some one's livelihood they have to be punished similarly.

5. **Country**: If people of different countries attack verbally, they too have to be punished similarly.

If some one curses his country or creed, society or his caste, then he has to get the degree punishment.

Gambling and conducting gambling was not a crime but there used to be a president and the gambling took place only in his place. There were also a lot of crimes connected to this and Chanakya has given a detailed explanation for this in 'Dhyut Samahvay' chapter.

Lawlessness is rampant today because there is no system of punishment is not executed immediately. Hence you find slander in books, magazines and memorandum and while giving speeches on the stage. The person who is slandered seethes silently but he doesn't have the guts to either say or do something. The puppets dance on the strings. Incidents of threat are happening at some place or the other every second but nobody is able to stop it. We can't even comprehend what's wrong with human beings now? What more destruction remains to be seen now? The societies, government offices, schools, universities, municipal corporation and panchayat should be given the power to punish instantly so that using bad language speaking ill of others can be controlled. Man has to be disciplined even if it has to be through force.

Fourth Case – Difficulties in Reformation

Chanakya has written a chapter on the redemption of obstacles in order to safeguard the ordinary citizens from the artisans, the farmers and the officers. In this chapter he has described in detail how these people trouble the ordinary citizens by taking various arms of power. He has also decided the punishments for such acts. Who has the time to worry or question the ordinary public in the present day when the nationalised and private banks loot people, the farmers and government workers get looted the moment they come out after clearing the money in the bank, when fake medicines are sold so rampantly in the market? Everyone is forced to live in fear and die crushed under the wheels of the vehicles. The drivers treat the punishment they get as some sort of awards. The loss of life of this magnitude was not heard of even during the times of war. People keep prophesizing that in the future years there will be so many disasters which will affect five crore people. Everyone is busy amassing wealth, there is no time to even look at someone else. Today we cannot find a civilized society or a rule or a discipline. Though it cannot be proved authentically, it is however true that in the present age the mortality of youth is five times more than that of old people.

The following are written in this unit and looking at it we can understand what a great visionary Chanakya was at his age that he could predict the modern happenings in those days itself.

1. The safeguarding of common public from the artisans.
2. The safeguarding of the common public from the merchants.
3. The safeguarding of the common people from the divine disasters.
4. The safeguarding of common public from secret plots.
5. Destruction of evil.
6. Knowledge about all those who deserve to be doubted.
7. Identification of dearth and murder.
8. Inspection and torment
9. Surveillance of the government departments and punishment
10. Partial killing and punishment

11. Complete murder and picturesque punishment
12. Punishment for having relationship with a virgin.
13. Punishment for extremities.
14. Punishment for rapists.

Fifth Case – Plan of Conduct

Maximum Wealth in the Treasury

The king can increase his treasury by levying taxes as he wishes, but Chanakya made conditions on that too. He forbade the excess levy from the border areas, forests and deserts. He said that at some places 20% of income should be levied while in some other place 10% and somewhere else 5%. He said that taxes have to be levied from businessmen, prostitutes and the animal rearers. If the needs are not fulfilled with this amount, then voluntary donations should be sought from the prosperous citizens. The treasury couls also be filled by gifting to Gods. A king can make two people fight, get one to kill the other and amass the wealth of the killer saying that he has committed a crime.

But this is neither possible nor proper for a farmer. He can fill his coffers only through hardwork and intelligence. Today's tradition of conducting business is to take a loan from the bank for the work. But the greatest danger in this is though the man uses his mind, body and man power and conducts business, he has to part with the majority of his income in the form of interest for the loan he has obtained from the bank. The actual remains constant and doesn't get depleted.

A businessman's treasury gets filled through the control of market: it increases when the quality of product is good and widely accepted. When the product is sold in large number, the income automatically increases. The farmer should follow those specific methods to fill his coffers. He should produce only those items which are useful to people, then people will prefer it and the demand and supply will be at par and his income increases.

If it is only sales and distribution, the warehouses should be filled or emptied accordingly. It has to be always kept in mind that the warehouses should never be filled completely or emptied fully, instead it should be filled or emptied as required. Only then can the profits be known and thus the treasury can be filled.

Workers who Cause Ruin

Those workers who are employed, paid and fed by the organization should be immediately removed if they are planning its down fall. The easiest way is to create a fight between two people. If such incidents happen against the administration or big organization, then there are a lot of ways of solving them. This work can be done by taking anyone's help. *Swapakshe, parapakshe va tushni dandam prayojayet.*

The Welfare of the Workers

The workers have to be paid well for their welfare so that they do not feel the need of money and lose interest in their work. Hence Chanakya fixed the salaries of people working in the royal palaces and other places. But he put in a condition that the salary will be paid according to the capacity of the king, kingdom, employer, strength of organization. The expenditure should not exceed the income and the organization run under loss due to the increased payment. Nothing should be done which will result in useless expenditure.

1. A sage, teacher, minister, priest, commander in chief, prince, queen mother and queen should be paid an annual income of 48,000 pann.

2. The gate keepers, the security guards of inner palace, the guards of armoury, the tax collectors, the president of warehouse should be paid the half of the above set ie. 24,000 pann.

3. The brother of the heir apparent, the leader, the police officer of the town, the president of the business establishment and the council of ministers should be paid half of the above ie. 12,000 pann.

4. To the head of a regiment or an engineer and the presidents who come in the second category should be paid 8,000 pann annually.

5. The commanders of various regiments have to be paid 4,000 pann annually.

6. To the teachers and animal rearers 2,000 pann should be paid as annual income.

7. Astrologers, authors, eulogizers, assistants to the priests and others of the same statur should be paid an annual income of 1,000 pann.

8. Painters players, poets writers, clerks etc., should be paid 500 pann.

9. Actors, dancers, singers etc., 250 pann.

Thus the scale of salary is reduced. For example, eventhough one may be a prince, his position or rank gets him only half. This is certainly a well thought out scientific plan.

This way the salary becomes 48, 24, 12, 8, 4, 2, 1, ½, ¼, 1/8.

But in the present days people working on the same job get different scales of salary. Therefore what can one say of people doing different work?

The Details of Workers Unions

1. A man who is well versed in worldly affairs has to work for the leader of the organization belonging to to a good race, is capable and intelligent.

Though the incapable man's past might be good but his future will not certainly be.

2. If some agreement has to be made, then it has to be legal and ethical.

3. Do only what the president of the organization orders.

4. Never sit beside the president while working. Neither be too far nor too near.

5. Never speak sarcastically, vulgarly or any falsehood.

6. Never speak out of turn or loudly.

7. Never clear the throat or belch while speaking.

8. Never speak to others in the presence of the president without first taking permission from him.

9. Never say yes or no in any situation.

10. Never take the role of the president or behave like him.

11. Never wear the jewels similar to the ones worn by the president.

12. Never speak with an eye closed or lips compressed or lifting an eye brow.

13. Never interrupt in the middle, while the president speaks.

14. Never fight with any relative of the president.

15. Never form a relationship with the women in the office, with the opponents or with the enemies.

16. Never keep repeating the same matter.

17. Never keep parroting the same words.

18. Relate important matters to the president immediately.

19. Tell the people around the president and the not the president if the matter is going to be advantageous to you.

20. Inform personally if it is about the welfare of others.

21. Always inform the important matters in right time and when necessary.

22. Good news has to be conveyed.

23. Never inform the bad news yourself but ask others to tell it.

24. Speak only the truth when questioned.

25. Remain quiet if you are afraid to answer.

26. Laugh when the president laughs but never guffaw aloud.

27. Inform the fearful news through someone else.

28. If you get the responsibility of some work, then you have to bear the repercussion calmly.

29. Always worry about personal safety, then worry about others' safety.

30. A president can either ruin you or provide you with everything depending on his mood.
31. Always be carful and cautious.

The Rules of an Organization

1. The workers should inform their master the profit remaining after subtracting the expenditure.
2. The worker should inform his master the actual incidents which occur both externally as well as internally.
3. If the master follows unethical ways, the workers should lure him to the ethical way by praising him.
4. The master has to be saved from the foreseen and unforeseen dangers even if the worker has to face the danger.
5. Always keep the master in good spirits after knowing the reasons for his joys and anger.

Leaving the Weak and Foolish Master

1. Leave the service of foolish master.
2. In the similar manner, ten capable ministers gave up the service of foolish and weak kings. This example has been given by chanakya. He has given a detailed description about this.
3. When the king said that the one who has to draw the water from a deep well, is drawing from a shallow well, many ministers quit their post and went away.
4. The minister Karnik belonging to Bharadwaja gotra left the king and went away when he heard that 'Krauncha bird' has flown away from the left side.
5. Acharya Deerghanarayan left the patronage of the king and went away when he saw a blade of grass in the hands of the king.
6. Acharya Ghotamukh left his king and went away when he heard that the clothes were all cold.
7. Seeing water being sprayed on an elephant, the Acharya Kinjalk left his master and went away.
8. Pishun left the king's patronage when he heard the praises of the chariot horses.
9. Acharya Pishun's son left the king's court when he heard the king's dog barking.
10. One should never work under a master who destroys wealth and respect.

11. If the master is angry, one has to send the explanation through his friend and work usefully until one's death.

12. It has been said that frequently changing the company or organization will result in bad report of character and the person will not be considered dependable. It happens a lot now a days. Hence the person who comes from another organization is not given a high post which requires secrecy in another organization. New employees are well paid but are not well placed where as the person who works in the same organization gets a lot of respect.

Method of Working During Danger

No one can comprehend either the worldly or the divine power. Sometimes a situation arises when the master is either kidnapped or dead and a capable heir is not ready. Then it becomes very difficult to run the organization which has many branches. If this happens due to some cunning plot, then even calling the council of ministers for a meeting is like inviting danger.

There are two ways to it, either hide the danger or reveal it. One has to decide on one way after a day's thought. The ones who are in danger will not accept it easily and the information about the danger has to be given to them. They cannot glorify death because they are afraid of falling into its snare. The one who plots, wishes to remain secret because if he reveals himself then there is fear of attack from all sides.

Chanakya has described various tactics to be used here, but the important point is all the affairs have to be managed well and successfully until the heir is selected and he takes up the responsibilities. If this post is given to a prince or the first born, then he should slowly be informed about the problem and asked to avenge it. If such a situation arises, please refer to aapatprateekaar prakaran. Whatever has to be done should be done during the time of difficulty as the strength and resilience is revealed only during the trying time. What is the use after the time is passed?

Chanakya wrote

Kaalam cha sakrudabhyeti yam naram kaala kaanshinam.
Durlabhah sa punah tasya kaalah karma chikishratah.

The long awaited moment comes only once. Once it is lost, it is lost forever, never to be regained. There is no point in beating the ground after the snake escapes. The snake has to be killed when it is close by.

To Prepare an Heir

It is the right time then to get a proper heir ready. A young son or a pregnant wife has to be given the most prominent post and the rest all other posts. The wages of the ordinary workers and the workers holding high posts have to be increased so that they are satisfied.

The heir's education should be extraordinary. He should have full knowledge in great qualities like education, modesty, law, politics, sociology and virtue. He should be informed of the situation only after he becomes competent. He should be informed of all the wealth, honour, prior decisions etc. Even after all these he has to be advised about righteousness and philosophy for some more time.

6

Sixth Case – Origin of Spheres

Seven Types

Below given are seven natures and tendencies of seven kinds of people. It is not possible to reign over them without knowing them, without forming a relationship with them, without keeping them happy or without being useful to them. These are the seven kinds of people, viz., aaster, administrator, public, office, treasury, regiment or army or workers, friend and enemy. Though friend and enemy are in the same section, if they are separated then there will be eight kinds.

1. **Master's Quality**: The master has many qualities which are attractive, wise and enthusiastic.

    He is of superior race, has Godly qualities, is filled with valour, is farsighted, is righteous, truthful, grateful, has high ideals, is enthusiastic, is a quick worker, is skilful, competent, can attract others, is firm, is filled with good qualities, is a family man and a follower of scriptures. These are called attractive qualities.

    Knowledge of scriptures, debates on scriptures, understanding, sharp memory, ability to reach the crux of the matter, one who gives up the unethical side and supports only the ethical ones. These qualities are called 'Wise qualities'.

    Valour, temper, and adeptness are the qualities of enthusiasm.

    A respectable master is one who is a good orator, is courageous, brave, superior, having restraint, excellent rider, annexer, saviour, one who knows both kindness and cruelty and takes revenge accordingly, modest, supporter during misfortune, one who understands the treaty, who is adept in warfare, sensible during conflict, having the ability of gaining from the enemies, much beloved, amicable, generous and respects the elders.

2. **The Qualities of an Administrator**: The qualities of a minister or an administrator or a judge or the council of ministers have been described eloquently during their election.

3. **The Qualities of the Public or Population**: The qualities of good population is known through its income and behaviour. Where the grains

are grown aplenty or where agriculture is done very competently, where the countryside is filled with bountiful trees and animal wealth- these are the necessary things for a decent livelihood not the items of luxury. Chanakya abhorred the luxurious things in any manner or form because luxury never lets one be healthy or refined.

The atmosphere of the land should be pure and the people healthy. The unhealthy people cannot work properly and will be immersed in debts. There cannot be any gains if people are already burdened with debts. The gains csn be found where both ordinary and extraordinary items are sold and where loving and pure hearted people reside.

4. **The Qualities of a Fort or an Office**: The office should be situated in such a place where the roads meet, should not be situated in an isolated place and should be in such a place where there is a heavy movement of people.

5. **The Quality of Treasury**: The treasury is that distinct place where the honest earnings of both our forefathers and oursis safeguarded. It should be filled with gold, silver, gems etc. It should have so much wealth thatit can be used for the safeguarding of family, relatives and workers during misfortune. This is called the wealth.

6. **Regiment or Army or Workers' Quality**: The workers who have been working since generstions are good, they are permanent and submissive, they work eagerly and are knowledgeable in their line of work.

7. **Qualities of a Friend**: A friend is one who is steady, submissive, one doesn't have rivalry with hi. He is filled with qualities like enthusiasm etc and is aperson who helps in the time of need.

8. **Qualities of an Enemy**: One who is not of good race, is greedy, comes from an unethical family, who goes against the scriptures, rules, is unworthy, addicted to vices, is not enthusiastic and performs tasks without any forethought.

Spiritual Knowledge

Peace is the reason for well being and exercise is the reason for welfare.

The exercise keeps the workers active and lithe. Peace destroys the obstacles on the path of attainment of the fruits of hard work.

There are six qualities of peace and exercise – treaty, war, conveyance, seat, alliance and dual feelings and these have the following three fruits – progress or growth, regress or downfall and average state of affairs.

Three Fruits

1. Growth or progress
2. Downfall or regress

3. Average state of affairs

➭ There are two methods of acquiring these three fruits. Mortal and immortal. Justice and injustice are human actions while fortune and misfortune are divine actions.

➭ These mortal and immortal actions are the two wheels on which the life makes its journey. The virtuous and non virtuous actions performed through luck is called 'destiny'. If the fruits of these actions are favourable, we call it fortune. If the fruits of these actions are unfavourable, we call it misfortune. If the unfavourable fruits of actions are what we get, then our state is indeed very unfortunate. The mortal actions are those which are performed through the strength of influence, strength of advice and the strength of enthusiasm. If the welfare, comfort is achieved through these then it is fortune, if it is not achieved then it is misfortune.

➭ The actions of destiny cannot be comprehended, therefore it is impossible to explain, it is foolish even to try it.

➭ A man is called a 'victor' if he is filled with self confidence, is wealthy and who follows virtue. The people around him are called enemies whereas the neighbours are called friends.

➭ The people having the clear qualities of enmity are called the foes. One has to win over a person with addiction. The weak enemy has to be won over too. The dependent yet strong king has to be troubled with various methods and his wealth and strength have to be reduced.

➭ The five types who a victor encounters ahead in his victorious journey are- enemies, friends, friendly enemies, friends of friends and friends of enemies. He leaves behind four kinds – they are destruction, lamentation, ruin and sorrow. The sphere formed with these nine is called the royal sphere.

➭ The enemy in the border of the victor's territory and the heirs of the enemy's race are the natural enemies. The one who revolts or makes others revolt is called an artificial enemy.

➭ The one who is slightly away from the border of the victor is a natural friend and his paternal and maternal cousins also become the natural friends. The one who seeks help for gaining wealth or livelihood is an unnatural or artificial friend.

➭ Strength is called might and the achievement is called happiness.

➭ There are three kinds of strength – strength of knowledge, strength of treasury and physical strength.

- In the same manner there are three kinds of achievements – achievements through advice, through the master, through enthusiasm.
- The man having these strengths is called superior and the man not having these is called mediocre.
- In the circle of this sphere, the circumference is made up of friends, the ones lose are enemies and the victor himself nucleus.
- The one who interferes between the person and his friends will be troubled and routed.

Seventh Case – The Six Qualities

The Aims and Weaknesess of the Measures; Place and Development

The agreement reached between two individuals, organizations, institutions, or states on any issue is known as treaty. To provoke and cause harm to an enemy is creating strife, boycotting is taking a stance, praising them is to take them for a ride, surrendering is establishing a connection, and simultaneously spreading strife and entering into treaty with them is akin to riding two horses at the same time.

Six Measures

1. **Treaty**: Two individuals, organizations, institutions or nations striking an accord on certain conditions is known as treaty.

    If it is felt that one is weaker than the enemy, treaty has to be entered into. If it is felt that one can make rapid progress, and the enemy will progress a little slower; own business interests will rise and that of the enemy would remain stable; even with equal progress, while one would be ascending, that of the enemy remain static; in such a situation, he should not worry about the progress or stability of the enemy. Even if the progress is equal, and both are making equal strides, then treaty has to be entered into with the enemy.

2. **Strife**: The enemy can be harassed in many ways including help from allies, creating obstructions and ignoring them.If it is felt that one is stronger than the enemy, then the method of spreading strife can be resorted to.

3. **Raid**: Attacking or mounting an offensive against another is known as raid. If it is felt that one is stronger than the enemy, all-conquering and extraordinarily powerful, then invasion should be made.

4. **Posture**: Whether enemy or ally, boycotting or ignoring the areas across the border is known as taking a posture or stance. If the strengths of the enemy is equal to one's own strength, then stance can be taken.

5. **Union**: To surrender oneself before an enemy is known as union.

    If one is utterly in a weak position, then surrender is the best way out.

6. **Twin-Pronged Approach**: To use simultaneously contradictory approach of reaching a treaty and spreading strife is known as twin or double-pronged approach.

   If co-operation is sought, this twin approach is effective.

   Only after assessing the situation and considering the effectiveness of each of the methods, decision has to be taken as to whether treaty, or spreading strife or outright invasion would be effective to successfully meet the situation.

Three Benefits

1. **Advancement i.e. Progress**: Out of the above described attributes one has to choose the right one to safeguard business, treasury, dependents etc. can achieve progress or can cause loss to the enemy; he has to ensure that he adheres to the chosen course. Using the right method itself is the cause for success.

2. **Decline i.e. Decay**: If the usage of any one of this would injure self-interest or is beneficial to the enemy, then definitely that attribute should not be used. Using the wrong method itself causes decline.

   When the decay is slower than the decay of the enemy, the one should not be perturbed. If the enemy's decline is rapid, then it would be proper to enter into treaty.

3. **Equilibrium**: By adhering to a particular attribute, if there is no perceivable effect on progress or decline, such a situation is known as stable.

Treaty: Weak Treaty

1. **Trap Treaty**: A weak king under suppression of army of a powerful king would be eager to strike a quick treaty. In such a situation the vanquished will have to part with wealth, land etc. Hence it is known as a trap treaty.

2. **Status Difference Treaty**: When the commander and prince are deputed to the enemy's palace for signing the treaty, the status of the signatories are not equal. While the enemy is represented by the head of the government, the king, the other side is represented by second line of administration. It is also known as self-protection treaty, because the king himself does not go to the enemy palace and protects himself from risk.

3. **The Fortunate Treaty**: If a king agrees to go personally or send his employees, armed force, etc. to assist a powerful king in any of his ventures, it is known as fortunate treaty – fortunate because even though he is weak , he is able to be ally of a powerful king. This is also known as treaty for self protection from invasion.

4. **Punishing Treaty**: When the powerful put up a condition of marrying the daughter of the weak as the term for treaty, it is definitely a punishing treaty.

5. **Ransom Treaty**: A treaty to release the top employees captured by a powerful enemy on payment of money.

6. **Satellite Treaty**: If it is agreed in a ransom treaty that the ransom amount can be paid in installments, the treaty is known as satellite treaty.

7. **Post-fix Treaty**: In a satellite treaty, if time and place are fixed for the payment of installments, it is known as post-fix treaty.

8. **Dowry or Golden Treaty**: If the installments are paid as per stipulation in the treaty, it is known as dowry treaty, as the victor and the vanquished develop friendship and closeness. Hence this is also referred in some place as golden treaty.

9. **Skull Treaty**: Where the treaty provides one time full payment, it is known as Skull treaty.

10. **Ill-Motive Treaty**: Treaty with bad intentions is known as ill-motivated treaty, wherein the weak and old horses and elephants are given after giving them poison with the result they die within two to four days of reaching the destination. In other words, substandard wealth is being given as a consideration for treaty.

11. **Defaulting Treaty**: If after paying a part of the amount, requesting the other party to be satisfied with this or avoiding the payment of the balance installments by giving some lame excuses, thereby making the intentions of non-payment of the balance amount clear is known as defaulting treaty.

12. **Planned Treaty**: To safeguard the interests of the Kingdom, resources and its subjects, parting a part of the land as consideration of the treaty is known as a planned treaty. Smart and cunning kings ensure that his spies are hidden in the area given who can cause turmoil in the area and later merge back with their own State.

13. **Infertile Treaty**: Parting with dry lands as consideration for the treaty with the ulterior motive of getting it back is known by this name.

14. **Produce Treaty**: Where the produce of fertile land is given as a consideration for treaty is known as produce treaty, as the produce are being parted.

15. **Highly Damaging Treaty**: In addition to the produce given as per the produce treaty, if anything more have to be given, it is highly damaging the interests of the the giver and hence known by this name.

16. *Land Parting or State Parting Treaty*: If the treaty specifies land to be given as a consideration, it is known as land parting or State parting treaty.

Treaty : Beneficial Treaties

Although Kautilya's Arthashastra is more applicable to the kings and related politics and is focused on their problems and solutions, and deals with the principles connected with them, people in all walks of life can assess their own situations and can choose their own options from the many guidelines contained in this treasure house. It has become all the more relevant now, as, even without enmity or former allies, the nations, organizations, institutions and individuals are in far-flung areas of the globe. They have different objectives and requirements and to achieve them are entering into several treaties, which in today's parlance are known by different names as contracts, memorandum of understanding, compromise, understanding, agreements, co-operation or collaboration. All these are in essence different forms of treaties.

1. *Specified and Unspecified Treaties*: These are two classifications of treaty. While in specified treaty, the State, time, and acts to be performed are clearly spelt out, in the case of unspecified treaty, these conditions are not clear. These treaties may have good or cunning intentions, which take several forms.

   If minor differences arise, the treaty may fall through.

Where the area of the State is specified –it is known as State specific treaty; where timing is specified – Time specific treaty; when act to be performed are clear – act-specific treaty. The last one has become very common in the modern world. A computer hardware company may cater to the need of an allied software company or divide the work into several parts and get the work executed. To create web site, again one has to enter into an agreement or understanding with the service provider. These are also called outsourcing of the work.

If one reflects on these matters, it will become amply clear that many of these agreements are based on the treaties expounded in this chapter.

Rules of Treaties

There are four rules of a treaty, viz., earnestness, strict compliance, active defilement and opaque act.

1. **Earnestness**: Treaties entered on the basis of cordiality, gift, disparity and punishment and as per the treaty, taking care of all his authorities, powerful or not, have an earnestness in the intention and hence this is known as the principle of earnestness.

2. **Strict Compliance**: After entering into treaty and willfully and gladly fulfilling all the terms promptly is the principle of strict compliance.

3. **Active Defilement**: Entering into treaty with rebels, and breaking other concluded treaty is the principle of active defilement.

4. **Opaque Act**: Entering into a treaty or agreement with a suspended employee or a friend, who have committed some offence, is on the basis of principle of Opaque Act. There are four classifications of this act. Whether the object is to intimidate or cause injury or whether the intention is really honorable will not be apparent to the other side. Only after getting all relevant facts and giving considered thought, one should enter into this treaty.

    a. Getting separated under a given situation and joining again under different circumstances.

    b. Getting separated without any specific reason and joining together without any reason.

    c. Getting separated on account of a given situation and joining back without any reason.

    d. Getting separated without any specific reason and joining back under special circumstances.

Who should not be allowed to come back? A person who has harmed you and joined the enemy and without causing any harm to the enemy should never be accepted back into the fold.

Who and what should be given up? The thinkers and teachers before Chanakya had opined that those who are not productive; who had lost his strength; a nation where education is being sold as a commodity; one who is depressed; where law and order is disturbed; such a nation should be given up. Kautilya, however does not agree with this thinking. According to him, only coward, angry and a non-starter should be given up.

Rules of Strife

Strife takes three forms. Open war, Covert war and Pollution war.

1. **Overt War**: War waged on a nation after due consideration of timing, is known as Open war. The Mahabharata war is a shining example of this.

2. **Covert War**: Showing a part of the force, as if there is huge one or through some other means intimidate, burning of forts, causing riots; executing assassinations, attacking at random many places and causing any other kind of troubles is known by this name.

    Now-a- days they call this Cold war.

3. **Pollution War**: Using poison or such other lethal matter and causing destruction through spies is known as pollution war. This also is prevalent in a large measure and goes by the name of Chemical warfare.

Uneven and Even Treaty

1. **Uneven**: Uneven treaties are of six types :

Entering into treaty with more powerful person by giving him equal share. Entering into treaty with more powerful person by giving him lower share. Entering into treaty with a weaker person by giving him a higher share. Entering into treaty with more powerful person by giving him equal share.Entering into treaty with equally strong person giving him a lesser share. Entering into treaty with more powerful person by giving him a higher share.

2.   **Even Treaty**: These are of three types. Giving higher share to stronger party. Giving equal share to equally strong person. Giving lower share to less weaker party.

3.   **Favourable Treaty**: If there is an approximate profit derived from the above two types of treaty, is then known as favourable treaty.

Other Types of Treaties

1.   **Treaty with a Friend**: This is self-explicit.
2.   **Golden Treaty**: The treaty made with a friend to get wealth from him is known as golden treaty.
3.   **Land Treaty**: The land has been created for owning by all of us by way of plots. When there is treaty with friend, the designated land should bear the correct number also.
4.   **Unoccupied Treaty**: When treaty is entered into with a friend, to build residence in unoccupied plot of land, then the treaty is known by this name.
5.   **Duty Treaty**: A treaty between two persons to jointly construct a manor house or start a new business or mutually beneficial project, it is known as Duty Treaty.

Allies and their Attributes

Allies and friends are six types: Eternal, amenable or contributory, temporary or transient, grand old, eminent, inseparable or ever supportive.

1.   **Eternal**: If on account of age-old friendship, are mutually protective of each other, it is known as eternal friendship. When this ally does not directly extending any help in kind, but makes a lively hood by looting the enemy, it is called weak eternal fried ship.

2.   **Amenable or Contributory**: This again is divided into three categories:

    a.   Full utility friendship: In this full support is given by extending the might, wealth, wisdom, land etc.

    b.   Utility friendship: Help is extended in the form of precious gems and stones, forest wealth and land.

    c.   Grand utility friendship: Help is given by supporting with all might and land.

From the point of help for disaster management, the contributory allies are of three kinds, viz., useful more useful and most useful. If on account of calamity or danger befalling a person and he becomes an ally or friend to overcome the situation he faces, the friendship is known as eternal weak contributory friendship. On account of help extended by him he is a contributory friend, but since the friendship will last only till he overcomes danger, it is weak eternal friendship.

3. **Temporary or Transient**: This friendship lasts only for a specific period of time or till a specific task is achieved.

4. **Grand old Friendship or Ally**: When age old family friendship is prevailing and is overwhelmingly strong, it is known by this name.

5. **Eminent friendship**: This is a stable and spiritually uplifting friendship.

6. **Inseparable Friendship**: A friend who always shares happiness and sorrow, always extends necessary help, who is never indifferent or condescending and does not desert in adversity is an inseparable friend.

Since he is constantly near at hand to extend ready help, he is also called an ideal friend.

One who helps a friend and his enemy or does not help for fear of consequences, or is extending his services to both is known as opportunistic friend.

Hence it is essential that all these factors have to be weighed before forging friendship.

Evam dushtuva dhuve labhe labhamshe cha gunodaym
Swarth sdhiparo yayat samhit: samvayikai

Advise on Starting Business—Where and When

The time of elephants and horses are over; there are items like petrol and the market is now flooded with various modes of transport. Only difficulty looming large is liquids like petrol will not last for ever and these vehicles even though brand new, will be of no use, whereas these animals of nature were not affected by shortage of grass and leaves. Although it is reported that automobile business is still profitable, there are accidents galore causing heavy and untimely loss of life and creating a large force of handicapped and crippled human beings. Hence there is a big question mark on the utility of this industry to society. How long should we tolerate this loss of lives on a daily basis?

The industry of gold, silver and precious stones are considered to be the second largest business. According to some ancient thinkers the mines yielding rare and high value stones are more profitable than the mines yielding ordinary gems; but according to Chanakya the customer of costly gems are a handful rich people, who purchase these items once in a way, whereas, there are plenty of clientele for ordinary gems ready to buy on a steady basis. In other words the market for rare and costly gems is limited whereas that for ordinary gems is large.

Business decisions should be taken quickly on the basis of the importance and location of the market, whether the hinterland is inhabited by affluent persons and there is possibility of good business. However on account of development of airways, railways and roadways, there is an increase in the number local merchants and thanks to these quick modes of transport, even in remote areas, towns and cities, business is flourishing.

Even today transport by waterways is considered good and economical. Waterways are of two types; one is point to point where the boats shuttle between two cities catering to the markets of both cities; the other is where the ship sails to predestined harbor. The roads are also of two kinds; one going to South and the other going to North. From the point of view of travelling convenience and population, the transport business to North is ever profitable.

Transport from East to West has to be assessed on similar lines.

Where income is less than expenses, then it is loss and just the opposite of this is profit and progress:

Alp aagam ati vyata kshayo: vrudhi viparyaye

Only by controlling expenditure and doing profitable business can one progress in all directions.

A thought on Business Associates

Associating with the right person is a burning problem in today's world. Everyone indulge in publishing inflated figures of production, sales and profits. Under these given situations, it becomes even more problematic to decide as to whose produce to be bought or to whom to sell own production. There are problems of recovery and overstocking of inventory. No one is walking on a straight path. Every year many suppliers are hot-listed and many contractors are blacklisted. But the morality has fallen so low that the same suppliers and contractors continue to get orders after changing their company's names. By merely adding the word "the" or 'New' to their old name, they are able to get into the approved list. By omitting or adding a mere hyphen, they are able to fool the computer. It is also possible to get approval by merely changing a letter!

There is a nexus between the marketing executive or the regional director and other customers which result in faulty selection of suppliers and contractors. Just for the sake of short term gains, wrong decisions are made. Even fixed profits are not made a part of the selling price; On the other hand price is fixed on basis of what the traffic can bear. The government. has made it mandatory to print the maximum retail price on the packaged product. In spite of this the consumers are being looted because MRP is highly inflated. Retail sellers are being enticed to over stock with the carrot of huge profit they can make. In towns and cities, the retail sellers are flooded with the inventory that they do not have any place to store products. In the case of textile retailers there are bundles of dumped stock, which are not even opened.

One more worrying factor is that all regional wholesale dealers procure the goods on credit and sell it on credit. For recovering the credit, they collect on an appointed date, a fixed percentage of sales made is recovered every week. Thus the market is quite unstable. The automobile company which boasts of highest market share of sales, in fact sell 95% of their sales on credit.

Hence, under this vitiated atmosphere, one has to look for genuinely good performance. There is no place for lies in business, however, only a handful of businessmen tread the path of truth. There is further contradiction in the situation. Earlier the products manufactured were durable and had longer shelf-life. Now the products manufactured do not last beyond three to five years. The computer technology makes radical changes every year. The morality has taken a new low with the report that it is the anti-virus software developers who spread the virus in the first place to create a market for their products, and the forecast is that every 24 hours, the anti-virus may become out of date and has to be updated every day; the fall out is that without internet connection, you cannot use the computer. There are no spare parts available for the products bought. This amounts to cheating of consumers.

In business all the stake holders, namely the manufacturer, distributor, the seller and the consumer should stand to benefit. But this is only a mirage. Within one week of purchase, the value is reduced to 50%. After the electronic goods reach home, they have absolutely no resale value. There are no rules and regulations; there is no stability, only outward glamour!

Circa World War and immediately thereafter, the situation was entirely different. Life was moving along in a definite pace. There were no such uncertainties. Today, neither the life nor the market is stable. Value of money has fallen by 90%. On the other hand there is an equal rise in the value of other items. As the multi storey and skyscrapers don the place that once was a fertile agricultural land, yielding food crops, the value of the land has shot up three thousand times! Animals and birds are facing extinction. Men are killed in various ways. The printed and electronic media are exclusively busy reporting these matters. There is no genuine empathy with the dead. Life is not safe in the villages or towns or cities, where people die like flies through weapons, automobiles, poisonous drugs, illicit liquor, fury, greed or hatred. There are lot of discussions on security personnel and security, but when the ultimate fortress, Pentagon can be bombed and shoes can be hurled on their President, where does the ordinary mortal stand?

Keeping security in view, the enemy camps were infiltrated with spies. There three categories: near the enemy, in the citadel of the enemy and in the military camp of the enemy. There was open warfare, wars were fought in battle-fields and were called war of exercise. The divine powers were primarily invoked and the enemy was vanquished with mental power without need of war and consequent loss of lives. Compare with the present style. Killing behind a cover; killing when person is sleeping. Today killer threatens after making children orphans; plays the game of kidnap and ransom and quietly bombs any place.

During those eras, invoking divine power or spells in war were considered most important. *Mantra-udhatr abhi uchaya*: Hiding the divine spell and prayer is beneficial. According to Chanakya a person who does not keep the magical spell and related prayers as a secret, will invite destruction. Just as the passengers in a ship are exposed to inevitable end if the ship breaks, the king will also face similar fate if the magic spell is leaked out:

Asanvrutasya karyani praptanyapi visheshataha:
Nischayam bipadhante binnaplav ivodhado

Methods to Augment Income

If the manufacturer is not able to appoint a number of friendly distributors, it will not be possible for him to become successful.

Associating with learned and eminent persons is a sure way to succeed. An eminent friend or employee can show the ways to economize on expenditure and bring in considerable increase in revenue. An expert can guide in innovation of new products and to manage efficiently.

Instead of depending exclusively on rainfall, farmers engaged in cultivation of food grains can be helped in construction of bunds and canals. Mining is considered to be a business with highest returns.

Forest resources rank next. A person blessed with the wealth of forests and gardens, will get maximum returns with minimum effort.

From dairy farm, the income will be without much effort, albeit insufficient. But agriculture is the best way to augment income as that is the basis for all life. Man cannot live without food grains, fruits, vegetables and bulbous plants, as it forms his basic food.

Greed is the cause of destruction of all goods. Man is never satisfied. Every business house has a mansion constructed in their agricultural land to take refuge when there is shortage of food grains; but, they give it a dignified name of farm house for rest and recuperation. Ultra-rich players, actors and singers all have agricultural lands. The only clan who do not own agricultural land is the agriculturists themselves. What little they own is mortgaged to the banks.

Anyone can marshal their resources and means with association of own relatives, friends, through education and with the blessings of elderly persons to augment their wealth.

Evam pakshena mantrena dravyena cha balen cha
Sampan: prati ni:gachetu par avagraham aatman:

It is absolutely essential that the learned administrators have to consider situations like progressive economy, regressive economy, the location, drought and rehabilitation and assess the right methods of cordiality gift, etc., to confront respective situations.

Vrudhi kshayam cha sthanam cha karshan chedanam thadha
Sarva upayan samadhyadru ytanu ya: cha arthashastravit

The administrator who uses these methods carefully can easily be victorious against the kings who are mired in ignorance and infatuations.

Evam anyo anya sancharam shatgunyam yo anupashyati
Sa vrudhinigalai: baddhai ariishtam kridathi psrthevai:

Eighth Case – Addiction to Vices

Vices and Retaliation

Vice literally means straying away from right path. Vice has repugnant qualities, which are not helpful and will be short on good qualities; these qualities will be used detrimentally; their sins will be on the rise; intolerance will also rise; with the result they get entrapped in anti-social activities.

Both mankind and divinity have passive and active vices. Not entering into treaty at the right time is a passive vice and getting entrapped by evil forces is active vice. Whichever vice is active, that can be overcome only by the corresponding contra of good quality. If on account of a particular vice, other vices grow, then that particular vice has to be dealt on priority.

The anger arising out of vices are of two kinds, hidden and external. The hidden anger is more dangerous than the latter.

Those who have not read the laws and are ignorant of them, and those who have studied them but are straying away from them, both in equal measure in their own way invite destructive effects.

Vice, by itself is a disease. If it is coupled with ego, it loses its balance and hurries towards colossal destruction.

An illiterate can become a victim of vices, because he does not understand its evil effect. Anger creates three kinds of vices which are called 'threesome' and desire causes four types of vices, which are known as 'foursome'. Both are dangerous, but vices arising out of anger are more dangerous.

Anger Related 'Threesome'; Foul language, tainted wealth and causing physical injury. Taking somebody's livelihood is tainted wealth, which again is of four kinds: Undue gain: not paying wages or salaries after getting jobs done. Undue gain: Usurping property by way of punishment given to victim; Destruction: creating obstacles and pulling down business. Loss of wealth: not safeguarding the acquired wealth gained by honest means.

Desire Related Foursome: Hunting expeditions, gambling, womanizing and alchoholism. These are all injurious to health and wealth. It depends on the addiction of the individual to understand which of these four evils is causing maximum injury.

It is only on account of these major frailties that desire and anger are considered the most abominable vices. Hence one should have self control on desire and anger and attain liberation from these vices. It is not possible to attain any kind of progress or prosperity with these dominant vices.

Tarmat kopem cha karmam cha vyasan arambham aatmavan
Parityej moolharam vrudhasevi jitendriya:

The Afflicted Classes

The divine power will unleash following miseries on the respective nation, society and individual:

1. Destruction by fire
2. Destruction by flood
3. Loss by spreading diseases
4. Death through poisonous alms
5. The fury of small pox

The Fountain of Vices

There are two towers of vices: Internal and external.

The Fiduciary Class

Various types of misappropriation and scams fall under this category.

It is bounden duty of administrators, directors and presidents of organizations to ensure that the stakeholders do not approach them for their satisfaction, progress, peace or happiness. In case, they approach they have to redresss their grievance expeditiously. This is their primary responsibility they are in a position to examine and take effective decisions.

Classification of Employees and their Weaknesses

Kautilya Arthashastra have many astounding revelations, but nothing can match that of psychology of employees dealt therein by Chanakya. It is said that the modern psychologists have made rapid strides on the subject, but in comparison with what is contained in this book, it appears that the western psychologists have to go a long way to achieve the standard of this ancient thinker.

Taking into account the psyche of the employees and behaviour arising there from, Chanakya has clsaissified the employees into 34 groups and also the type of work that can be entrusted to each category so that a square peg is not fitted into a round hole. Now-a-days soldiers of armed forces, employees and even students not only commit murder of their superiors and colleagues, but get to the extent of committing suicide. The management can read the book and can adhere to the systems propounded in this book. It is possible to stop the lacuna in selection only if after administering the test on reasoning, the prospective employees are administered a set of questions to be answered. The questions should be mixed up cleverly that the examinee cannot easily fathom what the intentions of examiner are. This is because it is not possible to sort out the mixed question package easily.

1. Undeserving, untruthful and showing pretences, through scornful means may win the undeserving honour and may get on with the job entrusted, but will be tortured within for the dubious method of getting appointed. He would be full of remorse.

2. Absentee who has not been paid wages and sick employee, who has been granted leave of absence would join back for duty, but has not recovered from illness.

3. New appointee and employee operating daily from far off. Of the two new appointee is better, because he shows earnestness in learning the job and wants to show and establish his capability on the job, whereas the one operating from a distance will be definitely tired.

4. Hardworking, lethargic on account of impoverished health, lack of integrity. The one with pooir health can recover from illness by availing sick leave, but the man lacking in integrity can never fulfikll the tasks entrusted to him.

5. Successful, unsuccessful enthusiastic and non-enthusiastic. A person who is unsuccessful willturn his efforts to turn his failure to success, but a person who lacks enthusiasm can never be corrected.

6. The unlucky employee who does not get sufficient time or complete assignment; Bad posting, where the person does not get the ideal place to work. Here the unlucky employee can turn roun d with a good performance if he is given time and means to execute the work, but the one with bad posting cannot achieve anything spectacular.

7. Positive, negative, depressed and buoyant, lacking in leadership skills. Out of these, a depressed employee could be given lessons on positive thinking and the one lacking in leadersjhip skills can be brought under a competent manager and devlop these skills.

8. Mischief monger, indulging in blame game and enmity hidden, who hides his happy, but the villainous character can show his colours any time and even commit murder

9. Fiery, laden with anger and divisive, who creates fissions. Of these the fiery person can be tackled whereas it is foolish to expect him to perform a good job.

10. Depressed, the one who is given trouble by the management and the oppressed, who is troubled by a whole lot of individuals. Of these, the depressed person can be tackled whereas the one who is troubled by many cannot forgive or forget his sufferings at the hands of many.

11. Nearness to enemy, meaning a person who works in enemy settlement ; deserter, the one who has un- derstanding with the enemy. The person working in enemy territory gains experience on account of confrontation with the enemy whereas the deserter can be of no help.

12. Single-siege, attacked by one side and multi-siege, surrounded on all sides. The one surrounded on one side or facing limited problems can overcome the situation whereas amperson surrounded on all sides with problems cannot show his capability or even his plans. Partly cut off, a person who has cut off his relations with a few persons; fully cut-off.

13. Partly cut off, a person who has cut off his relations with a few persons; fully cut-off, who has cut off relations fully with his people. By establishing new relations, the partly cut off can save the situation, whereas the other person will be drowning in thoughts of his worries, and cannot save himself from the situation.

14. Own derangement, who shows his madness only in his area; Mixed derangement whos is spread over many areas. That which is in one's own area can perhaps be better organized and retrieved whereas the one spread in many areas is beyond redemption.

15. Siding with enemy, keeping relationship with enemy and enemy, and followed by enemy, enemy is behind the individual. Person siding with the enemy can perhaps discharge his duties keeping in mind his future, whereas the person who is being followed by the enemy caanot discharge his duties without fear.

16. Least risk, the limited employees in headquarters and Unsupervised, those working without an immediate supervisor. If there is need on account of pressure of work, few additional hands can be given and complete the work at headquarters, whereas those without supervision will not be able to complete any job in given time.

17. Independent, worker without supervisor and Ignorant, those who are unaware of the rules and regulation of work. An independent worker can perhaps do a good job even without s superior supervising his work whereas the ignorant will not be competent to do any job

It is not difficult to understand the psychology of the employees and hence it is easy to salvage their morale.

Loss of Friendship

On account of the force of circumstances, on a particular situation a friend may cut his relaations or even cheat. This is known as loss of friendship. For love of wealth; sometimes out of ego clashes; sometimes out of jealousy and sometimes to take revenge on any matter, long standing friendship is broken. To make efforts to rebuild that friendship is akin to digging one's own grave. It will be better off to allow the friendship to be terminated for ever. The situation to cause a friendship to break arises only because of provocation, one-up-manship and usage of foul words. Hence such incidents should be avoided in the interest of long and lasting friendship

Nineth Case – Duty of Practice

Power or Strength

The real strength of an individual is not restricted to his innate skills and his own internal calibre. His strength assumes further dimensions from the DNA (or from his parent), from his association with relatives and friends and also from his teachers and mentors; from his employees and from those who are far and near. His final strength is then from all these contributors. If he is not using any of these powers, he loses that power, on account of which his strength gets diminished to that extent.

His internal strength does not comprise only his knowledge and experiences, but also of his willpower, convictions, influence and enthusiasm A few other thinkers have opined that an enthusiastic person can win over influential persons; but according to Kautilya, an influential person can easily win over an enthusiastic individual. However he also believes that the power of prayer and repetition of psalms are superior to the quality of influence.

Whenever an individual is confronted with a problem, he has to evaluate and take a decision of using the relevant quality required for meeting the situation. If the assessment is right, then he can solve the issue, even if he does not use few in the repertoire of his strength whereas if the assessment is not correct, usage of all his strength will be of no avail.

Nation

The word 'nation' is used to describe land or any specific part of land. From Himalayas to the Southern Ocean was known as The Empire. The head of governing this land was known as the King of Empire or simply The Emperor. Within this, a person heading a particular portfolio was called the Head of that particular field. Thus this part of area is quite vast and under comprehensive governance. There is diversity in the weather, natural resources and expectations. The given situation prevailing is such that for every 20 miles or 32 kilometres, the water tastes differently and for every 40 miles or 64 kilometres, there is change in the language spoken; there are areas of ever green gardens and mountainous regions; highly productive regions and draught stricken areas, deserts, plain land and oceanic regions.

In fact, the northern hemisphere, is spread across 8° North to 37° North, with the result that northern areas have severe winters and down south it is perineally hot. On account of these factors, it becomes a mini-world as what is available and produced all over the world, the food grains, textile and other mineral wealth are available in this minor part of the world. The diversity in nature, colour, clothing, language, business and ways of living are it highlight.

On account of these diverse advantages and disadvantage, the different areas of the nation are classified as prosperous, backward and medium.

If business is to be established in this nation or in a particular region of the nation, one has to properly assess the area, the needs and stability to start the business. Then only one will be successful, otherwise ignorance on these factors will cost heavily.

Time or Season

Seasons are divided into three, winter summer and rainy. Again they are subdivided into day, night, class, month, season, yield, century and era and others and have their own features. Taking into consideration the benefits and drawbacks of these divisions, seasons have been divided into ideal, not ideal or medium.

Various thinkers have attributed separate importance to the nation, season and strengths, however, in business and other aspects of living, equal importance have to be given to these three factors and then only begin new ventures, because all the three are having its own importance in their success. A person who considers all the three factors can only take a balanced decicion and achieve quick success.

Income through Taxation and Profits

There are 12 special characteristics of income and profits: responsible, irresponsible, blessing, punishing, transitory, personal levy, micro-gain, bonanza, future benefit, imaginative, attractive, and automatic.

1. **Responsible**: Income which can be easily accrued and which can be protected with ease; which can be never attached or snatched by enemy is known as Responsible.

2. **Irresponsible**: This is exact contra of responsible income. One who gets this sort of income or is solely dependent on it, will be financially ruined in quick time

If a person is able to understand that by getting this sort of income, he will put at risk his treasury, stock of foodgrains, and he will be able to get under his possession, the stock of foodgrains, chemicals, the harbor and business or line of business or is able to generate income in similar way, where there will be durability in the resource, his income will be large and steady.

3. **Blessing (Prasadak)**: The king, who converts immoral persons to follow moral ways and who is the cause for happiness of his subjects and himself and the resulting gain is known as Blessing.

4. **Punishing**: The exact contra to the gains out of blessing is known as Punishment. The depletion in wealth and incurring avoidable expenses by working under the instructions of a third person is also a type of punishment. All sorts of income earned through treacherous and dubious means fall under this category.

5. **Transitory**: Short term gain by short time work is called transitory income.

6. **Personal Levy**: The income derived exclusively from a sub-caste is known as personal levy.

7. **Microgain**: The gain made by giving only food and allowances in exchange of work is known as micro gain.

8. **Bonanza**: Large gain made on a single transaction is known as Bonanza.

9. **Future Benefit**: This is the gain which gives maximum benefit in the future.

10. **Imaginative**: The gains which will not be affected by any hurdles at present and future is known as imaginative source.

11. **Attractive**: The benefit derived by executing a transparent beneficial work is known as attractive.

12. **Automatic**: The regular income derived from friends and relatives without any condition is an automatic income.

If parties to a deal benefit equally, then such a deal should be struck. There should be no consideration of factors like nation, season, strength, means, likes and dislikes, victory or defeat. This has a very valuable and highly moral character.

Hurdles to Gain

1. **Immoral**: The hurdles in the gain made out of sensuality, anger and dishonesty is known as immoral gain.

2. **Shameful**; The hurdles in the gain derived out of charity and shame fall under this category.

3. **Sub-Human Feelings**: The gain derived through betrayal haunts a person and thus becomes the hurdle for this kind of illicit benefit.

4. **Overbearing**: The gain derived from a person having superiority complex and given with a sense of condescension is marred by this overbearing attitude.

5. **Mortal Fear**: The gain which has been derived from a person solely out of fear in the hereinafter, has this hurdle of mortal fear.

6. **Highly Unfair**: Profits generated out of arrogant and unjust deal, suffer from this category of hurdle.

7. **Humiliation of Acceptance**: The gain derived in a state of poverty, and jealousy fall under this category of hurdle.

8. **Against Conscience**: Gains made out of illicit business suffer from this hurdle.

9. **Passivity**: The hurdles caused by distrust, fear and non-exposure of the enemy are known as Passive hurdles.

If one cannot face the severity of winter, summer and rainy seasons, gains will be affected. Before starting a venture, if the stars, date and timing are not carefully fixed, the activity will not prosper.

However, according to Chanakya, for the success of the venture, if one equips himself with necessary capital, required materials and will power, then it may not be necessary to go by the position of stars, etc.

Nakshatru ati puchnatham balam arth ati-vartatey
Adho haartasya nakshatram kim kariyanti tarka:

Without capital and required materials, whatever may be the efforts of the individual, it will all be futile. Money begets money and wealth is the means of creating more wealth just like an elephant only can captivate or capture another elephant. Do not be under the impression that the phrase 'Money begets Money' is a western concept.

Na adhna prapuvantya arthanu nara yant shatai: api
Artha: arthe: prabhadhyante gaja: prati gajai: iva

Internal and External Obstacles

The internal and external obstacles are of four types.

1. Obstacles created by foreigners and our own people.

2. Those created by our own people with assistance from others.

3. Those created by foreigners and actively spread by foreigners.

4. Those created by own people and actively spread by them.

There are two types of obstacles or hurdles created by the opponents and enemies; pure harm and pure enmity.

The obstacles created by harmful and harmless means is known as mixed obstacles. Obstacles created by ally and enemy are known as ally mixture or enemy mixture.

Classification of External and Internal Obstacles

1. **Dangerous Wealth**: The wealth that is dissipated by laxity and is being diverted to the development of enemy; the wealth that is returned after receiving; the wealth which vanishes gets and is wasted is known as dangerous wealth.

2. **Disastrous Wealth**: The fear generated by wealth which is acquired by self or with assistance may cause disastrous repercussions is known as Disastrous wealth.

3. **Suspicious Wealth**: The suspicion caused by the wealth, whether it is safe or disaster-prone and keeps a person always on tenterhooks is known as suspicious wealth.

If the wealth and its different classes are postulated then three sub groups emerge and similarly if they are not postulated another three sub groups are created making a total of 6 sub-groups. These are known by the term postulated sixers.

Meaningful wealth: Destruction of the enemy.

Unrelated wealth: Helping someone else with the wealth destruction of ally of the enemy.

Meaningful destruction: Helping the neighbour of the enemy

False assurance destruction: promising a weak enemy with help, without ever extending the promised help. Meaningless destruction: Promising help to powerful enemy and not extending the help.

4. **Feudal Wealth**: If wealth flows from all sides in one stroke, it is known as feudal wealth.

5. **Suspect Feudal Wealth**: When there is opposition to the flow of feudal wealth, it is known as suspect feudal wealth.

6. **Calamitous Feudal Wealth**: Means fear of enemies surrounding all the four sides.

7. **Suspect Calamitous Feudal Wealth**: If it is suspected that the allies are also creating obstacle in addition to fear from enemies it is known by this name. Effective steps can be taken to appease the allies to overcome these obstacles.

8. **Dual Danger to Wealth**: Means hurdles caused in getting wealth from both sides.

9. **Dual Accumulation and Destruction of Wealth**: Means that while you get from one side and equal loss from the other side.

10. **Dual Suspicious and Calamitous Wealth**: Means while on one side there is calamity, on the other side there is doubt in getting wealth.

11. **Calamitous and Suspicious Feudal Wealth**: The obstacles are similar to that of the previous one.

Remedial Measures for Internal External Challenges

It is difficult to confront these obstacles in one stroke, hence these have to be redressed individually. Both skills and courage in equal measure is required. For taking adequate steps to meet the threats, one has to understand the following three trios:

A. **Trio of Wealth**: Wealth, duty and desire

B. **Trio of Calamity**: Perversion, immorality and sorrow

C. **Trio of Suspicion**: Inability to differentiate between wealth and perversion, duty and immorality and desire and grief.

Son, brother and other relatives have to be dealt with in a harmonious way and should be given gifts.

In respect of royal staff and other important personalities the method of giving gifts and creating differences.

In respect of others, the methods of creating disparity and of punishment can be used.

A. This kind of remedial measures are known as ascending methods.

B. The usage of this from the top to bottom is known as descending methods.

C. It will be quite appropriate to use these methods interchangeably according to situation with dealing with allies and enemies. The usage by permutation and combination of these methods is known as 'effective mix'.

These methods which are brought into use to meet all challenges, small or big, are again classified into three categories.

A. **Imperative**: Only one method and none others, will enable to successfully confronting the problem.

B. **Options**: Whether the problem can be overcome with one method, or some other options has to considered.

C. **Combination**: Only by combining one method with other options can the problem be overcome. These combinations are in groups of two or three or four making a permutation and combination of 15 measures. These can be used in reverse order also. We have listed the measures in the ascending order:

1. Cordiality, gift, punishment, disparity
2. Gift, punishment. Disparity
3. Cordiality, punishment, disparity
4. Cordiality, gift, disparity
5. Cordiality, gift, punishment.
6. Punishment, disparity

7. Gift, punishment   8. Cordiality, punishment
9. Gift, disparity   10. Cordiality, disparity
11. Cordiality, gift   12. Cordiality
13. Gift   14. Punishment
15. Disparity

If the objective is achieved through a single measure, it is known as single solution. If two or three or four methods are used they are known as dual, triangular and quadrangular solutions respectively.

Although these principles are means to overcome all the threats to wealth, duty and desire, the ability to overcome that related to wealth is considered to be most significant.

Fire, flood, diseases, contagious small pox, rebellion, faulty charity and demonic creations are divine hurdles for mankind. To meet these challenges one should be god fearing and surrender to these powers and treat respectfully the Brahmins who are fluent in moral teachings. As mentioned in Atharva Veda, one should work for establishing peace and harmony. They should also follow the teachings of saints, sages and great men to establish lasting peace in the universe.

Tenth Case – Association

The entire chapter has been written about the methodology of war. Since such wars don't take place now, there might not be any use of it. But for the benefit of the readers, the chapter and sub chapters' information is given which make one understand what is written in there.

1. Construction of a cantonment.
2. Measurement of the cantonment.
3. Safety of the armed forces during the attack.
4. Variety of deceptive warfare.
5. Encouragement to the armed forces.
6. Usage of others armed forces.
7. Terrain comfortable for the war.
8. The work of various branches of armed forces.
9. Creation of platoon, class and strategy.
10. Allocation based on the strengths of forces.
11. The division of cavalry unit.
12. The warfare using the four forces – horses, elephants, chariots and infantry.
13. Natural strategy, Altered strategy, and Anti strategy.
14. Secure strategy, Crow's strategy. Disaster strategy etc.

11

Eleventh Case – Plan of Society

The eleventh methodology which deals with society/corporation, compiled in seven chapters in Kautilya's Arthashastra, is the smallest one. This methodology explains the greatness of a society and it also says that during a favourable time, the society has to be used for peace as weel as charity and during an unfavourable time for dissent and punishment.

There is a discussion on how one has to make use of the secret service for the benefit of the society, the benefit of the army and the benefit of friends. Ther is also a discussion on punishment. There is an extensive explanation on how to use this to demoralize the society.

12

Twelfth Case – Weakness

The twelfth methodology is also small in which there is a description on how a weak king should behave when he is attacked by a powerful king and the methods he can use to avenge his defeat. This chapter and sub chapter deals with this strategy.

1. System of sending envoys
2. Secret warfare/ Subversive warfare
3. Killing of the Commanders-in-chief
4. Helping the royalty
5. Secret usage of weapons, fire and acids for killing
6. Destruction of Essence and broadcast
7. Victory through cunning and foul means
8. Gaining victory through cunning annexation

Thirteenth Case –
Longevity of Fortress/Organization

Chanakya has described in the thirteenth case, on how to keep control on people, workers and related merchants and has also described the cunning tactics to be used to defeat the adverseries. It contains details about how to annex in a cunning manner, propagandize one's false divine powers, through the state of dream talk about divine speeches and divine visions.

The deceptive methods said by Chanakya for annexing a kingdom can be used on any organization for the take overs. Any organization can be taken over using these wrong examples. But we have the historical evidences, the wise sayings of the sages and saints and the witnesses who say that we should not follow these paths. There might be an instant profit or a minute's comfort but the lineage of the one who follows this, gets destroyed. This could also be one reason why this is not discussed while talking about annexation. Even if there is instantaneous advantage, one cannot destroy the entire lineage just for one's enjoyment or to show power.

Chanakya has thought deeply on these cunning methods just like how he has thought of judicial ways. Chanakya has decribed in his judicial methodology that the end result of a deed – good or bad- will be different. Hence we cqnnot think of anyone even half as magnificent as Chanakya in the present day. He never hankered after wealth, never allowed avarice to come close to him and never even looked at sensuous pleasures. That is the reason for his stupendous achievement and immortality. *Kirthih yasya sa jeevati*.

The chapters, sub chapters and units in this case are as follows:

1. To generate, to deceive
2. To entice the king through cunning means
3. The residence and work of secret service
4. To surround the fort of the enemy
5. To rule over the enemy.
6. Usage of dwarfs and poison

7. To surround

8. To unman, destruction

9. Acquisition, pacification

Acquisition – Pacification

To establish peace in the kingdoms won over.

To take control of an organization or business concern.

The Advantages or Achievements of Attack and Take Over

When there is a take over, it is not just the organization which is taken over, but the responsibility and duty of it is also taken and the most significant thing is yhat the entire workforce is also acquired. If a kingdom is taken over, then the people of that kingdom are acquired. The hopes, aspiration and doubts of these people are also acquired. Hence the person taking over and the administrator should have the following in mind while taking over.

When taking over a kingdom, try to hide the faults of the king who has been defeated or in danger and overwhelm his quality with double the qualities of the conqueror.

The kingdom and its people have to be brought under control through righteousness, work, blessing, forgiveness, waiving of loans, donations, respect etc.

Always keep the supporters on your side. Depending on the extent a supporter has helped you, repay his help with an award of equal size.

Portray behaviour, demeanor, attire, language and conduct which merits trust from others.

There are three kinds of advantages in this form of take over.

1. **New advantages** : The advantages secured should be safeguarded and steps should be taken to improve upon those advantages.

2. **Past advantages**: The past advantages are when the said person had lost the organization once before but regained it after recovering the loss.

3. **Paternal advantage**: If the kingdom or the organization became some one else's due to one's father or grand father and if the person acquires it again, then it is called paternal advantage.

The new administrator should bring into force all those ethical procedures which are not in vogue in the new work place or administrative place. People should be encouraged to follow the virtuous methods. Unethical behaviour should not be allowed to take root and if such people are found, they have to be curtailed with strength, cunningness and intelligence.

> *Charitram akrutham dharmya cha anyaih pravartayet.*
> *Pravartyam cha adharmya krutham cha anyai nivartayet.*

Fourteenth Case – Treatise

This methodology and its contents deal exclusively on ambush attacks and is related to security matters. It also brings out the depth of knowledge of Chanakya on poison-related matters. In today's world nobody could imagine the extent of knowledge on poison that Chanakya had. In olden times also nobody had the level of information on various types of poison. Even the herbs on which discussions are made in this chapter no longer exist. The subject is not restricted to only poison; references are also made to herbs, which when administered will make the victim not to feel hunger for 15 days or even a month.

On the one side, he deals with methods for making the hand cuffs and iron chains stronger and on the other hand he discussed about poisons which can cut iron chains! He was indeed a complex and Rare breed.

This chapter consists of the following headings and sub-headings:

1. Assassination of enemy

2. Art of alluring; change in the facial expression.

3. Medicinal and magical spell usage.

4. Retaliation of ambush and safety.

By following the teachings of Chanakya, the administrator can secure himself, his dependents and their employees from the poisons and medicines discussed herein. They can also use the poisonous gas and water on the enemies.

Athai:krutva pratikaram sva sainyanam atmana:
Abhitranshu prayanjit vish dhumam ambu deshanam

15

The Fifteenth Case – Bases of Principles

This chapter not only contains description of various tactics of 'The Science of Wealth', but also makes two proclamations. One was that it was Vishnugupt, alias Chanaka who freed the world from Nand dynasty, has written this book also. It has to be seen here that Chanakya does not say that he destroyed the Nand dynasty, but that he liberated earth from Nand! This appears to be very appropriate statement because all the evils and atrocities of Nand dynasty had spread to the feudal lords and also the society at large. That is why he had said that 'Like King – Like citizens or "as the king is disposed, so the subject will also be disposed !"

Yen shastram cha shatru cha nandrajgata cha bhu:
Amarshena udhuta anyashu ten shastram hadam krutam

The second proclamation was that since other scholars had differences with the views expressed in his book **Arthashastra**, Chanakya had written these formulas and their explanations.

Dushtva vi pratipatam shastreshu bhashyakaranam
Satyam eva vishnugupt: chakar sutram cha bhasahyam cha

He also made a third proclamation that only these constitute the elements of Arthashastra (science of wealth and meaning) and are effective in the practice of this science.

Dharma arth va kamam pravarthayati paroti cha
Adharma anarth vidveshanidam shastram nihanti cha

Strategy of Arthashastra

The sustenance of mankind is known as wealth. The land attached with man is also known as wealth. The science describing the methods for procuring this land and protecting the land is **Arthashastra:**

Manushyanam vrithi: arth:; manushyavati bhumi: iti artha:
Tasya pruthivya labh palan upay: shastram arthashastram hati

Arthashastra consists of the following 32 different strategies. We request writers to understand in depth and use these in their literary works.

1. **Authoritative**: The explanation given with authority is known as Authoritative.

2. **Presentation**: Presenting the science in full by dividing it into several topical chapters is known as Presentation.

3. **Combination**: The scheme for sentences is known as Combination.

4. **Substance**: The bare meaning of verse is known as Substance.

5. **Submission**: The arguments for in support of acquisition of wealth is known as Submission

6. **Objectives**: The statement made in brief sentence is known as Objective.

7. **Directives**: The statements made in detailed sentances are known as Directives.

8. **Advice**: The statements given for strict observance of practice is known as Advice

9. **Quotation**: The statement saying that 'such and such a person had said this' is known as Quotation.

10. **Establish**: Establishing a new point with what has already been proved is known as Establish

11. **Region**: Proving a new point with what is to be said ahead is known as Region.

12. **Anology**: To establish what is unseen with what is already seen is known as Anology.

13. **Wealthy**: That which has not been said and can be acquired only through wealth is known as Wealthy.

14. **Doubt**: When the same matter is viewed differently by opposing groups, it is known as Doubt.

15. **Context**: Where the opposing groups agree on the meaning, it is known as context.

16. **Contradiction**: Giving contradictory instructions on an issue is known as Contradiction.

17. **Completion of Sentence**: That which completes a sentence is known as Completion of sentence.

18. **Assent**: The sentence which is not opposed is known as Assent.

19. **Elucidation**: To reaffirm what is already agreed through different tactics is known as Elucidation.

20. **Wordless**: To establish the meaning of a word through wealth or forcible means is known as Wordless, because agreement is reached without discussion and by other means.

21. **Exemplification**: Citing some examples, proving a point is known as Exemplification.

22. **Shrinkage**: In order to explain any rule in a simple and lucid manner, if the subject had to be narrowed down, it is known as shrinkage.

23. **Autosignal**: Using the words not used or signaled by opposing group is called Auto signal.

24. **Eastern Side**: The sentence being contradicted is known as Eastern side.

25. **Northern Side**: The sentence which rebuts Eastern side is known as Northern side.

26. **Solitaire**: The wealth that cannot be sacrificed by any nation or at any time is known by the name Solitaire.

27. **Incomplete Explanation**: If it is said that it will be explained later, it is known as incomplete explanation.

28. **Excessive Outlook**: If it is said that a matter ihas already been proved earlier, it is known as Excessive Outlook.

29. **Disjointed**: To say that a particular mission can be achieved this way or it should not be pursued upon is known as Disjointed.

30. **Options**: To say that a particular mission can be achieved this way or it can also be achieved is known as Options.

31. **Complete**: To say that execution of a particular mission can be done in a particular way or in a different way is known as complete.

32. **Assumption**: to do a work that has not been specifically told is known as assumption

These are not restricted to Arthashastra only. While writing a book or while delivering a discourse or speech, the above points should be carefully borne in mind. While writing on any subject or fiction or treatise, the writer should not only read these 32 points over and over again, they should thoroughly understand and practice them, before writing and then only their work will achieve a level of standard and responsibility. On the other hand, if they follow the style of modern writers, their writing will be frittered, flow of language will be affected and will resemble a boiling pot, feelings will be scattered and without sequence. There will be no clarity of thoughts and topics will get mixed up in the presentation. Modern writers are not able to focus on a point for a long period and go deep into the thought being discussed and are not capable to bring out these in their books. There are two main reasons for this lacuna in their writing; they do not read fully all the related works on the subject; they do not get live experience and without doing sufficient research on the main theme, they start writing. If only they had gone through Chanakya's analysis on the subject, they would not have made these mistakes.

SECTION-5

IMMORTALITY AND SALVATION, REMAINING STORY

1. Chanakya's Steadfast Activity
2. Chanakya's Journey and Salvation

1

Chanakya's Steadfast Activity

It is in the present time and the rostrum, where we had to stand and comprehend the past and the future, because whatever happens will have to be at the present time. We can neither visit the past or go to the future. Whatever little knowledge we can derive, it is from the entry of Chanakya to Pataliputra and the establishment of the Maurya empire therein. The happenings before or after those two events can be seen, imagined or understood on the basis of illuminations emanating from that era. This period was marked by Chanakya's continued benevolent activities, from which we can conclude that from the beginning to the end he was perenially in action mode.

After taking the pledge Chanakya diverted his full attention and power for the destruction of Nand dynasty. But this pledge was made by an Act of God. His earlier objective was only to weave all the States under one ruler. Once this objective was achieved Chanakya started working in that direction. His force now did not consist of only a handful of youngsters nor was it restricted to an young army commandant; he was now a Minister under an Emperor, responsible for training and commanding huge army of Magadh Empire.

The fear of Chankya and the mighty fame of Chandragupta were so overwhelming that nobody dared to disobey their orders. Chanakya was past master in taking full advantage of such a situation.

Annexation and Expansion of Maurya Empire

Because of his extensive travel throughout the Empire, his eagle eyes grasped the problems and conditions of the nation, whereas administrators failed to see all these. As a result, he took full advantage of his intense knowledge and aided by reports received from his spies,he lost no opportunity in expanding the Empire. Creating the nation, organising and strengthening became his focal point. He was prepared to stake everything for achieving this mission.

In the history of India, that period was marked by conquests and transition. One State was collapsing and another was born. The area conquered by Alexander was still under the Greeks. Under the rule of Selucus Nicotar, Greeks were still occupying that area. Chanakya's aim was to snatch that vast area from their clutches aand stamp his authority.

Acquisition through Marriage

Chanakya was not in favour of waging war and thereby weakening himself nor did he want bloodshed. Marriage alliance was one way of achieving this, so that his purpose will be achieved without any loss for him or his people. He knew everything about Helen, the beautiful daughter of Selucus, whose original name was Cornelia. He also knew about Chandragupta's leaning towards a village belle, Chitra. (Poet and theatre personality Jaishanker Prasad, in his drama "Chandragupta" had dealt at length on this love angle. In a few places, this was accepted as a fictionalised character)

Armed with all this information, and having known the mind set of Selucus, Chanakya decided that by marriage of Helen with Chandragupta his State can be merged with Maurya Empire. This would result in all gains without any pain.

Chanakya informed his desire to his dear disciple and Emperor. Chandragupta was crestfallen on hearing this suggestion, bnut he could not utter anything in contrary to his Guru. He had to stand by his Guru in this too. Although he knew pretty well that nothing is hidden from Chanakya, he still wanted to disclose everything to him. He was very much ill at ease. However he informed his position to Chanakya and left the decision to him, knowing fully well that decision has already been taken and further it became clear to him that Chanakya was not contented with getting Magadh under their rule. When they had nothing they got Magadh and now when they had everything, there was no end to desire.

Selucus was not the one to accept all the requests without a fight. Hence Chanakya had to invade. Selucus lost comprehensively, agreed for the marriage and ceded four Provinces viz., Kabul, Jandhar, Herat and Makeran.

The Greek historian, Apeas had given vivid description of the war and the treaty. Megasthanese in his book 'INDICA' had given the rest of the details.

Chanakya did not stop with this. He had his eyes on another State also. The king had only one daughter by name Doord. He had decided upon marriage once again to get that State too by way of dowry. He announced the marriage proposal. Chandragupta put forth his view and got overruled once again. Chandragupta married Doord also, got the State merged and the border and security of the Empire further expanded.

Further Chandragupta once again explained to Chanakya that Chitra was still longing for him and was looking forward for the marriage. To fulfil his vow to Chitra, he married her too with the blessings of Chanakya, whose mission was now more or less accomplished.

Explanation: Marriages are considered a sacred life long relationship. Hence all relationships arising out of marriage were also maintained life long. In the royal families marriage was considered on par with signed and sealed treaty and none would break such a sacred treaty.

Similar relationships exist in business also. Business houses also come closer after marriage, and much stronger business house emerge from marriage. Even today small or big business houses, through marriage become co-owners or partners in new ventures.

Moral : Business relationship treaties and partnerships should be well founded for getting confidence and making progress.

Annexation through Treaties

Chanakya in his treatise 'Kautilya Arthashastra' (Kautilya's Economics), while disussing about kings, organisations, etc., dealt at length annexation through treaties. His basic belief was that treaties do not last for ever; but are based on transient situation, compulsions of governance and depends on the ruler. According to him, when necessary, one can enter into a treaty in view of weakness and when that necessity ends in any which way including when occasion arises by waging war that State or State can be merged with their own.

When Chanakya had waged war on border areas, and was successful in winning a few areas, the State of Parvatharaja was critically situated, that he had to establish good relations with him. This was based on the assessment that he could not win a battle against him. Further his focus was on overcoming Dhananand and he could not afford to have enmity towards another king. Chanakya collected all information related to the social, political, economic and armed strength and weaknesses and then fixed the time and place for a meeting with Parvatharaja.

Chanakya along with Chanddragupta, and his army Chief Bhadradutt met the king. He briefed about the current situation and expressed his desire for treaty. Parvatharaja examined the proposal in depth and finally gave his consent. The treaty provided for mutual help, non waging of war with each other and facility for the army to pass through each others' territory without any restriction. The third point was most important for Chanakya.

A few years passed. Maurya Empire was on a strong footing. Many small States became part of the Maurya Empire on their own free will. A few were subdued through aggression. Now the existence of independent State of Parvatharaja was an eye sore for Chanakya. His state was a much needed passage for strengthening his Empire. Chanakya decided on annexation of this State.

Chanakya broke the treaty by alleging that the demands were high and unbusiness like. Then he was silent for 6 months so that the king would become lax and treat the remark as passing one and not take the threat seriously. Parvatharja could not think that war would be waged breaking the treaty and hence failed to keep himself ready to face the threat. All on a sudden, the Maurya Empire invaded the state. A battle of unequals ensued; while one was not battle ready,while the other was fast, effective and well trained. Parvatharaja could not array his forces effectively to fight vast and efficient army, and had to surrender meekly. His state became part of Maurya Empire.

Explanation: Before acquiring any business organisation, one should have full information like production capacity, gross and net profit and on assessing decision should be taken. Lack of clarity on these would be counter-productive.

If it is established that net profit will increase and goodwill will increase with the acquisition, then a favourable decision can be taken.

It will be desirable to weaken the organisation to be taken over, so that acquisition can be done cheaply. If the cost of acquisition is high borrowing from the market had to be resorted at high cost resulting in doubling the cost of acquisition resulting in loss of benefit from such acquisition.

Moral: Knowledge of the market, the needs of the consumer and the acceptability of the product are the key factors that decide the future of the organisation.

Protection of Chandragupta

Many people do not understand that Chanakya was ceaselessly active because of his lean, slender and healthy body with the result he was never exhausted by work. Chanakya was many sided genius with unequalled dedication, unshakable determination with steady focus on job at hand. Besides he was a devoted wealthless soul, who led a simple and straight life but was a strong believer in high thinking. As a result he was healthy and active throughout his life. He was indomitable and continued to protect Chandragupta and expansion of Maurya Empire, ensured appointment of senior officers, trained the officers to be ever alert and ensured formation of a strong and ever expanding Empire.

Chandragupta was a front behind whom Chanakya strengthened administration and also demolished the Nand dynasty merging it with the Empire. Along side he also went about methodically to extend the border. Kings of smaller States and provinces became part of the Maurya Empire. It was not that everyone had welcomed the development. But the fact of the matter was that Maurya Empire had become so strong and powerful that nobody dared to speak or stand against them. This was a fertile ground for the undercurrents of differences to grow and spread. There were several people who were having grudge against the Maurya Empire and Chandragupta and they had hatched a plan to assassinate Chandragupta.

Chanakya's spy network was so wide spread that he was getting information in time of the developments from around the world and he was taking necessary steps to confront the situation. Nobody escaped from his eagle like observation. His active agents were posted near the suspects. No doubt, the survivors from

Nand dynasty were given good facilities, sufficient wealth to lead lavish life, without having to do any work. Yet they were disgruntled and were hatching a plan to restore their kingdom and were bent upon assassinating the Emperor. Chanakya could not digest this information.

Once one of the King's spies came posing as a messenger to meet Chandragupta. Doubts arose about the spy in the mind of Chanakya; he did not lose much time in knowing the truth as his spies gave full details about the fake spy and the plot to kill the Emperor by giving a drink laced with poison. Chanakya decided to nab him red-handed.

While arrangements were made for the spy to meet the king, steps were on to nab him. As the spy went to meet the king, Chankya with his men hid behind a curtain biding their time. They were ready and prepared for action.

It seemed that there were only the Emperor and the messenger in that room and they began discussing secret matters in a cordial manner. The people hidden behind the curtain saw that the messenger started praising high quality of the syrup of his State and produced a bottle of syrup and two silver glasses. While handing over the syrup filled glass to the Emperor, he calmly mixed it with the poison he had hidden in his ring. The Emperor accepted the glass graciously and was about to drink, when Chanakya emerged with his men and stopped the Emperor. He ordered the spy to be arrested and informed the king the truth about the drink. The spy was forced to drink the syrup from the very same glass. The Emperor was shocked to see the result; but Chanakya remained calm, though boiling with anger inside.

Explanation: Courage comes from internal strength of the mind while doing any work. Only a courageous mind can analyse the information coming to them. They can explain them lucidly and can take appropriate action at the right moment. These qualities get them the desired result. Higher the courage, higher will be the gains and results.

Suppression of Hatred: An Aid for Security

Chanakya was ever alert in monitoring his employees and officers to ensure that they did not have any dealings with enemies or competitors, which may result in conspiracies being hatched and if so they had to be nipped in the bud. According to Chanakya, irrespective of the position of the employees, big or small and irrespective of their salaries being big or small, , the responsibility of preventing their leaning towards enemies or competitors lies not only with the chief, but also with those managers, who control them from near.

'Avam Swavishyaye Krutya Cha Vichikshen
Paropajapatu Sauirakshetu Pradhanan Kshudakam Api

This was necessary to ensure that secrets do not go to others or stake holders belonging to prospective business or State do not get the wind of developments and with this knowledge turn to others for a better deal. Even in the earlier times, people were thwarting the efforts of one group and were joining another group. In today's situation these things happen on a higher scale and with more frequency. Enticing employees of others to work with them by offering higher salary and facilities or rewarding by regular salary to those, who while working with others, pass on critical information are prevalent on a large scale.

It was Chanakya's opinion which holds good even today, that the success of any organisation, institution and management depends wholly on collecting information and based on this, tqake prompt and effective steps. This holds true during time of war or countering rebellion or even during peace time for development. In those olden days, when spies were either walking or riding horses from place to place, Chanakya had put in place a system for getting messages promptly and give response to the situation through a system of lights.

For this system to be effective, the most crucial aspect was locating convenient heights from which light can be transmitted to another height. This kind of communication, however was prevalent in India even before Chanakyas time. While using this system, Chanakya, to counter its shortcomings, brought changes to improve and make the system more effective.

There was such a system from Pataliputra, across North of river Ganges right upto the foothills of the Himalayas.Some of this arrangement have stood the test of time, although some part of it was lost. From the the fort of Kumharar to Hajipur, then to the Stupa of Kesaria, then to Nandangarh Laurea and the to Chanaki Garh the system of communication was in place. Whatever messages were being sent from the Palace, were received by these channels and were promptly replied.

Kumharar fort sank, as a result of which the tower was buried. Even during the time of Mughals there were reference of this arrangement. During the British rule. the efficacy of this tower was tested for commercial use; although the trial was successful , they did not persist on this line of communication.

Now the Governments have given mobile phones to employees of commercial organisations for the purpose of getting quick information. However absence of towers covering all areas are causing problems. They are not able to solve this problem and with all technological advances, are not able to cover all areas for mobile communication!

Birth of the Heir

The attempt on the life of the Emperor through poisoning has been discussed earlier. There were several such attempts at regular intervals subsequently also, which left Chanakya worried. He realised that there cannot be an end to these conspiratory attempts. If there was even a little lapse in the act of saving or timing, the conspirators will succeed in their mission, and all time and efforts that has gone into the making of a strong emperor, would go waste.

There was no doubt in Chanakyas mind on the physical attributes of Chandragupta; he was an expert in all forms of warfare, had the capacity to destroy any army singlehandedly. There was no doubt that he will be the victor. Nobody could confront him and defeat him. No one, however, can understand fully a conspiratorial mind. If anyone wanted to kill him by treachery, it was difficult to take counter steps, because, by nature, Chandragupta was not in the nature of doubting people.

Taking all factors into consideration Chanakya took a tough decision: that of administering a daily dose of poison to Chandragupta and make his physical constitution resistant to all poisons. The poison was made by Chanakya himself personally and he explained in detail to the chief cook about the entire procedure. For the first few days mixing of poison in the food was done under his direct supervison to ensure that there were no lapses and later it was done by the cook himself. The emperor was being given varieties of poison. Initially the cook was apprehensive, but later became confident on seeing that the poisons were not having any effect on the Emperor. Even then he knew that a small lapse will be fatal.

However unexpected events happen without any warning and even the most alert person cannot escape its clutches. Even Chanakya could not escape Chandragupta came under its clutches. There was loss at that very moment and its effect was also felt in the distant future.

Chandragupta had three queens – Helen, Doord and Chitra. The marriage had taken place under three different situations. The marriage with Chitra took place last, as she was loved by Chandragupta. The first marriage with Helen, daughter of Selucus took place because the areas won by Selucus were to be received. Next Doord, the sole princess of Royal House was married, as her State was to get merged as she was the Crown queen of State.

Queen Doord became pregnant. It was the ninth month of her pregnancy. The queen was weak and was also scared of her first pregnancy. As a result the Emperor was spending more time with her. Emperor was looking after her with great care. Then the unexpected happened.

As usual, poison administered food reached the Emperor. On account of his extreme love, he requested the queen to share food with him. The chief cook was shocked on seeing this. What should have happened was that the food for the queen, suiting her condition should have been brought quickly; or he should have jumped on the plate and tumbled the contents. Instead of this, he ran to Chanakya to inform him the tragic development. Chanakya ran to the place; but by then it was too late. In the meanwhile the queen had consumed one or two morsels of food . Her delicate body could not withstand the poisonous food.

When Chanakya reached the spot, he could see the effects of poison on the queen. He realized that it was impossible to save the queen, but the heir she was carrying had to be saved. The baby had to be removed before the poison reached the womb.

Chanakya had no time for informing the doctors and giving the very antidote. Every second was priceless. Whatever was to be done was to be done then and there. Chanakya took the decision of removing the child from the womb through surgery. The female attendants of the queen were busy with their work, as the queen was sinking. Chankya, though alert, could not comprehend the happenings. Surgery was conducted in this acrimonious situation.

Chanakya had definitely studied surgery; it was also possible that he had some experience also, but to deliver a baby through surgery? He was a stranger to this situation. But Chanakya had confidence in his training and practice. With his sharp memory and concentration gained through his knowledge, he performed the operation successfully with a steady hand. The baby boy was removed from the womb. The queen could not be saved as on one hand the poison was having its effect and on the other he could not stop the blood flow due to surgery.

The child also had absorbed a drop (bundh in Hindi) of poison, but Chanakya saved the child through treatment and as the child had a bundh, he was named Bindusar. He later became famous by the names- Bimbisar and Bindhusar.

The child was also brought up by Chanakya; when the child grew up, his education, direction and training were imparted under the direct supervision of Chanakya. When he became a youth, he became a more capable and competent Emperor than his father.

Chandragupta entrusted during his lifetime itself the Empire to his son and headed to the forests for meditation. Bindusar also extended the same amount of respect to Chanakya and under his direction he was managing the Empire.

Result: Decisions taken under difficult circumstances have an effect on the future course of events. Balance of mind and firm determination are the most important requirements of those defining moments .

Retirement from Service : Give the Dues to the Enemy

Chanakya had the twin objectives of expansion and security foremost in his mind and was giving importance to efforts required to achieve them. He was keen on expanding the Maurya Empire throughout the Aryavartha and wanted to give it the status of a powerful Empire; he was also keen on security of both the government and citizens of the State. Pondering over this, he came to the conclusion that so long as prime minister of Nand was free and alive, there will be a threat to Chandragupta and security and progress of the Mauryan Empire.

But Mudrarakshas was quite learned and possessing high moral values on account of which he could not be assassinated even though it was quite easy. He was a valuable treasure. His capabilities had to be fully utlised. Chanakya also knew that once Mudrarakshas gives Chandragupta his whole hearted approval, then he would back the development and security of the Maurya Empire with all faculties at his command.

Chanakya was desirous of retiring from service. He had his own plans. He wanted Mudrarakshas to come forward and serve the Maurya Empire. In order to fulfill this Chanakya began weaving his web. The web was so comprehensive that either he had to join Chanakya or commit suicide. The Sanskrit drama 'Mudrarakshas' produced by Vishakadutt was mainly based on this theme. The final moments described below are as per the dramatist's imagination.

Chanakya was waiting impatiently for the message and his spy who was the bearer of the message. He became restless and started brooding about the thought process of Mudrarakshas at that very moment. In which direction would his brain be working. He had tightened the rope around his neck through his spies. It was impossible for him to escape from the iron grip of Chanakya. He had no escape route.

His most trusted colleague and chief of espionage, Purushdutt was seen at a distance rushing to him. Chanakyas anxiety had reached such a point that he too ran towards his chief to know the details. In a sup pressed voice, without taking any name he asked: What? What happened? What is he doing now?

In a confident tone Purushdutt replied: In an hour's time he will commit suicide.

Immediately Chanakya screamed: No! It should not happen! It will be the worst defeat. He is a minister far superior to me. He is an invaluable treasure. I cannot afford to lose him. Did you give him the message that he should meet me.

Purushdutt informed him what he knew: On getting your humble invitation, he was flushed with fury and shouted: He can kill me. I can kill myself, but I cannot meet that cruel and cunning Chanakya.

Chanakya said in a courageous and thoughtful tone: It is not a question of my character or destiny. The question is the security of the King, the State and its citizens. His life is more important than mine.

Purushdutt had a straight question: Then why did you drive him to commit suicide?

Chanakya's confidence was ebbing: So that he would come to me. But this is not the time to discuss these matters. This is the time to save him.

At that time another spy came. Chanakya took couple of steps towards him and asked: Tell me Mukesh, what have you to say?

Mukesh said: At first I could not understand. But he is coming straight here to see you. His hands are empty and he is totally at peace. I have accompanied him. I could not leave him alone.

Chanakya was pleased and raising his hand: Aha! Let Almighty be pleased! The Goddess of Victory is standing outside with a garland! Praise the Lord!

Mukesh murmured: He has come!

Both of you go and welcome him, Chanakya ordered.

They were both astonished and said in a voice: What? However, without expecting any reply, they moved towards the shadow of uncertain future course of events. Then three of them returned.

Chanakya bowed with all humility and welcomed the famed Premier Mudrarakshas.

He then bowed before him and garlanded him with folded hands.

Mudrarkashas responded to the welcome thus: Your behaviour is intended to add insult to injury.

Chanakya said in the same humble tone: You are a noble soul, Premier Mudrarakshas. Today and at this moment, you are not a vanquished individual, on the contrary, you are the Prime Minister of the Mourya Empire. I welcome you.

There was no change in Mudrarakshas. This is another joke that hurts.

Chanaky's humility did not change: "No! Certainly not! You have just now replaced me and got this post. You are victorious".

Mudrarakshas did not make any effort to hide his anger and surprise: So long as Chanakya is there there cannot be another victor.

Chanakya clarified: Chanakya will not be seen anymore. Just now he has relinquished his office, and has handed over the Office to Premier Rakshas with his whole heart. In the absence of your enemy, Chanakya, you manage the affairs of the State on your own accord. I know you love your motherland and its citizens and you were always submissive to the king. This is a well deserved prize for the great services rendered by you.

Mudrarakshas was dumbfounded for the first time: I do not believe this.

Chanakya opening up invited him: Individual belief and disbelief are ordinary matters. Take up the post and start your operations. But before that meet the Emperor Chandragupta and inform him of your appointment and taking over of the responsibility of the Office. Come with me Prime Minister.

Explanation: It is very common in these modern times, that no president or director or chief operating executive of any organization is ever willing to give up his office and to give the reponsibility to hard working and capable person. There are instances where people fight amongst themselves for sticking on to the chair overlooking the damage caused to their business and organization. They pin their hopes on their ability to make good the losses, but on account of their physical and mental deficiencies, that will not happen. They should hand over the post and power to other deserving persons.

Effect: Individuals should be free of greed, especially the greed of power. Personal gains should be sacrificed for the benefit of the organization.

Handing over in a gold plate, as it were, the most important post occupied by him, to a person who was inimical and was driven back to the wall, must be unique and strange instance in the history of mankind. In this act, personal gains, enmity and earlier impressions were totally cast aside, and individual's character, qualities, capability, enthusiasm towards work and gains to the nation were given importance. Whatever he had in his mind was done by Chanakya. He had handed over the post to the most capable individual to take on from there and do whatever had to be done. He did not give importance to his own feelings, because only he can say or only such an individual can say that for the family's benefit the individual benefit, for the society's benefit, the family's benefit and for the benefit of the nation, the benefit of the society should be sacrificed. It was essential that a qualified and capable individual to occupy that post and Chanakya just did that.

Even though, sacrificing a post may not be agreeable to the people of the modern society driven by greed and ambition and used to seeing people promoting their own self interest, it is still true that one has to think of the benefit for all. If the nation and all others are safe and prosperous, individual's safety and prosperity are automatically taken care. Today, when life is endangered everywhere, and human beings are crushed by speeding vehicles; are being killed by bullets; bomb explosions destroy their very foundation, then of whose security are we talking about?

Chanakya's Compositions

After installing Chandragupta firmly as Emperor; integrating the entire nation in a thread; making Mudrarkshas as the Premier and relinquishing himself from services, Chanakya engaged himself in writing, and came out with immortal classics. He had seen it all: emerging, dissipating, decaying, stinking, well developed, fragrant, prosperous, impatient, restless, indulgent, controlled, democratic, dictatorial, unjust, ethical, corrupt, selfless individual, Society and State. He was a treasure house of these experiences. He had thus accumulated knowledge on both philosophical and business related issues. He had the capability and expertise to mould philosophy to business and vice versa because he was always in the midst of or very near to raging storm. Silence or inaction were not his virtue. If there was no tumult near him, it was only on account of fear caused by his towering personality.

He created for himself the required environment for writing and also ensured that he will get continuous flow of continuous and uninterrupted news.

He used several pseudonyms for his poems and literature. He was Vishnugupt, Vishnusharma, Vatsyayan and Kautilya. Whether he wrote under any other names is not known. His life was an enigma shrouded in mystery, that nothing in this regard can be said with certainty.

With the march of remorseless time, it becomes difficult to say whether some of the verses were written by Chanakya or someone else. Some of the researchers even give credit to Chanakya books authored by others. It is also accepted that Chanakya was reading all the literature then available, and in his books too he had included some of the thoughts of these books. In Kautilya Arthashastra, he had cited many ancient thinkers and propagated secularism. Hence it is not surprising to see verses from Mahabhaarata, Puranas and Manusmriti. It is quite possible that Chanakya had included these, or someone else had added these in his works. The verses below can be found in Chanakya's *Nitishastra*, and also in *Hitopadesh*, *Markhandeya Purana* 37/23; *Barah Purana* 153/26 and Mahabharat's Shanti paarva:

Nasthi vidhyasamam chakshu: nasthi satyamam tapa:
Nasthi ragasamam dukham nasthi thyagasamam sukham

There are six verses like these, but it does not make any difference whether these are retained or expunged. What matters is not the full text, but storehouse of Chanakya's classical treatise.

Chanakya has threaded his knowledge and experience in verses and given to posterity. On the one hand, he was liberated, without any tension or pressure in writing, and on the other side, he had kept open his quick and sharp eyes active, with sharp wisdom explained and elaborated which enabled creation of such classics.

1. **Chanakya Niti** : The importance of moral science becomes clear from the fact that Sri Krishna had proclaimed in Gita that whoever seeks victory should first have morality: *Niti: Asmi Jigistam* I From the Vedic Ages to Harshavardhan period there was a tradition of writing moral verses, teaching these verses . Brahma, Indra, Vishnu, Sriram, Srikrishna, Vedvyas, Brahaspati, Shkra, Markhandeya, Bharadvaj, Vaishampayan, Budha, Mahavir, through Chanakya this tradition was prevalent upto Bhatrahari. These moral verses were written mostly in Sanskrit's Anushtup Chanda.

The achievement of Chanakya in this phase, has been given a traditional acceptance that a poetic-thinker should guide mankind for achieving internal and external growth and purity; to confront every situation in life successfully and to lead enriched, peaceful and happy life. In order to prove his point, has extensively embellished his works with similes and metaphors. He has explained in depth with authority to meet different facets: At the time of treaty, in religious congregation, during arbitration, in the face of controversies.

Moral science is considered as the main source of all knowledge and the credit for consolidating this, goes to Chanakya. From the ancient times, thinkers and pets have recycled these thoughts, which is the foundation of Moral Science.

Nana shastr uddutham vakshaye rajsaniti samuchayasm
Sarvaa-bij idam shastram chanakyam sarasangraham

Chanakya Niti Shastra consist of 70 chapters and each chapter has 18 to 22 verses , thus making a total of 336 verses. Truth, clarity and simplicity are the main features of these verses. He has only put forth his views, without reference to any event. These are simple and brief. On account of these qualities, they have become extremely renowned and immortal. They have withstood the test of time too.

The highlight of Chanakya Niti is that he had only focused on imparting knowledge. There is no narration or explanation; only the essence of principles has been given in these verses. Thus the statements are simple and straight and so natural that it touches and enlightens the mind and no one can ignore them. Their truth and enlightenment have the power to transcend the time and are true even today and will be applicable for the future too. It is appreciated by humanity for its pragmatic approach. He has not touched upon anything else other than educating mankind. This was possible only for a totally dedicated soul

This was a major contribution of Chanakya and it was claimed from ancient time, that even a fool can become a master by reading this.

Moolsutram pravakshayami chanakyena yadothditam
Yasya vigyan matrena murkho bhavit pandit:

2. **Old Chanakya—Part one**: Old Chankya Part I is written in normal literary style. It consists of 8 chapters. It could be seen as another version of Chanakya Niti.

3. **Old Chanakya – Part two**: Old Chanakya Part II iis written with figure of speech. However in the available copy of the book, Niti Shastra is dealt with.

In the available copies of both the parts of Old Chanakya formulae of moral Science and the recitation of rules of morality are dealt with, but it does not go well that two different books deal with the same subject. It could not have happened in those times. It is quite possible that since the original writings were not available, the same thoughts were put in these books, as they are quite similar. No books of Chanakya embellished with figures of speech is available to the present generation.

4. **Collections of Chanakya's Thoughts**: In this there are 300 ANUSHTUP collections, divided into three parts of 100 each. Besides dealing with politics, this shows the way to lead simple life. In the last verse, he has recommended for becoming a resident of Kashi (Benares). He has described the essence of 4 different aspects of living — Truthful Living, Living on the banks of River Ganges , The Worship of Lord Shiva and Becoming a Resident of Benares:

Asare khalu sansare saram chatu: satyam
Kasyau vasa: satam sango ganga bha: shambu sevanam

5. **Simple Chanakya(Laghu Chanaya)**: This consists of 8 chapters, each chapter again consists of 8 tom 10 verses. This was not available in India, but was very popular in Europe. Even now, it is not freely available in India. The belief that the Greeks had joined the forces residing in the Emperor's palace or joined with priests were not prevalent there.

6. **Chanakya's Political Science**: This consists of 534 verses. This again is divided into 8 parts. This book was found in Tibet. In the Middle Ages, , when India was plundered and burnt, many books disappeared and many were found in other countries or in the border towns of the then Indian nation. Traversing through China, Mangolia, Java and Bali, theses books appeared back in India. As can be made out from the heading, this book deals in depth about politics. This is considered as a precursor to Kautiya's Arthashastra, which gained huge popularity and this book became part of Arthashastra.

7. **Chanakya Formula (Chanakya Sutra)**: The knowledge propagated by Chanakya in verses are considered as formula. This art of ancient writing is given to the world by Bharat and is a pride of this country. There are more than 500 verses in this book.

Kautilya Arthashastra (Kautilya's Economics): Kautilya Arthashastra has been universally accepted as Chanalya's book because at the end of the book Chanakya wrote a verse wherein a brief proclamation about the elimination of Nand dynasty from the face of the earth and it conclusively proved that this book is written by none other than Vishnugupt also known as Chanakya:

Yen shastram va shatru cha nandrajgat cha bhu
Amarshen udhutha anyashu ten shastram idam krutam

Today people are interested in separating politics from religion. These have remained mere proclamations. In reality, politics and religion cannot be separated. It might have so happened that on account of political interference, religious practices have been affected. Chanakya's firm belief was that religion and politics have deep rooted relationship and they cannot be separated.

Judicial Reflections(Nyay Shastr Mimamsa): This book is in the form of a discourse on judicial matters and is accepted as written by Chanakya. It depends on individual's leanings whether to accept it or deny.

Vatsayana's Kamasutra: It has been accepted that the famous Kamasutra by Vatsayana is written by Chanakya. Incidentally Chanakya belonged to Vatsayana clan. The teachings of this book can neither be accepted with whole heart nor can it be easily turned down.

Panchatanta : Vishnusharma : Panchatantra is also attributed to Chanakya, which deals with adavice for well being, and gains from friendship. The essence of this book is now not merely taken as anology in name but extends to languages and feelings. In addition, there is a collection o famous verses of Chanakya in this book not as example, but as main source.

On going through these books, it becomes clear that Chanakya has written more than 3000 verses. There is no point in wasting our time or energy to find out who had created these verses. One has to get the benefit of the wisdom hidden in these verses and shape our life and habits accordingly. This is what is essential.

Whoever be the author of these works, it is a fact that lot of ideas for practice are given. It is quite possible that it has been modified to improve and give more depth to these thoughts or it is also possible that it has been edited. The maturity in these thoughts and its practicality are the main benefits for us. Irrespective of our ability to identify distinctly the author of these verse, their wisdom is passed on to us.

After his permanent retirement from active services, he was immersed with his books bequeathing his wisdom and experience to posterity. Being Chanakya, his continuous action did not stop with this. His sharp and sleepless eyes were ever focussed on the Maurya Empire, and was contended about its safety and growth. His spies were active and he gave necessary orders to them from his dwelling place. His dwelling place was not a fort of Royal Palace, but a humble shade of a banyan tree amidst Mango groove which was sufficient for him and his works.

Without any self interest, for attaining salvation from the cycle of re-births, through his actions and writings, Chanakya made his objectives clear:

- ↪ Have a clear understanding of life
- ↪ Make everyone high on morality
- ↪ Create an ideal society
- ↪ Ensure welfare of common man
- ↪ Acquire wisdom and knowledge, discharge your duties through right action and lead an enriched life.
- ↪ Lead the way to have happiness, peace and prosperity.
- ↪ Well being and progress of mankind.
- ↪ Leading mankind towards salvation

2

Chanakya—Journey & Salvation

Whatever Chanakya said for the kings also hold in good measure for intellectuals and it would certainly fit him, for Chanakya lived his whole life as he preached, never for his own self, but always for others. Chanakya had said that in the happiness of his people lies the happiness of the ruler or administrator, in their prosperity lies his prosperity too. The ruler should never look for his own progress or prosperity; instead he should realise that his happiness should come out of the satisfaction of his subjects.

Chanakya made Chandragupta the Emperor. He strung all states into one nation, appointed Mudrarakshas as the Premier. relieved himself of all responsibilities and engaged himself in writing. He created number of immortal classics; in another direction, through competent reformers. he devoted attention towards the welfare of the people so that they realise their potential and become an ocean of happiness.

Objectives of Man's Life—Duty, Wealth, Desire & Moksha

Through his work, he had established that his entire life was devoted to these objectives of life namely ***Dharma. Artha, Kama & Moksha***. which can only be loosely translated as above. He never drifted from these aims of life. He was only concerned about his duties which he performed day and night with full vigour and single minded devotion. As for the need of wealth, for a normal living, wealth in the form of materials only were required and there is nothing to be gained by accumulating coins. He was getting these materials in sufficient quantity for feeding quite well all the people dependant on him, whatever be their numbers; there was never a shortage. It is quite astonishing that a person who was not having any wealth was giving lessons to all for attaining prosperity. He was leading such a simple life that he was never in need of wealth. However he was quite confident that if wealth was required, he has to only request any one from anywhere and sufficient wealth will be at his disposal. He will not even be aware as to who brings or the source of wealth brought to him. The crux of the matter is he will get the wealth if required. He always performed his duty and also gave lessons in observance of duty and charity and to lead a good life resulting in his getting salvation. After getting the well deserved Moksha, Chanakya is only a thought. A very strong belief which can blow up or hold in good stead. A positive thought which can change the directions and state of living. a thought that brings in change, a thought which can give power, a rare treasure that can make an individual strong.

Chankya achieved his objectives. There was struggle, but he was always crowned with success. In each and every field he was successful and thereby established his greatness. No person either in the past or in the future could ever match him. His teachings are for humanity forever and is not limited by time or place. That is why it is being read, taught; that is why it was followed then and is being followed and respected even today. Chanakya's name always evokes wide spread respect. His teachings have always given worldly knowledge and self-satisfaction.

Chanakya's philosophy is deep, complete precise and full of wisdom. He has displayed such clarity of thought and justice that knowingly or unknowingly various governments in large parts of the world have framed their rules and regulations based on his thoughts. This is the main reason that amongst the writers of our ancient age Chanakya's writings are the most taught and accepted as most thought provoking. His writings are available in all the languages of the world and a continuous stream of books and essays appear in the literary world. Now even subject wise books written by him are on sales.

Detatched Yet Engaging Personality

In every place and in every task the victor Chanakya! In every situation the overwhelming personality. the fearless Chanakya! Determined, firm and ever alert Chanakya! Governance and Organisation guru Chanakya! Fearless, calm and skilful Chanakya! Without wanting a quid pro quo, expectations will be fulfilled by Chanakya! Whatever he got or accumulated were distributed by Chanakya! A scholar of all subjects, Chanakya! How deep were his attachments! How great were his detachments! How matchless were his beliefs! How alert he was towards non-belief! How matchless were his dedication to duty! How sharp were his defence and punishment! So balanced! Firm on the middle path! Unequalled! Matchless! With everyone and marshalling everyone!

Self Willed Death: During the lifetime of Chandragupta, Bindusar became the Emperor. Chandragupta retired to the forests. Chanakya's relatiomship with his second disciple Bindusar remained unchanged. Bindusara also held him in high esteem.

Bindusar had a minister named Subandhu., who developed enmity towards Chanakya. He also came to know the mysteries around the birth of Bindusara. He informed Bindusara that Chankya was responsible for the death of his mother. Bindusara enquired with a few of the women helpers who also confirmed the minister's information. Bindusara was provoked to extreme anger against Chanakya.

A few of Chanakya's spies informed him that the Emperor has developed bitter anger against him. Chanakya then sent a message to Bindusara to the effect that when as an Emperor he has resources to the roots of a truth, why should he base his decisions on statements of mere mortals. Rumours have no base.

Chanakya was ill at ease even after sending the message to the Emperor. Then he took a difficult decision with ease, the decision to fast unto death. Heart of hearts he might have had some repentance and a sense of atonement. However, he was deeply hurt by the fact that his disciple has misunderstanding about him.

Announcing his self willed death, he sat atop a huge manure dump and began his fast without touching either food or water.

On seeing the message from Chanakya, Bindusara was shocked. He realised his folly and felt perhaps his Guru was not responsible for death of his mother. He started his investigation into the matter. It was a matter of coincidence that the midwife who was present when operation was performed at the time of his birth, was alive. She was summoned. She confirmed that his mother was not administered any poison, but on her own volition she had consumed poison. She had food with the emperor. It was none other than Chanakya who had saved him through operation.

Bindusara's rage turned towards cantankerous Subandhu. He beheaded him with a slice of his sword. He was worried that the Guru had heard of his angry disposition towards him and what could be going through the mind of the great man. Commanding his forces to follow him at a distance, he went alone riding his horse. Almost immediately, his bodyguards reached him.

It was too late when he arrived at the manure dump. Chanakya had given up food and water. Neither the humility nor the pleadings of Bindusara and others had any effect on Chanakya. He stuck to his determination like a rock. He did not change his decision.

Bindusara stayed back. The army cleared the area by cutting down all trees and made it neat and clean. This news flew across all the four sides. The villagers around came running with flowers. Disciples ran and brought garlands and decorated the dump. The fragrance emanating from the dump spread across all directions. In the midst of those flowers Chanakya went into a deep trance, and later attained Samadhi in an unperturbed sitting posture.

Priests chanted Vedas and conducted rituals of Mahamrtyunjaya; (Victory over death). The disciples also joined the chanting. Musicians brought their musical instruments and the music reverberated around the place. Drums, cymbals, violin, mridang, veena sarangi and flute went full blast. The sound of instruments gave a festive atmosphere. The sound of music were putting an end to the fear of death and hope was being generated for a new beginning.

It was indeed a unique sight. On the death of an elderly person, there is a tradition in India of sounding musical instruments at the funeral procession; But here sound of musical instruments was before the death, which heralded Chanakya's purity in life. This was not death, but a journey. He breathed his last and his last expiration mingled with the air in atmosphere; his soul departed to the nether world and thus his journey was complete. His soul was liberated and he attained the ultimate salvation.

Moral: Only through the duties performed, fame earned, the wealth saved and prestige earned life will be meaningful. Life spent on amassing wealth and spending lavishly on material luxury have no meaning whatsoever!

Lesson: One has to spend life in serving others and death should be immemorial.

Journey: Liberation, Salvation, Immortality

Chanakya's journey was completed by giving up the body wilfully. He attained liberation from life, resulting in salvation, by attaining which he was freed from the cycle of rebirth. By sacrificing his body, he is not away from us as,his thoughts are actively alive even today. That is immortality—immortal classics, immortal teachings and immortal wisdom. In Chanakya's departure from here lies a new beginning. Whoever understands and follows his teachings will begin a new life.

It is a wrong notion that remorseless time separates people. Time in fact unites people through the ancient traditions and men who had become part of history. It binds our future, our nation and generations. Time offers opportunity for all. We are not united; we have developed fissures; we are not duty bound. For these ills we cannot blame time. Even today we have a mutual connection with Chanakya. This connectivity encourages us to attain wisdom. From other's immortality we are inspired to go in the same direction and attain immortality. Similarly from the liberation and salvation of another soul we tend to tread the same path.

The immortal systems and sayings of Chanakya have such a quality that if anyone chooses to follow the path and aims propounded by Chanakya without straying, he will be phenominally successful and will not be found wanting in wealth or power. They can stand the test of time. In order to achieve this Chanakya's works have to be read over and over again and those tough teachings can be mastered only through hard labour with a single minded devotion and determination.

Chankya's immortality establishes that through his creative writing, he does not belong to any time-frame; he is beyond the limitations of time frame; he now belongs to all the time to come, for all eras and to all mankind, wherever they may be. Thus he has become a victor of time.

Chanakya was an individual in the world. He strode the earth and had a strong platform. His tremendous success in life is not lesser than the glory of planets of the universe. By becoming a thought, a treasure, he is still striding the earth like a colossus with a strong base and shedding enlightenment. He is no more an individual, but an idol.

Gyani acharya chanakya namo namaha (Salutations to Chanakya)

Sarve Shubha

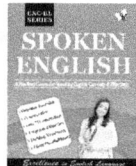

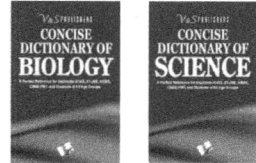

www.ingramcontent.com/pod-product-compliance
Lightning Source LLC
Chambersburg PA
CBHW072117020426
42334CB00018B/1627